# CHURCHILL
# AND MALTA

Malta is a little island with a great history. The record of the Maltese people throughout that long history is a record of constancy and fortitude. It is with those qualities, matchlessly displayed, that they are now confronting the dark power of the Axis.

The Right Hon. Winston S. Churchill, C.H., M.P.

Foreword to *The Epic of Malta*, 1942

DOUGLAS AUSTIN
FOREWORD BY SIR MARTIN GILBERT

# CHURCHILL AND MALTA

First published 2006, this edition 2014
by Spellmount, an imprint of The History Press

The Mill, Brimscombe Port
Stroud, Gloucestershire, GL5 2QG
www.thehistorypress.co.uk

British Library Cataloguing in Publication Data.
A catalogue record for this book is available from the British Library.

ISBN 978 0 7509 6069 4

Typesetting and origination by The History Press
Manufacturing Managed by Jellyfish Print Solutions Ltd
Printed in Malta by Gutenberg Press

# *Contents*

# *Preface*

In September 1922 Winston Churchill purchased Chartwell Manor, a house with medieval origins surrounded by 80 acres of land on the greensand hills of Kent near Westerham. It continued to be his principal residence until his death in January 1965, and it was there that he and Mrs. Churchill raised their family. It then reverted by the terms of a previous arrangement to the National Trust and it is now open to the public between April and October each year. On display in the house are many of the thousands of gifts that Sir Winston received during his long life. Among these there hangs in his Study an elaborate silver shield mounted on a black oval base. It is described in the Chartwell Guide Book as 'A shield bearing the arms of Malta, given by the people of the island.' This statement is incorrect in several respects and the author has with the help of Mr. Michael Refalo, Mr. Antoine Attard and Fr. George Aquilina, O.F.M. in Malta, and papers held in the Churchill Archives held at Churchill College Cambridge, pieced together the story of this gift.

In July 1945 the Rt. Hon. Winston Churchill lost the General Election called at the end of the war and became leader of His Majesty's Opposition. In May of the following year he received a letter from Lt.-Col. Agius, Trade Commissioner at the Malta Government Office in London, asking if he would be prepared to accept a gift from a Maltese citizen. Lt.-Col. Agius wrote that Mr. Edward Ceravolo wished to present a piece of Maltese silver to Mr. Churchill 'whom he considers the saviour of the world from slavery and paganism.' Churchill said he would be 'greatly honoured' by such a gift.

Edward Ceravolo had lived in Valletta throughout the bombing of 1940-43 and he owned and managed the 'Splendid' bar in Valletta. Although the building is no longer a bar the colourful sign of the 'Splendid Lounge Bar' still hangs on the corner of 34 Archbishop Street. During the Second World War this bar was the haunt of many British and Commonwealth servicemen and Edward Ceravolo named a number of his special drinks after wartime battles. Early in the war he bought two fine examples of Maltese silver that had been made by Antonio Attard, a well-known and highly accomplished silversmith who had had a workshop on St. Paul's Street in Valletta. One was a model of Kingsgate, the old entrance to Valletta. The other was a shield depicting an elaborate and finely crafted array of medieval weapons surrounding a coat of arms. These are not the arms of Malta but rather those of Grand Master Jean Parisot de la Valette. It was he who at the age of 71 had led the resistance of the Knights of St. John and the people of Malta against the Turkish armies of Suleiman the Magnificent in the Great Siege of 1565. Edward Ceravolo had initially thought of presenting the Kingsgate model to Churchill but later decided that the shield would be more appropriate in view of Churchill's role during Malta's second Great Siege of 1940-43.

Edward Ceravolo came to England several months later and on Wednesday 24 July 1946 he called on Churchill at his room in the House of Commons, accompanied by Lt.-Col. Agius and Mr. H. A. Bonavia from the Malta Government Office. Edward Ceravolo presented the shield to Churchill saying that it was a 'token of his admiration of Mr. Churchill's leadership of the British nation during the war'. He also gave Churchill for Mrs. Churchill, who was not able to be present, a bouquet of red and white roses—Malta's colours. After examining the shield Churchill responded by saying: 'It is really lovely. I shall keep this in my home and treasure it as a memorial to Malta's great heroism.'

Churchill then made arrangements for a signed photograph of himself to be framed in walnut at Aspreys, the London jewellers, and on 4 November he sent this to Edward Ceravolo together with a box of his special 'Churchill' Havana cigars. His covering letter, written at Chartwell, read as follows:

Dear Mr. Ceravolo

I am sending you herewith a photograph which I have signed, and some cigars, as a small measure of recognition of your kindness in presenting me with the beautiful Maltese shield. This, which now hangs in my study here, is a continual source of pleasure to me, and the care and craftsmanship which produced it have my warm admiration. It will also be a perpetual reminder of Malta's gallantry during the war.

Yrs sincerely,
Winston S. Churchill

The shield still hangs today in a place of honour in Churchill's Study at Chartwell where he placed it in 1946. The signed photograph, in its walnut frame, that Churchill sent to Edward Ceravolo in November 1946 is now in the care of Fr. Aquilina, O.F.M., Archivist of the Franciscan Order in Valletta to which it was bequeathed by Mr. Ceravolo's nephew. The many thousands of visitors who each year pass through Chartwell thus have this valuable and historic reminder of the close ties forged between Winston Churchill and the people of Malta, particularly in the stern days of the Second World War.

# Foreword by Sir Martin Gilbert

In the vast panorama of Churchill's life, his relationship with Malta is a bright light, as bright as the paintings that he did of Valetta harbour. Douglas Austin has traced this relationship from Churchill's first visit in 1907 to his sixth visit in 1945 and beyond. At the centre of the story is Churchill's understanding of what he called 'Malta's gallantry during the war', which had so impressed him.

Even before his first visit, Churchill had glimpsed Malta on the sea voyage to India, at the age of twenty one. His first, 1907, visit has intrigued me since, forty years ago, I was working my way through the 1907 files of the Churchill papers. Douglas Austin's pages about that visit have finally satisfied my curiosity.

Like everything Churchill set his mind to, there is a wealth of gems: personal, historical and constitutional, in this 1907 visit alone, the brightest being Churchill's 'Malta memorandum', uncovered by the author in the files of the old Colonial Office, and examined fully here for the first time. The first wartime assault on Malta came with Mussolini's bombers in 1940. As Douglas Austin shows in fascinating detail, it was from that moment that Churchill made every effort to protect and defend the island, as it took its part in the long, hard and often harsh struggle with Italy and Germany in the Mediterranean.

Churchill's part in that struggle is finely presented in these pages, from which one can see clearly why Malta was awarded the George Cross, a remarkable and unique honour for a place. Churchill understood, as he telegraphed in early 1941 to the Governor, the scale and nature of the 'magnificent and ever-memorable' defence of Malta by the 'heroic garrison and citizens'.

That heroic defence of Malta, and the extraordinary story of the Malta convoys and their escorts, of courageous sailors and intrepid airmen, is an integral part of Britain's war story. 'We are absolutely bound to save Malta in one way or another', Churchill informed his Deputy Prime Minister, the Labour leader Clement Attlee. The terse six words: 'The Navy will never abandon Malta', are among Churchill's greatest wartime instructions; and they were carried out.

This book is a tribute, not only to Churchill's concerns and achievements across the Maltese scene, but also to its defenders, and to its civilian citizens, each of whom was, by the very nature of the war, a combatant. The research is copious and impeccable; the result is a book that is both true history and high drama.

# *Acknowledgements*

My thanks are due first to Sir Martin Gilbert who has kindly written the foreword to this book. The footnotes within will make clear how much I owe to his remarkable scholarship. I also wish to thank Professor David French for his continued support and encouragment. For their help in providing information about the gift to Sir Winston Churchill of the Malta Shield, which still hangs in his study in Chartwell, I am indebted to my good friends Fr. George Aquilina, O.F.M., Mr Michael Refalo, and to Mr Antoine Attard who is the grandson of Antonio Attard who made the Shield. I am also grateful for the help given me by Mr Neil Walters, the National Trust House Manager at Chartwell, not least for making arrangements for me to include a new photograph of the Malta Shield.

Throughout this study numerous quotations have been made from official British government records now lodged at the National Archives at Kew. These documents and the map entitled 'Malta: Showing airfields in April 1942' (plate section no. 22), which is taken from the Official History, 'The Mediterranean and Middle East, Vol. III', are Crown Copyright and are reproduced with the permission of the Controller of HMSO and Queen's Printer for Scotland.

Numerous quotations have also been included from books, memoranda and letters written by Sir Winston Churchill, some of which form part of the Churchill Papers, which are now held at Churchill College Cambridge. The copyright holder is Winston S. Churchill, administered by Curtis Brown Ltd, and permission to quote from these documents is hereby gratefully acknowledged.

The copyright holders of the photographs included in this volume are as follows and the author is pleased to acknowledge their consent for their use in this volume. Imperial War Museum, London: picture numbers 4, 12-19, 21, 23, 25, 27, 29; Richard Ellis Ltd, Valletta, Malta: 2, 6, 8, 9, 11; Churchill Archive Centre, Broadwater Collection, © Winston S. Churchill, administered by Curtis Brown Ltd: 3, 5; Library of Congress: 1, 7, 20, 26, 32; *The Times*, Malta: 31, 34; National Trust: 30; author: 10, 33, 35-38.

Finally, I wish to acknowledge and pay tribute to the staff and volunteers at Chartwell for the high regard in which they hold the memory of Sir Winston Churchill and the warm welcome they give to the many visitors to Sir Winston and Lady Churchill's home.

The author records with great sadness the deaths of Michael A. Refalo in June 2011, and of Fr George Aquilina OFM in Spetember 2012.

# *Introduction*

Sir Winston Churchill visited the island of Malta on six occasions. He first sailed in to the Grand Harbour of Valletta on the evening of 2 October 1907 when at the age of 33 he was Under-Secretary of State at the Colonial Office. His last visit took place in January 1945 when, as Prime Minister, aged 70 and on his way to the Yalta Conference, he arrived at dawn on his special Skymaster aircraft. During the inter-war years, too, his eyes were on several occasions drawn to the island by the march of events. But it was during the Second World War that Malta most urgently claimed his attention. This was particularly the case when a few weeks after he had become Prime Minister in May 1940 Mussolini declared war on Britain and launched his bombers against Malta. From that moment as the war in the Mediterranean began with the crash of bombs and guns on the crowded civilian communities around the historic Grand Harbour Churchill was determined that every effort should be made to defend the island and its people and that Malta should play a full part in the defeat of the Axis powers. By the time he paid his last visit to Malta in the closing months of the war he was able to judge, despite severe human loss and physical damage, how well that part had been played. As he had written in 1942, 'Malta is a little island with a great history. The record of the Maltese people throughout that long history is a record of constancy and fortitude. It is with those qualities, matchlessly displayed, that they are now confronting the dark powers of the Axis.'[1]

In the following pages the author has drawn together out of the long life of one of the busiest men of the early twentieth century the story of Winston Churchill's involvement with the people of Malta. Because in his long career he held so many Cabinet positions and always devoted himself with great energy to the task at hand he was able to look at the affairs of the Maltese people from two points of view. At the Colonial Office in 1906 and again in 1921 his concern was for the civil administration of the island and its political, social and economic development. Although he was throughout his life a firm believer in the British Empire and Commonwealth he was also convinced that people would rather govern themselves poorly than suffer the 'better' rule of others. This was undoubtedly his view as early as 1906 and it was reflected in the undertaking during the Second World War that Malta would receive a new Constitution as soon as the war was won.

Malta's other role as a unique imperial fortress in the Mediterranean commanded his attention when on two widely separated occasions he held the office of First Lord of the Admiralty. It was this strategic role that inevitably dominated his thoughts and decisions when he became Prime Minister during the Second World War. Before 1940 it would not be correct to suggest that Malta engaged his attention for long. It was otherwise after he had become Prime Minister and Mussolini had made his cowardly decision, in what Churchill later denounced as 'the rush for the spoils', to begin the bombing of a crowded, inadequately defended island. From that moment the plight of the Maltese people and of its military garrison was never long out of his thoughts. Moreover, official Government records and his own voluminous personal files on Malta, from which many papers have been quoted in this study, make clear that many of the key decisions relating to the defence of the island and its development as a powerful offensive base can be attributed to him. Without his forceful insistence that Malta, despite the savage bombing which its people and defenders were compelled to endure, had a unique role to play in the fight against the Axis powers in the Mediterranean it is possible that the island might have been forced to surrender.

As far as possible the story presented here is unfolded in Sir Winston's own words, official and private, as they were spoken or written at the time. This is especially important for the war time years since Churchill's own memoirs of the Second World War were, as has often been observed, written under considerable constraint, not least because he was unable to reveal the secret intelligence which guided or determined many decisions. In the latter chapters of this study, therefore, the author has based his account largely upon official government records, particularly those of the Prime Minister's Office, the War Cabinet and of the Chiefs of Staff Committee. Throughout this study much use has been made of Churchill's own letters, memoranda and contemporary documents, extracts from many of which are printed in the official biography of Churchill and the associated Companion volumes. The author, like all recent writers about Churchill, owes an enormous debt to Sir Martin Gilbert for this magisterial work. No one can write about Churchill with any hope of accuracy without constant reference to these volumes. Several members of Churchill's family and many of his friends, colleagues and personal staff have also recorded their personal memories of him. Where appropriate, extracts from these works have been quoted to show how they remembered him. The attached bibliography indicates the main sources that have been consulted in this study.

The narrative set out in the following pages spans a period of half a century. During these years despite dangers and hardship the Maltese people moved steadily towards self-government, independence and, more recently, membership of the European Union. Although the last miles of this long journey have been travelled after Winston Churchill's death he would surely have applauded as Malta took her place in the community of nations. That the Maltese people should choose to remain within the Commonwealth and to carry upon their national flag the representation of the George Cross awarded to Malta by King George VI in April 1942 would undoubtedly have given him particular pleasure.

[1] Foreword to *The Epic of Malta* (Odhams Press, London, n.d., c. October 1942).

# CHAPTER I

# First Visit to Malta, October 1907

*He should see the hot stones of Malta, baking and glistening on a steel-blue Mediterranean.*

Winston Churchill, *My African Journey*, p. 1

In September 1896 Winston Churchill, a twenty-one year old subaltern in the 4th Hussars, passed within sight of Malta on his first voyage to India but his troopship, the SS *Britannia*, did not call at Valletta on that passage. While at sea, 'Between Malta and Alexandria', Churchill sent his mother, Lady Randolph Churchill who had given her son a new telescope, a detailed description of the voyage.

> The monotony of the voyage and of the view is relieved by frequent glimpses of land—at one time off Cape Finisterre—Cape St. Vincent or the lights of Lisbon—at another of Malta or the African coastline. We pass many ships & my telescope is in great demand and constant use. It is a very powerful glass and will be very valuable in India.[1]

It was not until eleven years later that, in the evening of 2 October 1907, he set foot on Malta for the first time. He was on his way to a private hunting expedition in East Africa, which subsequently became the subject of his book, *My African Journey*, but his visit to Malta was undertaken in his official capacity as Under-Secretary of State for the Colonies. He had been appointed to this, his first ministerial position, by Sir Henry Campbell-Bannerman in the Liberal administration which the latter had formed in December 1905. As Churchill crossed the Malta channel on the SS *Carola* between Syracuse and Valletta on that autumn evening he had every right to feel pleased with his achievements in the previous eighteen months.

The Liberal Party had been out of office since 1895 but when in December 1905 Arthur Balfour, the Conservative Prime Minister, resigned King Edward VII invited the Liberal leader, Sir Henry Campbell-Bannerman, to form a government. The new Prime Minister at once offered Churchill, who had moved from the Conservative to the Liberal benches in 1904, the Financial Secretaryship of the Treasury. However, Churchill sought and was, after some delay, granted the less important position of Under-Secretary of State for the Colonies. As he wrote to his friend, Lord Hugh Cecil, at the time, 'I had some difficulty in securing my wish as it involved considerable alteration in other minor offices.'[2] In his biography of his father Randolph Churchill has suggested that Churchill's preference for the Colonial Office was due, at least in part, to the fact that the new Secretary of State, Lord Elgin, was in the House of Lords. It would consequently fall to Churchill to represent the department in the House of Commons. As Financial Secretary, on the other hand, he would have served under the Chancellor of the Exchequer, Herbert Asquith.[3] In the general election that followed in January 1906 the Liberal Party won 377 seats and the Conservatives only 157. Churchill himself, standing for the first time as a Liberal, captured North-West Manchester from the Tories.

With this overwhelming majority the new administration could do much as it liked although, particularly in the field of foreign policy, it acknowledged some obligation to maintain a bi-partisan approach in the interests of continuity. Ministers, however, felt less bound to abide by this principle in matters of colonial policy where they believed that the Tories had eroded the spirit of justice and fair play. Churchill fully shared these views. As early as 1904 he had lectured Joseph Chamberlain, a former Colonial Secretary, that if the empire held together it would be 'because it is based upon the assent of free peoples, united with each other by noble and progressive principles; because it is animated by respect for right and justice . . . an agent of human progress and of international peace.'[4] Upon taking office Campbell-Bannerman's government had put principle into practice by securing the grant of self-government to the former Boer republics of Transvaal in 1906 and to the Orange River Colony in the following year. The detailed work on the transition of these territories from Crown Colony status to full self-government had fallen to Lord Elgin and to Churchill, his Under-Secretary. It would be difficult to imagine a greater contrast than between these two men whose only common characteristic seemed to be their membership of the Edwardian ruling class. The white-bearded, Oxford-educated, 9th Earl of Elgin was then 58 years old. His grandfather had been responsible for removing the 'Elgin marbles' from the Parthenon, and his father had achieved great distinction as Governor of Jamaica, Governor-General of Canada, and Viceroy of India. He in turn had been Viceroy, 1894-99. He was, however, unusually shy and rarely spoke in Cabinet and then only on his departmental responsibilities. When he was initially recommended to Queen Victoria for the Viceroyalty she observed that 'he is very shy and most painfully silent . . . He would not command the respect which is necessary in that office.'[5]

Churchill could never have been accused of being shy or silent. Although then only 31 years old, he had already gained wide publicity—self-publicity, many said—as a soldier, journalist, biographer, and rising politician. Reticence and modesty were not part of his personality and he attracted admiration and loathing in almost equal measure. Alexander MacCallum Scott, a fellow Liberal MP, had already in 1905 published the first of many biographies of Churchill and in this he observed that his subject was 'probably the best-hated man in England after Joe Chamberlain.'[6] This judgement owed much, but not everything, to Churchill's defection to the Liberal Party in 1904. MacCallum Scott added, however, that Churchill was 'confidently spoken of by his admirers as a future prime minister.' John Morley, at that time Secretary of State for India, and a close political ally, thought that, after Joseph Chamberlain, Churchill was:

> . . . the most alive politician I have ever come across—only he has not got Chamberlain's breadth nor his sincerity of conviction. But for ceaseless energy and concentration of mind within the political and party field, they are a good match. They make other folk seem like mere amateurs.[7]

Churchill had already met Elgin in India in January 1898. He was at that time a mere 2nd Lieutenant in the 4th Hussars, while Elgin was Viceroy, but he had stayed with the Elgins for several days at Government House in Calcutta. Churchill had recently been attached to the Malakand Field Force on the North West Frontier of India, and had been 'Mentioned in Despatches' for his involvement in the fighting there. These experiences became the subject of his first published book, *The Story of the Malakand Field Force*. Churchill, exhilarated by this experience, had hurried to Calcutta hoping to be attached in some capacity to the Tirah Expeditionary Force.[8] In this he was unsuccessful and he must have thought it most unlikely that eight years later he would be working with Elgin at the Colonial Office.

Inevitably, Elgin had some initial misgivings about his junior colleague but resolved to make the relationship work by taking Churchill fully into his confidence. The latter in his first ministerial appointment plunged into the work with tireless energy and enthusiasm, often writing memorable minutes on the many papers that crossed his desk. He and Elgin frequently disagreed. On one of Churchill's memoranda that concluded with a resounding, 'These are my views', Elgin quietly minuted, 'But not mine'.[9] Once each had taken the measure of the other a constructive, if never close, working relationship developed. Edward Marsh, Churchill's Private Secretary, later described this relationship as one of 'qualified esteem'.[10] After Elgin had left office in April 1908 he told his successor, Lord Crewe:

> When I accepted Churchill as my Under Secy I knew I had no easy task. I resolved to give him access to all business—but to keep control (& my temper). I think I may say I succeeded. Certainly we have had no quarrel during the 2½ years, on the contrary he has again and again thanked me for what he has learned and for our pleasant personal relations. I have taken a keen interest in his ability and in many ways attractive personality.[11]

This oddly paired couple despite their temperamental differences success-fully steered the Government's proposals for the new Transvaal constitu-tion through Parliament in the summer and autumn of 1906. As noted above, one of the political advantages of Churchill's position was that, since Elgin was in the House of Lords, it fell to him to present and argue the Government's plans in the Commons. However, even he could hardly have expected to present the Cabinet's Transvaal proposals at the end of July 1906. He later told Violet Bonham-Carter, Asquith's brilliant daugh-ter and a life-long friend, 'how astonished and overjoyed he had been when he was sent for by the Prime Minister and asked, quite unexpect-edly and at a fortnight's notice, to undertake it.'[12] The speech Churchill made in the House of Commons on 31 July, meticulously prepared, as were all his speeches then and later, was warmly received at least on the Liberal benches. His concluding, but fruitless, appeal to the Opposition that 'we can only make it the gift of a party; they can make it the gift of England', was an early example of Churchill's gift for finding the apt and long-remembered phrase.[13] Shortly before he left London in October 1907 he received a letter from the Prime Minister. Referring to Churchill's con-tribution to the new constitutions in South Africa, Campbell-Bannerman wrote 'a large part of the credit of it must be always attributed to you.'[14]

At the end of the Parliamentary session in the summer of 1907 Elgin wel-comed Churchill's plans to spend the autumn months on a hunting expedi-tion in East Africa since this would give him the opportunity to study various problems at first hand. Nevertheless, Elgin had not expected Churchill to have time to send back to London so many letters and memoranda and he later wondered how 'a purely sporting and private expedition . . . drifted into so essentially an official progress.'[15] After leaving London Churchill had attended the French army manoeuvres and then, accompanied by his cousin, the Duke of Marlborough, had spent some time hunting on Baron de Forest's estates in Moravia. They had then parted and Churchill made his way south to Syracuse where he boarded the SS *Carola*. He landed at Valletta on the evening of 2 October. There he was joined by Edward Marsh whom two years earlier he had appointed as his Private Secretary. Marsh later recounted in his memoirs that when Churchill had offered him the position he had some misgivings which he expressed to Lady Lytton. She, as Pamela Plowden, had once been unofficially engaged to Churchill and after listening to Marsh she told him: 'The first time you meet Winston you see all his faults, and the rest of your life you spend in discovering his virtues.'[16]

Two years older than Churchill, Edward Marsh was the great-grand-son of Spencer Perceval, the only British Prime Minister to have been assassinated, and his upbringing and education were financed by what he called the 'murder money' that Parliament had voted after Perceval's death for the benefit of his children and descendants. Following a fine aca-demic career at Cambridge 'Eddie' Marsh entered the Colonial Office and was a First Class Clerk in charge of the Africa Department before being appointed as Churchill's Private Secretary. During the following thirty years until his retirement in 1937, Sir Edward Marsh, as he later became, served as Private Secretary whenever Churchill held office. He became a close friend of Churchill's family and was godfather to Churchill's second daughter, Sarah. For his part Churchill quickly formed a strong attachment to Eddie Marsh and in August 1908 wrote to him that 'Few people have been so lucky as me to find in the dull and grimy recesses of the Colonial Office a friend who I shall cherish and hold to all my life.'[17]

Upon his arrival at Valletta Churchill was, as he wrote to his younger brother, Jack, 'installed in much state in this wonderful old Palace of the Grand Master of the Knights of Malta'.[18] During a characteristically busy week he inspected the dockyard, the military positions, the schools and hospitals, but, as he wrote to Lord Elgin before leaving Malta, the '*pièce de résistance*' of his week there was his meeting with the elected Members of the Council of Government on 4 October.[19] Churchill was fully aware that he was stepping into a political and constitutional hornets' nest when he undertook this visit. The full story of this complex situation properly belongs to Maltese constitutional and political history. Suffice here to say that in 1903 the Malta Constitution of 1887 was revoked after a long dispute about the degree of autonomy to be granted to the elected Maltese Members of the Council of Government in respect of purely local matters. Imperialists in London, such as Joseph Chamberlain, were apt to quote in defence of their position a saying attributed to the Duke of Wellington that 'you might as well give a constitution to a man-of-war as give it to Malta.'[20] The naval importance of Malta at that time is more fully explored in the next chapter.

On the day after Churchill's arrival in Valletta the *Daily Malta Chronicle* printed a lengthy address by Augusto Bartolo, the son of the newspaper's Anglophile editor, arguing for greater Maltese control of local affairs. 'Malta Lacks a Constitution', he insisted. Shrewdly he also drew attention to the disparity between the British Government's treatment of Malta and the Boer republics.

Can anyone believe that that same England which . . . has given an autonomous government to conquered South Africa, should obstinately refuse to grant the management of its domestic affairs to our Malta . . . which entered the British Empire of its own free will, relying on the honour and good faith of the British Nation?[21]

Churchill hardly needed this reminder of his part in securing the grant of self-government to Transvaal and the Orange River Colony. He might also have recalled that in his speech to the House of Commons on 31 July 1906 he had said, 'No one can contend that it is right to grant the forms of free institutions, and yet to preserve by some device the means of control.'[22] Many Maltese political leaders would no doubt have argued that this was an accurate description of the situation in Malta.

Churchill met the elected Members and representatives of the nobility, the Malta Bar and the Chamber of Commerce at the Palace on the morning of Friday 4 October. Most of the Members offered their views and proposals, after listening to which Churchill made a lengthy reply that was printed in the local press. He began by saying that he was there to listen, and could not give any promises or pledges. He then made reference to the arrangements that had been made after the withdrawal of the Constitution in 1903. He told his listeners: 'I do not feel any astonishment that you do not like them; indeed, if I were in your place, I should not like them, but Lord Elgin must be confronted with clear evidence that a new situation has arisen before he can be induced to reconsider the present state of affairs.' He welcomed the earlier decision of the elected Members to resume their seats in the Council of Government and continued: 'I shall be glad if it be possible to make some arrangements which would be more in accordance with your wishes and secure to you a more effective voice in purely local affairs.' He concluded by declaring that 'the door is not closed on the constitutional question.'[23]

Later the same day, while the details and the apparently cordial atmosphere of the meeting were still fresh in his mind, Churchill wrote a lengthy letter to Elgin. After describing his activities, he wrote:

> I am bound to say that their complaint—viz that they were never conquered by England, but that now we spend their money without allowing the Maltese any sort of control—is a vy real & to me at least a vy painful one. . . . My line was that 'the last word has not been spoken' & that it rested with them by frank cooperation with the Government to establish a case for the reconsideration of the question.[24]

Several days later Churchill and his party boarded the cruiser, HMS *Venus*, which the Admiralty had put at his disposal, and sailed for Cyprus. He then prepared a longer memorandum setting out the proposals he had promised Lord Elgin and this was duly despatched to the Colonial Office.

In many of the numerous biographies of Churchill the reaction of the Colonial Office officials to this memorandum has attracted much attention, its contents almost none. Sir Francis Hopwood, the Permanent Under-Secretary, wrote to Churchill that 'I am nursing up the Malta Memorandum until your return, as it must be dealt with with considerable circumspection.'[25] A month later, however, Hopwood, having received from Africa a steady stream of letters and memoranda, sent a letter to Lord Elgin which was highly critical of Churchill.[26] 'He is most tiresome to deal with & will I fear give trouble—as his father [Lord Randolph Churchill] did—in any position to which he may be called. The restless energy, uncontrollable desire for notoriety & the lack of moral perception make him an anxiety indeed.' He went on to write:

Churchill should have reserved his points until he returned home—anybody else would have done so both out of caution or at the dictation of personal convenience—Marsh gives a vivid description of 14 hours work in one day upon these memoranda in the heat & discomfort of the Red Sea.

Elgin, too, was critical of the numerous memoranda that Churchill sent home, writing to Lord Crewe, 'I believe most of them hopelessly to be unpracticable at least as they stand.'[27]

Churchill's Malta memorandum, carrying the pencilled date 'January 1908', is to be found in the Colonial Office files at the National Archives at Kew.[28] Churchill began by referring to his discussions in Valletta. He noted that the views of the elected Members, often given little weight by the Governor's official staff, had been 'quite unexpectedly endorsed' by the representatives of the old Maltese nobility, the Bar, and the Chamber of Commerce whom he had also met. These special interest groups expressed in even stronger terms than the elected Members did their indignation at the constitutional position. They were, they declared, 'strangers in their own island'. Churchill rejected the 'fortress Malta' argument employed by Chamberlain, characterising this as an 'extremely inadequate argument upon which to dismiss the claims to any measure of self-government even in respect of their own purely local affairs'. He felt unable to recommend a return to the 1887 Constitution, but went on to suggest a revision to the proceedings of the Council designed to put the Maltese elected Members in a majority whenever the issue in question was a purely local Maltese matter. It would be for the Governor to determine whether an issue for consideration was local or imperial, and Churchill recognised that this might lead to controversy. Nevertheless, he expressed the hope that goodwill on both sides would prevail, and reinforced this by proposing that in every case where the Governor ruled that a question was an imperial one a report should be made to London to ascertain the views of the Secretary of State. Clearly, this proposal did not fully square the circle but Churchill argued that it was worth a trial; it would, he felt, 'mitigate a very real grievance and actual injustice'.

Churchill's scheme reflected a genuine sympathy for the Maltese position with regard to local issues, without conceding overall London control on matters of imperial concern. However, as he recognised, its practicability required goodwill on all sides, and he may have been encouraged by his visit to believe that this might be forthcoming. In urging co-operation he had reminded the elected Members that 'If everybody in England was to strain his privileges and rights to the utmost letter of the law, the British Constitution would become unworkable in a week.'

Churchill's absence in East Africa which kept him out of England until mid-January 1908 meant that formal consideration of the proposals set

7

out in his memorandum did not begin until his return. By then, however, political changes were imminent and on 10 April Churchill left the Colonial Office to take up his first Cabinet appointment as President of the Board of Trade. At the same time the Earl of Crewe succeeded Elgin as Colonial Secretary. With Churchill's departure from the Colonial Office the impetus for any change in Malta's governance slowly evaporated. A full two years later, after numerous memoranda and minutes, all recorded in the Colonial Office files, the only change was an amendment to the Constitution providing for two of the Maltese Members of the Council of Government to be appointed to the Governor's Executive Council. The elected Members found this unsatisfactory and resigned their seats.

Long before then, as we have seen, Churchill had left the Colonial Office. It was not until 17 January 1908 that he returned to London from his African expedition having already been made aware that the Prime Minister's health was failing and that his resignation could not be long delayed. In the event Campbell-Bannerman resigned on 3 April and several days later Asquith succeeded him. On 8 April he offered Churchill the position of the Presidency of the Board of Trade, with a seat in the Cabinet, and Churchill, after some initial hesitation, accepted. It was this promotion that, for the time being, brought to an end his direct involvement with the affairs of Malta.

There remains, however, an intriguing possibility that deserves attention. When Asquith, even before Campbell-Bannerman's resignation, was beginning to think about appointments in his new administration he had a meeting with Churchill on 12 March 1908. Two days later Churchill sent him a letter with his thoughts on the three possible appointments that they had discussed, viz. the Colonial Office, the Admiralty and the Local Government Board. In his letter Churchill made quite clear his aversion to the Local Government Board and the difficulty he felt about considering the Admiralty caused by the fact that his uncle, Lord Tweedmouth, was the incumbent First Lord. With regard to his present appointment he wrote:

I *know* the Colonial Office. It is a post of immense importance, but largely disconnected detail: & I have special experience of several kinds which helps. During the last two years practically all the constructive action & all the Parliamentary exposition has been mine. I have many threads in hand and many plans in movement.[29]

He went on to add that, compared with a move to the Local Government Board, 'I would rather continue to serve under Lord Elgin at the Colonial Office without a seat in the Cabinet'. He, nevertheless, concluded by saying that he would serve 'where you wish' and on 10 April accepted Asquith's offer of the Presidency of the Board of Trade.

One is inevitably left to wonder what the effect on Malta's constitutional development might have been had Churchill remained at the

Colonial Office, especially had he, rather than Lord Crewe, succeeded Lord Elgin as Secretary of State. Despite the misgivings of some officials in London and Malta, it seems likely that he could have persuaded Asquith and the Cabinet that the proposals set out in his memorandum should be given a trial. Moreover, his evident sympathy for Maltese grievances might well have ensured that his overall supervision of the Governor's discretion to regard an issue as an imperial one was exercised in such a manner as to meet the Maltese demand for control over purely local matters. Evidence of Churchill's views about British colonial rule can be found in many of the Colonial Office papers. In a letter to the King describing the new Transvaal constitution he wrote: 'Any intelligent community will much rather govern itself ill, than be well governed by some other community.'[30] At the end of his thoughtful study of Churchill's early years at the Colonial Office Ronald Hyam offered this assessment of Churchill:

> He had a generous and sensitive, if highly paternalistic, sympathy for subject peoples, and a determination to see that justice was done to humble individuals throughout the empire. He had this sympathy to a degree which was rare among British administrators, and even politicians, at this time.[31]

It is more difficult to judge how the elected Members might have responded to Churchill's proposal had it been implemented. But it seems at least possible that the mutual goodwill, which appears to have been created during the Valletta discussions, might have persuaded them that the proposed new voting procedure was a meaningful step forward and well worth a trial. What is, nevertheless, clear is that, after Churchill's promotion to the Board of Trade in April 1908, lethargy replaced 'tireless energy' in the corridors of the Colonial Office. Nothing, therefore, came of Churchill's initiative and by 1911 the constitutional impasse in Malta was as firmly established as it was before his visit to the island.

This first experience of Malta and his meetings and discussions with leading men in the island thus gave Churchill a direct view of the realities and complexities of British colonial rule in the early years of the twentieth century. Although he expressed no doubts about the need to retain overall British control for imperial and military reasons he saw no justification for denying the Maltese people an acceptable constitution and the right to decide their own local affairs. His inclination, not then widely shared in the Colonial Office, was to broaden the sphere in which the Maltese might govern themselves through leaders of their own choice. At this time, however, this basic inclination did not prevail. Nevertheless, the fact that Churchill's first direct experience of Maltese affairs was related to civil and political issues rather than to military considerations gave him an early insight into Maltese political conditions and aspirations. This would influence the future decisions he took when he held positions related to imperial defence. Such a perspective was required when, five years later, he next visited the island.

## Notes

[1] Randolph S. Churchill, *Winston S. Churchill: Companion Volume I, Part 2 1896-1900* (Heinemann, London, 1967), WSC to Lady Randolph Churchill, 18 September 1896, p. 679.

[2] Randolph S. Churchill, *Winston S. Churchill: Volume II, Young Statesman 1901-1914* (Heinemann, London, 1967), pp. 106-7. [Note: The volumes of the official biography of Winston Churchill, of which the first two were written by his son, Randolph, and the other six by Martin Gilbert, are henceforward referred to as *Churchill.* The accompanying Companion volumes of related documents are referred to as *Companion* with the relevant volume and part number.]

[3] *Churchill, Vol. II*, pp. 106-7.

[4] R. Hyam, *Elgin and Churchill at the Colonial Office* (Macmillan, London, 1968), p. 50, footnote 3.

[5] Ibid., pp. 17-18.

[6] A. MacCallum Scott, *Winston Spencer Churchill* (Methuen, London, 1905), p. 241.

[7] Quoted in Hyam, *Elgin*, p. 502.

[8] *Churchill, Vol. I* , p. 368.

[9] Hyam, *Elgin*, p. 494.

[10] C. Hassall, *Edward Marsh: Patron of the Arts* (Longmans, London, 1959), p. 122.

[11] *Companion, Vol. II, Part 2*, Elgin to Crewe, [?] May 1908, p. 797.

[12] V. Bonham-Carter, *Winston Churchill As I Knew Him* (Eyre & Spottiswoode and Collins, London, 1965), p. 137.

[13] D. Cannadine (ed.), *The Speeches of Winston Churchill* (Penguin Books, London, 1990), p. 30.

[14] *Companion, Vol. II, Part 1,* Campbell-Bannerman to WSC, 9 September 1907, p. 667.

[15] *Companion, Vol. II, Part 2*, Elgin to Crewe, [?] May 1908, p. 797.

[16] *Churchill, Vol. II*, p. 111.

[17] *Companion, Vol. II, Part 2*, WSC to Marsh, 20 August 1908, p. 836.

[18] *Companion, Vol. II, Part 2*, WSC to Jack Churchill, 3 October 1907, p. 684.

[19] *Companion, Vol. II, Part 2*, WSC to Elgin, 4 October 1907, pp. 684-7.

[20] Quoted in H. Frendo, *Party Politics in a Fortress Colony: The Maltese Experience* (Midsea Publications, Valletta, 1991), p. 5.

[21] *Daily Malta Chronicle*, 3 October 1907.

[22] Cannadine, *Speeches*, p. 30.

[23] *Daily Malta Chronicle*, 7 October 1907.

[24] *Companion, Vol. II, Part 2,* WSC to Elgin, 4 October 1907, p. 686.

[25] *Companion, Vol. II, Part 2*, Hopwood to WSC, 15 November 1907, p. 698.

[26] *Churchill, Vol. II*, Hopwood to Elgin, 27 December 1907, p. 228.

[27] *Companion, Vol. II, Part 2*, Elgin to Crewe, [?] May 1908, p. 797.

[28] NA CO 158/360/3351, WSC to Elgin, January 1908.

[29] *Companion, Vol. II, Part 2*, WSC to Asquith, 14 March 1908, pp. 754-6.

[30] *Companion, Vol. II, Part 1,* WSC to King Edward VII, 15 August 1906, p. 559.

[31] Hyam, *Elgin*, p. 503

## CHAPTER II

# *The Malta Conference, May 1912, and Its Consequences*

*We cannot possibly hold the Mediterranean or guarantee any of our interests there until we have obtained a decision in the North Sea.*

Churchill letter to Lord Haldane, 6 May 1912

Winston Churchill's second arrival at Valletta was markedly different from the first. In 1907 he had disembarked late at night from the Syracuse ferry. Five years later in the morning light of Wednesday 29 May 1912 he sailed into the Grand Harbour as First Lord of the Admiralty standing on the bridge of the gleaming 3,500-ton Admiralty yacht, HMS *Enchantress*. Alongside him stood, among others, the Prime Minister, Herbert Asquith, and his daughter, Violet. In her book, *Winston Churchill As I Knew Him*, Violet Bonham-Carter has described being summoned on deck by Churchill as the *Enchantress* approached Malta.

> The Island we were approaching looked like one vast fortress, a great heap of battlemented stone built between sky and sea. We sailed into the most wonderful harbour I could have imagined or dreamt of. —'harbour of harbours'—strongholds and fortresses piled up on every side, Men of War hoisting their colours with bugle calls from every deck. Grandees of all sorts began to arrive in pinnaces—all the Admirals in the first, followed by their Flag-Lieutenants, then Ian Hamilton with a military contingent and finally Lord Kitchener looking quite splendid, treble life-size—but alas! dressed as a civilian in a Homburg hat.[1]

Much had happened in Churchill's official and private life since his previous visit to Malta but, by his own account, by far the most important event was his marriage on 12 September 1908 to Clementine Hozier. Her father, Sir Henry Hozier, who had died a year earlier, had been Secretary of Lloyds and in that capacity was well known to the commercial and shipping community in Malta. As a result Mr. Giovanni Messina, President of the Malta Chamber of Commerce, wrote to Churchill on 31 August 1908:

As a token of the Chamber's respectful homage and hearty greet-
ings, I beg, on my behalf and that of my colleagues, you would
condescend to present for its acceptance to Miss Clementine Hozier a
reproduction of a Gozo sailing boat . . . wishing you and Miss Hozier
a happy and prosperous life.[2]

Clementine stood beside her husband as *Enchantress* steamed into the
Grand Harbour on that May morning.

In the years since joining the Cabinet as President of the Board of
Trade Churchill had become Home Secretary in February 1910, and
then, in October 1911, had been appointed by Asquith as First Lord of
the Admiralty exchanging positions with Reginald McKenna. In the first
volume of *The World Crisis*, his subsequent history of the First World War,
Churchill described his visit to Asquith's Scottish residence, and his joy
at being offered the Admiralty.

The fading light of evening disclosed in the far distance the silhou-
ettes of two battleships slowly steaming out of the Firth of Forth.
They seemed invested with a new significance to me.

'I was to endeavour' he added, 'to discharge this responsibility for the
four most memorable years of my life.'[3] His joy was not shared by the
many supporters of the Navy. This was due in large part to his vehement support of Lloyd George in 1909 when the latter, as Chancellor, had
opposed McKenna's plans to build six new dreadnought battleships. To
support McKenna Admiral Sir John Fisher, the First Sea Lord, orchestrated
a campaign in the press with the slogan, 'We want eight, we won't wait!'
Churchill himself attracted widespread criticism. Lord Knollys, the King's
Secretary, wrote to Lord Esher on 10 February 1909:

What are Winston's reasons for acting as he does in this matter? Of
course it cannot be from conviction or principle. The very idea of his
having either is enough to make anyone laugh.[4]

A fierce struggle within the Cabinet ensued before agreement was reached
that only four would be laid down in 1909-10 but with the understanding
that four more might be ordered later if circumstances warranted. The
subsequent news that both Italy and Austria had announced their intention to build new dreadnought battleships then triggered the construction of the additional four British ships. As Churchill later wrote: 'The
Admiralty had demanded six ships: the economists offered four: and we
finally compromised on eight.'[5]

Since 1909, however, and particularly after the Agadir crisis in the
summer of 1911 had brought Britain and Germany to the brink of war,

Churchill had become convinced of the need for a powerful modern Navy. Moreover, during the crisis a conference summoned on 23 August by Asquith to consider what actions would be necessary should war with Germany break out revealed an alarming discrepancy between the war plans of the War Office and those, such as they were, of the Admiralty. It was these considerations that persuaded Asquith that a change at the Admiralty was essential and that Churchill should replace McKenna as First Lord. As Geoffrey Best has written: 'There was indeed a very great deal to do, and Churchill had been put there to do it. The largest navy in the world was no longer quite the best, and the world had become a riskier place.'[6] It was, consequently, matters of imperial defence that brought Churchill to Valletta on 29 May 1912.

Violet Bonham-Carter in the book quoted above has left a vivid impression of the social aspects of this high-level visit. There were numerous receptions, official visits, inspections, and, in the evenings, banquets and dances. On Friday 1 June she, together with her father, Churchill, and all the Admirals embarked on the battleship HMS *Cornwallis* to witness firing at sea. She recounted how, after a prolonged period of shooting at a towed target four miles away:

> Winston was itching with impatience to know how many 'hits' had been scored. I shall never forget his face when Admiral Poe broke to him that there had been—*none!*—'Not *one*? *All* misses? How can you explain it?'—The Admiral's reply did not have a soothing effect: 'Well—you see, First Lord, the shells seem to have either fallen *just* short of the target or else gone just a *little* beyond it.' I will not describe what followed . . .[7]

However, the main purpose of the visit was to confer with Field Marshal Lord Kitchener, at that time Commander-in-Chief and Agent-General in Egypt, about Mediterranean security. Kitchener arrived at Valletta from Alexandria an hour before Churchill on the cruiser HMS *Hampshire*. Tragically, it was on the same cruiser that he was to lose his life four years later when it struck a mine as it left Scapa Flow while taking him on a mission to Russia.

By May 1912 a complex and threatening naval situation had developed.[8] Not long after Churchill had moved to the Admiralty Anglo-German naval rivalry, which was initiated in 1898 when Germany had decided to build a battle fleet, was intensified by advance notification of the proposed German Naval Law of 1912. This provided for further expansion of the German battle fleet. The threat posed to Britain by this growing modern fleet was underlined, firstly, by a proposed increase in German naval personnel that would allow a large proportion of these capital ships to be kept in full commission, and secondly, by plans to widen the Kiel Canal to allow more rapid concentration of the High Seas Fleet in the North Sea.

Diplomatic attempts to seek a *rapprochement* with Germany having failed, Churchill proposed to meet this threat in two ways. Firstly, when presenting the 1912 Naval Estimates to the House of Commons on 18 March he announced the Government's intention to maintain a superiority of 60% in dreadnought battleships over the German fleet as then planned and to lay down two new keels for every additional ship built by Germany. Secondly, however, the growing concern about a surprise attack across the North Sea made it imperative, in Churchill's view, that Britain's capital ships and, equally importantly, its trained officers and ratings be concentrated in Home waters. This meant the recall of the Atlantic Fleet based at Gibraltar and two of the six battleships hitherto based at Malta. The other four would be moved to Gibraltar to form the Fourth Battle Squadron. From there they could, in theory, operate in either sea. However, on 6 May Churchill made clear in a letter to Lord Haldane, who was then Secretary of State for War, his central argument for the new distribution of the fleet.

> We cannot possibly hold the Mediterranean or guarantee any of our interests there until we have obtained a decision in the North Sea. The War-plans for the last 5 years have provided for the evacuation of the Meditern as the first step consequent on a war with Germany, & all we are doing is to make peace dispositions wh approximate to war necessities. It would be vy foolish to lose England in safeguarding Egypt.

He went on to write that if another fleet of dreadnought battleships could be provided for the Mediterranean 'the attitude of the Adm'y will be that of a cat to a nice fresh dish of cream.' He did not, however, regard this as 'practical politics'.[9]

Churchill's plan to concentrate against the escalating North Sea danger was only a continuation of a policy initiated by the Admiralty in the early years of the century when the German naval challenge had first arisen. This had resulted in the withdrawal of battleships from the China and American stations and in the steady reduction of the battleship force at Malta from fourteen to six. However, the Admiralty's removal of these remaining battleships from Malta attracted fierce criticism in Parliament and the press. Such a withdrawal, it was argued, thereby increased the risks to British interests in the Mediterranean and, in particular, to the security of Egypt and of the direct route to India and the Far East. Moreover, in this sea, too, dangers were escalating since Italy and Austria, who were formally allied to Germany in the Triple Alliance, had both, as noted above, begun the construction of modern dreadnought battleships. A growing outcry that the Mediterranean was 'being abandoned' reflected strong emotional elements as well as strategic judgements. Sir Julian Corbett, the official British naval historian of the Great War, later wrote that:

It had become a canon of British policy—consecrated by repeated experience—that our Mediterranean Fleet was the measure of our influence in continental affairs, and the feeling was only increased since the road to India lay that way, and Egypt and Cyprus had become limbs of the Empire.[10]

Behind the scenes Lord Esher, an influential member of the Committee of Imperial Defence (CID), had, as early as January 1912, written to Asquith urging the maintenance of naval strength in the Mediterranean. On 30 May he had also written in the same vein to King George V who, as a young naval officer, had served with the Mediterranean Fleet at Malta during the 1880s. Esher argued that Churchill's statement had been 'dust in the eyes of the public' since the Fourth Battle Squadron to be based at Gibraltar would be needed in the North Sea and could provide no security in the Mediterranean.[11] In a subsequent memorandum of 17 June he again objected that the new fleet distribution would impair the security of Malta and Gibraltar and concluded:

What is in dispute is whether the Naval power of Great Britain should not provide both (a) for reasonable security in the North Sea, and (b) for the maintenance of those interests in the Mediterranean, inclusive of the safety of Malta.[12]

A possible escape from the counter-claims of the North Sea and the Mediterranean seemed to be offered by an arrangement with France. The French Navy, although large and highly professional, was outdated. Its first dreadnought battleship was not laid down until 1910 and it could not hope to match the German High Seas Fleet. On the other hand, France had a vital interest in keeping open the sea passage between her possessions in North Africa and southern France, and the French fleet, if concentrated in the Mediterranean, would match any potential Austro-Italian combination. These considerations suggested that an arrangement under which the Royal Navy concentrated in the North Sea and the French navy in the Mediterranean would be mutually beneficial. The possibility of such an understanding, however, ran into the objection, quite apart from the prevailing public attitude towards 'abandoning the Mediterranean', that many Ministers, and Churchill himself, were strongly opposed to any steps that might appear to turn the *Entente Cordiale* into a formal alliance with France.[13]

This necessarily condensed account of a complex and steadily worsening naval situation provides the background to the Malta Conference with Kitchener in May 1912. It had initially been intended to make this a formal meeting of the CID but Asquith had decided that this would attract too much attention and the talks were, therefore, described as informal. It was entirely appropriate that these talks should take place at Malta. In the previous century since Malta had become a British colony many millions of pounds had been spent adding to the defensive works inherited from the Knights of St. John. As a result Malta had become the Royal Navy's principal base outside the UK, the home port of the Mediterranean Fleet, and the guardian of the shortest route to India and the Far East. The Conference met to consider the whole question of Mediterranean security and not just the defence of Malta, but these two matters could not be considered in isolation. As was to be shown more clearly in the Second World War, although mere possession of Malta could not guarantee the control of the Mediterranean, such control was not possible without the active participation of forces operating from the island. Its occupation by a hostile power would inevitably close the Mediterranean to British traffic and make the defence of Egypt more hazardous. Consequently, any plans to retain British use of the Mediterranean, or to deny it to any other power, must make provision for the security of Malta.

The defence problem facing the British authorities in Malta was determined by geography since the island lies in the narrows of the central Mediterranean between Tunisia and Sicily. The nearest British territory was over 1,000 miles away at Gibraltar whereas Sicily is only 60 miles distant. Italy was formally allied with Germany in the Triple Alliance and her acquisition of Tripolitania and Cyrenaica at the end of her war with Turkey later in 1912 further added to Malta's isolation. The immediate responsibility for the defence of Malta lay with the War Office, and the Governor was always a senior military figure. As C-in-C of the garrison he came under the orders of the War Office, although as representative of the Crown he reported to the Colonial Office. The War Office provided a garrison of regular infantry supported, in the case of Malta, by a local militia unit, the King's Own Malta Regiment (KOMR), and also coastal and field artillery. Over the years since Malta had become a British colony and a major naval base frequent inspections and reports had led to the construction of an elaborate defensive system. Coastal guns of increasing size, calibre and range had been installed at key points around the coast.

However, in the days before the emergence of air power, the ultimate responsibility for the defence of Britain's overseas possessions lay with the Admiralty. But in accepting this responsibility the Admiralty made clear that:

> [The Admiralty] claim the absolute power of disposing their forces in the manner they consider the most certain to secure success, and object to limit the action of any part of them to the immediate

neighbourhood of places they consider may be more effectively protected by operations at a distance.[14]

What this meant was that, should Malta be attacked, the Admiralty would assemble a sufficiently powerful force to relieve the island. Until then the island must depend on its local forces. This Admiralty plan to relieve Malta if attacked was not appreciated by the press and the public. They took the view that Malta's continued security required a strong battleship force at Malta itself rather than 1,000 miles away at Gibraltar. Only this, it was argued, would deter any hostile attack. The harsh reality that, far from acting as a deterrent, such a force, tied up in harbour, might prove to be a tempting target for a surprise attack was demonstrated in the Second World War at Oran, Taranto, and Pearl Harbor. As we shall see later, when Malta appeared threatened by Italian air attack at the time of the Abyssinian crisis in 1935 the Mediterranean Fleet was prudently removed to Alexandria.

The War Office and Admiralty prepared detailed papers and with these before them Asquith, Churchill and Kitchener debated the problem of Mediterranean security on board HMS *Enchantress* moored in the Grand Harbour. Among the papers presented by the War Office was an analysis that concluded that the proposed withdrawal of the Malta battle squadron would enable the Italian army to land a force of 35,000 troops. To counter an invasion on this scale would require the addition of as many as eight battalions to the Malta garrison. Only adequate naval defences would avoid this necessity.[15] Inevitably, therefore, Kitchener protested strongly about the proposed removal of the battleship squadron and the consequent dangers to British Mediterranean interests and Churchill, under pressure from the Prime Minister, was forced to make some concessions. He now proposed to replace the six withdrawn battleships with two, or preferably three, more powerful dreadnought battle-cruisers to be based at Malta, supported by cruisers, torpedo craft and submarines. This appeared to meet the War Office's suggestion that local naval defences be strengthened if a major increase in the size of the garrison were to be avoided. In addition Churchill stated that the Fourth Battle Squadron at Gibraltar would cruise as much as possible in the Mediterranean. However, and this was Churchill's main requirement, it 'will be available for service elsewhere if seriously required in peace, or in case of war.'[16]

In these proposals can be detected the influence of Admiral of the Fleet Lord Fisher. Although he had retired in January 1910 from the position of First Sea Lord he had subsequently established an influential, if at times stormy, relationship with Churchill. Moreover, he had come aboard *Enchantress* at Naples for discussions with Churchill and the Prime Minister a few days before the Admiralty yacht steamed on to

Malta. Fisher had for some years been pressing the advantages of fast heavily armed battle-cruisers as well as of destroyers and submarines. The latter were referred to in some quarters as 'Fisher's toys'[17]. Since the provision of such units to replace the departed battleships formed the key element of the provisional agreement with Kitchener one must assume that this was the outcome of Fisher's discussions with Churchill in the bay of Naples.

Asquith and Churchill left Malta on *Enchantress* on 1 June and Kitchener returned to Egypt on the following day. Despite the brief duration of this visit Churchill had found time to visit the dockyard and before he left he issued a statement praising the efficiency of the yard and promising that the navy had every intention of making full use of its facilities and that all necessary steps would be taken to ensure its security.[18] After returning to England on 10 June 1912 Churchill circulated to the CID a lengthy analysis of the whole Mediterranean security question together with a copy of the draft agreement with Kitchener.[19] The main arguments of these papers were, firstly, Churchill's insistence that North Sea superiority was paramount. Secondly, however, he made the point that 'the influence and authority of the Mediterranean Fleet is going to cease, not because of the withdrawal of the Malta battleships, but because of the completion of the Austrian and Italian Dreadnoughts.' The only immediate solution to the problem of Mediterranean security was to adopt the role of the weaker power, that is, defence by torpedo. Malta, consequently, would be strongly reinforced with destroyers and submarines. In Churchill's view, 'if Malta and the Malta Channel obtain the reputation of being a nest of submarines and torpedo craft, and is effectually so defended, it would not be worth the while of Austria or Italy to risk either battleships or transports in an attempt to capture it by a regular attack.'

An arrangement with the French, allowing the concentration of the French fleet in the Mediterranean, offered the only escape from this strategic dilemma, and Churchill urged that 'a definite naval arrangement should be made with France without delay', albeit one that 'would only come into force if the two powers were at any time allies in a war.' He then proposed that this strengthened French Mediterranean force be supported by the immediate transfer to Malta of two dreadnought battle-cruisers as agreed with Kitchener. Perhaps recognising the strength of the Mediterranean lobby, Churchill circulated a supplementary memorandum on 22 June. In this paper he pointed out that, although nothing could be done in the following four years to meet a threat from an Austro-Italian battle fleet, the Admiralty could by 1916, albeit at a cost of an additional £15-20 million, provide a Mediterranean force of eight battleships which he thought would be sufficient to match any Austro-Italian threat.[20] Lord Esher, however, continued his fierce opposition to the 'abandonment of the Mediterranean', noting in his diary on 6 June 1912 after a conversation with the King, 'We are making a tremendous fight for sea command at all times in the Middle Sea and we have got to win.' [21]

The whole problem was debated at a day-long meeting of the CID on 4 July 1912.[22] Among those attending were Admiral Lord Fisher and the Chief of the Imperial General Staff, General Sir John French. Churchill opened the discussion by summarising all the arguments described above, maintaining that the retention of the six pre-dreadnought battleships in the Mediterranean would be 'merely a useless and expensive symbol of power'. To this Esher and McKenna, supported by Harcourt, the Colonial Secretary, pressed their opposing arguments. Sir John French summarised the findings of the War Office studies noted earlier and concluded that the loss of naval control of the Mediterranean would require a radical re-organisation of military defences at Malta and in Egypt. Admiral Fisher disagreed. He thought that adequate security was provided by the Fourth Battle Squadron at Gibraltar and that a force of destroyers and submarines at Malta would mean that 'no battleship could move in the Mediterranean'. Several other references were made to the safety of Malta. When Churchill insisted that 'it was beyond our power to maintain a separate war against Austria and Italy in the Mediterranean at the same time as against Germany', Harcourt replied that 'he supposed that in these circumstances the loss of Malta was probable.' Churchill responded by saying that the island had provisions that would last for at least four months but questioned whether Italy would consider it worth risking such a hazardous operation as the invasion of the island.

Later in the afternoon discussion Sir Edward Grey, the Foreign Secretary, prompted perhaps by a lunch time note from Lord Esher, made a critical intervention. He said that diplomacy could help in the Mediterranean if Britain maintained there a fleet equal to a one-power standard against any other Mediterranean power, excluding France, as long as that fleet was free to operate in the Mediterranean as required. Such a force would, in his view, be best based at Malta although this was not essential. Freedom of movement, however, was 'and should be emphasised on every occasion.' To this Churchill could only reply that this fleet must then 'be left out of account in the North Sea.' The lengthy discussion was brought to an end when the Committee accepted the following Conclusion proposed by the Prime Minister:

There must always be provided a reasonable margin of superior strength ready and available in Home waters. This is the first requirement. Subject to this we ought to maintain, available for Mediterranean purposes and based on a Mediterranean port, a battle fleet equal to a one-power Mediterranean standard, excluding France.

It will be clear from this analysis that Churchill had won only partial approval for his plans. The CID had accepted his view that in the North Sea lay the gravest risk to the country. However, it had declined to endorse his further argument that Mediterranean defences should be scaled down if this was necessary to the achievement of the main objective. Consequently, Churchill was forced to divert to the Mediterranean two, and later four, dreadnought capital ships that he had planned to retain in home waters, and at the same time to construct a new battle squadron for Mediterranean service. It appears from a letter written at the time that Churchill's plans did not have the full support of all his Admiralty colleagues. Balfour's Private Secretary, J. S. Sandars, after speaking to the First Sea Lord, Sir Arthur Bridgeman, wrote to Balfour telling him:

I asked Bridgeman how Winston was getting on in matters of naval policy. Bridgeman replied that they had hoped that after the mess Winston made over the Mediterranean arrangement he would be more careful & less impulsive.[23]

Two reasons can be advanced for Churchill's failure to carry the CID with him. Firstly, as he had written to Haldane in May, he did not think it 'practical politics' to demand a completely new battle squadron for the Mediterranean over and above the force required for the North Sea. In making this judgement he was perhaps mindful of the arguments he had levelled at McKenna's naval programme in 1909. In the event the CID, under pressure from Esher, had authorised this additional squadron, although, as we shall see, Churchill, in attempting in 1914 to persuade the Cabinet to vote the monies to honour this pledge, was forced to the brink of resignation.

Secondly, it seems clear that Churchill had failed in the view of his colleagues to give sufficient weight to the wider political implications of his proposals. Upon his appointment to the Admiralty he had, characteristically, become totally absorbed in naval business. As he himself wrote of his years at the Admiralty in *The World Crisis*:

These were great days. From dawn to midnight, day after day, one's whole mind was absorbed by the fascination and novelty of the problems which came crowding forward ... Saturdays, Sundays and any other spare day I spent always with the Fleets at Portsmouth or at Portland or Devonport, or with the Flotillas at Harwich. Officers of every rank came on board to lunch or dine and discussion proceeded without ceasing on every aspect of naval war and administration.[24]

This complete absorption in departmental matters had its disadvantages. In this case his overriding concern to achieve safety in the North Sea seems to have dulled his perception of the wider consequences of his proposals in the Mediterranean. Several years later, after Churchill had left the government, Lord Esher said of Churchill:

> He handles great subjects in rhythmical language, and becomes quickly enslaved by his own phrases. He deceives himself into the belief that he takes broad views, when his mind is fixed upon one comparatively small aspect of the question.[25]

It was perhaps for this reason that Esher was able to convince the CID that the security of the Mediterranean was also a vital British interest, and it is significant that Grey's intervention in the afternoon discussion appears to have been decisive.

Finally, it is interesting to compare Churchill's arguments about Mediterranean security in 1912 with the position he adopted twenty-eight years later. As we shall see, in June 1940 when he was finally Prime Minister he vetoed his First Sea Lord's plan to abandon the Mediterranean, taking then, as befitted a Prime Minister, a wider view of strategic choices. With his remarkable memory he must then have recalled the discussions of 1912.

During this second brief visit to Malta Churchill had no opportunity or reason to enquire about constitutional developments in the island. As a member of the Cabinet he was aware that little had changed since his previous visit but, if he regretted this, his concern now was for the external security of Malta as a vital naval fortress and guardian of the passage to the east. If some Maltese were disappointed or indeed aggrieved at the lack of constitutional development others were no doubt aware of the employment and income that 'Fortress Malta' brought to the island.

## Notes

[1] V. Bonham-Carter, *Winston Churchill*, pp. 267-8.

[2] The Churchill Papers, Churchill Archives Centre, Cambridge, CHAR 1/74/65. [Subsequently referred to as CAC.]

[3] Winston Churchill, *The World Crisis 1911-1914* (Thornton Butterworth, London, 1923), pp. 68, 70.

[4] *Churchill, Vol. II*, Knollys to Esher, 10 February 1909, p. 517.

[5] Churchill, *World Crisis*, p. 37.

[6] G. Best, *Churchill: A Study in Greatness* (Hambledon and London, London, 2001), pp. 43-4.

[7] V. Bonham-Carter, *Winston Churchill*, p. 270.

[8] For more detail see Winston Churchill, *World Crisis*, pp. 94-120; P. Halpern, *A Naval History of World War I* (UCL Press, London, 1994), pp. 1-20: R. Hough, *The Great War At Sea 1914-1918* (Oxford University Press, Oxford, 1986), pp. 37-52.

[9] *Churchill, Vol. II*, WSC to Haldane, 6 May 1912, p. 588.

[10] Sir Julian Corbett, *History of the Great War: Naval Operations, Vol. I* (Longmans, Green & Co, London, 1920), p. 7.

[11] *Churchill, Vol. II*, WSC to King George V, 30 May 1912, p. 581.

[12] Quoted in Vice-Admiral Sir Peter Gretton, *Former Naval Person: Winston Churchill and the Royal Navy* (Cassell, London, 1968), pp. 133-4.

[13] *Churchill, Vol. II*, WSC to Asquith and Grey, 23 August 1912, p. 596.

[14] NA CAB 8/5, ODC Memorandum 417-M, 'Imperial Defence: General Principles affecting the Oversea Dominions and Colonies', 7 July 1910.

[15] The relevant War Office papers are in NA CAB 5/3, Memoranda 91-C and 92-C, May 1912.

[16] *Churchill, Vol. II*, 'Note of Draft Agreement concerted with Lord Kitchener', [n.d.], p. 589.

[17] Churchill, *World Crisis*, pp. 73.

[18] *Daily Malta Chronicle*, 3 June 1912.

[19] NA CAB 4/4/33, CID Memorandum, 'The Strategic Position in the Mediterranean Sea', 2 July 1912.

[20] *Companion, Volume II, Part 3*, WSC Memorandum, 22 June 1912, pp. 1570-2.

[21] Viscount Esher (ed.), *Journals and Letters of Reginald Viscount Esher, Vol. III, 1910-1915* (Ivor Nicholson & Watson, London, 1938), p. 94.

[22] NA CAB 2/2, 117th CID Meeting, 4 July 1912.

[23] *Churchill, Vol. II*, Sandars to Balfour, 10 October 1912, p. 629.

[24] Churchill, *World Crisis*, pp. 118-9.

[25] Esher, *Journals, Vol. IV*, Esher to Sir Douglas Haig, 30 May 1917, pp. 120-1.

# CHAPTER III

# *The Approach of the Great War*

*We propose to hold the Mediterranean with a force of those very large, very strong, battle-cruisers which are a different kind of force altogether from any that will be found in the Mediterranean.*

Churchill Memorandum to the Committee of Imperial Defence, 6 July 1912

The scene had darkened perceptibly when Churchill, still First Lord of the Admiralty, sailed into the Grand Harbour on his third visit to Malta in May 1913. The third chapter of the first volume of his history of the First World War, *The World Crisis*, is prefaced with A. E. Housman's well-known verse:

> On the idle hill of summer
> Sleepy with the sound of dreams
> Far I hear the steady drummer
> Drumming like a noise in dreams.
>
> Far and near and low and louder,
> On the roads of earth go by,
> Dear to friends and food for powder,
> Soldiers marching, all to die.[1]

On this last pre-war Mediterranean cruise HMS *Enchantress* again carried a large party, which included the Prime Minister, Lady Asquith and their daughter, Violet. Also on board were Clementine and Churchill's mother, the former Lady Randolph who had re-married in 1901 and was now Mrs. Cornwallis-West. Churchill later wrote that *Enchantress* had become 'largely my office, almost my home', and that he had 'spent eight months afloat in the three years before the war.'[2] On this occasion *Enchantress* had visited Athens and cruised in Greek waters before reaching Malta on 22 May 1913. In the week that followed there was the customary busy round of official ceremonies and receptions, interspersed with inspections of ships, the dockyard, and the observation of naval gunnery practice at sea.

Churchill would have immediately noticed a significant difference since his last visit. Moored in the Grand Harbour were as many as four powerful dreadnought battle-cruisers, HMS *Indomitable, Inflexible, Invincible* and *Indefatigable*, each mounting eight 12-inch guns and capable of steaming at 28 knots. This force, in terms of gun power and speed, was far superior to the six pre-dreadnought battleships they had replaced. As has been seen this was the result of the CID's decision in July 1912, against Churchill's wishes, that the Mediterranean should not be stripped of battleships, but it was only a temporary measure until a new battle squadron could be based at Malta. Churchill had warned that this could not be accomplished until 1916. However, as he had also promised, battleships were frequent visitors at Malta especially when tensions created in the eastern Mediterranean by the Balkan Wars prompted the Cabinet to order the Third Battle Squadron to the Mediterranean from Home waters. Moored in Valletta's harbours there might be at times as many as seven battleships, four battle-cruisers, four armoured cruisers, thirteen light cruisers and fourteen destroyers. Malta was the only British base in the Mediterranean that could accommodate and service such a large force and this was the consideration that had persuaded the CID that the Malta should be the base for a squadron of capital ships.

Churchill announced the formation of the Malta battle-cruiser squadron, to be supported by four of the latest armoured cruisers, to the House of Commons on 22 July 1912 when he presented Supplementary Naval Estimates. The addition of £990,000 to the March figures brought the 1912 total to just over £45 million. The need for the additional expenditure was the result of the passage of the new German naval law. Churchill also assured the House that the Government intended to lay down two capital ships for every additional German ship, the 'Two Keels for One' policy demanded by the navalists. The press warmly, indeed fulsomely, received Churchill's statement. *The Western Daily Mercury*, for instance, a paper widely read in the area around the Plymouth dockyard, wrote:

> Within the scope of a few months he has gained a mastery of his mighty subject as no predecessor has shown since the dim days of Lord St. Vincent. . . . His eyes are fixed on Germany as he speaks.[3]

In a memorandum of 6 July Churchill made clear the Admiralty's plans to send two battle-cruisers to Malta in November and a further two in April 1913.[4] He explained the rationale for these provisional arrangements to the CID on 11 July.

> We propose to hold the Mediterranean with a force of those very large, very strong, battle-cruisers which are a different kind of force altogether from any that will be found in the Mediterranean ... We think this method of confronting an enemy's battle fleet by a cruiser force of the greatest strength is the best substitute for a stronger line of battle ... That is what we propose to do in the meanwhile, and of course to develop our destroyers and submarines so as to make good the defence both of Egypt and of Malta.[5]

The War Office in particular welcomed these arrangements since they removed the need to strengthen the garrisons at Malta and in Egypt about which Kitchener had warned at the Malta Conference in May.

The risks in the Mediterranean were eased to some degree by concurrent decisions taken by France. Churchill had already pointed out the need to reach some kind of naval agreement with France and in July he told the French Naval Attaché in London of the Admiralty's plans for the Mediterranean. He also advised him that 'France would be wise to aim at a standard of strength in the Mediterranean equal to that of Austria and Italy combined.'[6] In August the Cabinet authorised naval discussions with France while stressing that these would not constitute any binding obligations. A month later the French Admiralty transferred the Brest squadron of six pre-dreadnought battleships to Toulon, largely to ensure the safe passage of troops from North Africa to France. It was this battle fleet that the British battle-cruiser force was designed to complement until the new British battle squadron became available.

There was, however, much resistance to any notion of an 'arrangement' with France. Despite the realignment of British strategic and diplomatic interests demonstrated by the *Entente Cordiale* in 1904 a century of hostility to France permeated the attitudes of the public and of numerous public figures. Lord Esher's successful opposition to Churchill's Mediterranean proposals rested, in large part, on his distrust of any arrangement in that area which depended on France. As he wrote to Balfour on 1 July:

> Any attempts to rely on 'alliances' or the naval forces of friendly Powers, are bound to prove illusory. Britain either is not or is one of the Great Powers of the world. Her position in this respect depends solely upon sea command, and sea command in the Mediterranean.[7]

Such distrust was to prove well founded in the Second World War when, as we shall see, the surrender of France left the Royal Navy alone in the Mediterranean. Churchill, too, expressed some anxiety about the implications of these arrangements to Sir Edward Grey, the Foreign Secretary. In a letter of 23 August he wrote:

> The point I am anxious to safeguard is our freedom of choice if the occasion arises and consequent power to influence French policy beforehand. That freedom will be sensibly impaired if the French can say that they have denuded their Atlantic seaboard and concentrated in the Mediterranean on the faith of naval arrangements made with us ... Everyone must feel who knows the facts that we have the obligations of an alliance without its advantages and above all without its precise definitions.[8]

Meanwhile the potential threat posed by Italy and Austria was increasing. The conclusion in October 1912 of her war with Turkey gave Italy control of Libya and Cyrenaica, with the ports of Tripoli and Tobruk, and possession of the Dodecanese Islands in the Aegean. These developments led Sir Edward Grey to warn Italy in November that any attempt by Italy to construct a naval base in the Aegean would compel Britain to do the same.[9] The first Italian dreadnought battleship, the *Dante Alighieri*, carrying twelve 12-inch guns in four triple turrets, was commissioned in September 1912 and two more were under construction. Austria, her ally in the Triple Alliance, was also building dreadnought battleships. The first, the *Viribus Unitis*, joined the fleet in October 1912, and two others were under construction. These, too, carried twelve 12-inch guns in triple turrets. In both navies these new ships were supported by several modern 12-inch semi-dreadnought battleships, which could take their place in the battle line, and by numerous smaller warships. The fear in London that these growing dreadnought fleets might concert their actions in the event of war was confirmed by the signature of the Triple Alliance Naval Convention in October 1913. Plans were made to concentrate at Augusta on the east coast of Sicily and stocks of coal and other supplies were established there. A joint codebook was also agreed.[10]

What gave rise to even more concern in London and Paris was the German decision to support her Triple Alliance allies by establishing a naval force of her own in the Mediterranean, the *Mittelmeerdivision,* under the command of Rear Admiral Wilhelm Souchon. Only two ships were allocated to this force. One was a modern light cruiser, the *Breslau*, but the other was a fast, modern battle-cruiser, the *Goeben*. Although carrying only ten 11-inch guns she was considered a match for any of the British battle-cruisers and had a slightly higher speed. Germany's contribution to the combined Triple Alliance Mediterranean naval force was, therefore, a significant one, in both material and psychological terms, despite its small size.

Churchill's principal achievements in the year between his two visits to Malta as First Lord were, firstly, the decision to build a squadron of fast battleships carrying newly designed 15-inch guns. These five ships, HMS *Queen Elizabeth, Warspite, Barham, Valiant,* and *Malaya*, fought at Jutland as the Fast Division, and were still the mainstay of the fleet when Churchill once again became First Lord of the Admiralty in 1939. Of all these ships HMS *Warspite* is perhaps the best known and she will appear frequently in the following pages. The seventh British warship to bear this name she was launched at Devonport on 26 November 1913 and Churchill stood among those who watched as she took to the water.[11]

Churchill's second bold decision, and one of perhaps of even greater long-term significance, was to switch the navy from coal to oil, and the subsequent acquisition of a controlling interest in the Anglo-Persian Oil Company. In *The World Crisis* Churchill wrote of these decisions:

The fateful plunge was taken when it was decided to create the Fast Division. Then, for the first time, the supreme ships of the Navy, on which our life depended, were fed by oil and could only be fed by oil. The decision to drive the smaller craft by oil naturally followed upon this. The camel once swallowed, the gnats went down easily enough.[12]

However, these bold and far-sighted decisions, on top of the directive to the Admiralty to provide a battle squadron for the Mediterranean, came at a cost which increasingly worried some members of the Cabinet and their supporters in the House. Within days of the Mediterranean decision Churchill warned the Chancellor of the Exchequer, David Lloyd George, that the Malta battle squadron would cost an additional £9 million over the five following years. Anticipating objections to this increased expenditure, he wrote:

The expense, so far as men and maintenance are concerned, might be added to the total estimates without seriously aggravating the problem; but if the capital cost of the three additional battleships has to be borne by this country, it would appear to place an undue strain on the taxpayer to raise the money by annual finance.[13]

As narrated in the preceding chapter the CID, at their all day meeting on 4 July, had overruled Churchill by directing that there be provided for the Mediterranean a battle squadron equal to a one power standard, excluding France. The interim deployment of the battle-cruiser force to meet this directive has been described above, but the provision of the battleship squadron presented greater difficulties. Responding to the British Government's request that they contribute to imperial defence the Australian and New Zealand Governments had each provided a battle-cruiser and the Federated States of Malaya a battleship, the new 15-inch gun *Malaya*. The Conservative government of Canada was also willing to help and this seemed to offer the solution to the problem caused by the Mediterranean decision.

In an Admiralty memorandum of 6 July 1912 Churchill had proposed that by the spring of 1915 a Malta-based battle squadron be formed to replace the battle-cruiser force.[14] This would comprise four dreadnought battleships, two of the most recent pre-dreadnought ships, and two battle-cruisers. However, the removal of these eight capital ships would in 1915 leave insufficient ships in Home waters to satisfy the 60% superiority over the German fleet to which the Admiralty was also committed. After making allowance for the increased power of the new 15-inch *Queen Elizabeth* class, which would be completed by 1915, and the Royal Navy's continuing, though diminishing, superiority in older battleships, Churchill concluded that it was necessary to lay down without delay four more battleships over and above the four already committed for 1912-13.

On 11 July the CID again met to discuss the whole matter and this meeting was attended by a delegation of Canadian Cabinet ministers led by their Prime Minister, Robert Borden.[15] Churchill explained the naval problem in great detail. The provision of the Mediterranean squadron in 1915, even after reducing the required dreadnought superiority in Home waters from 60% to 50%, would leave the Admiralty 'three or four ships short'. 'We ought,' he went on, 'to lay down now three more ships over and above the four we are building.' Britain could, and would, if necessary, provide these additional ships but there was a danger that this might provoke further construction by the Triple Alliance countries. However, Churchill explained:

> If we could say that the new fact was that Canada had decided to take part in the defence of the British Empire, that would be an answer which would involve no invidious comparisons . . . If it is the intention of Canada to render assistance to the naval forces of the British Empire, now is the time when that would be most welcome and most timely.

The upshot of this discussion was that in the following December Borden introduced in the Canadian House of Commons a Naval Aid Bill which included the construction of three battleships as an urgent defence requirement. However, in May 1913 this Bill, which had passed the House in February, was rejected in the Canadian Senate where the Liberal opposition had a majority. Churchill immediately warned the Cabinet of the implications of this setback and the Cabinet agreed that Canadian default could best, and most economically, be repaired by accelerating three of the five ships of the 1913-14 programme.

The Canadian Liberal Party's opposition to Borden's plans was, no doubt, the principal reason for Canada's failure to provide the ships for which Churchill had hoped and, to some extent, planned, but Borden's position was seriously undermined by developments in London. In early December 1913 Churchill had outlined the Admiralty's plans for the 1914-15 Naval Estimates, and these, even assuming three Canadian ships, exceeded £50 million. These proposals attracted growing opposition among Ministers. More seriously, the Chancellor, Lloyd George, was reported in an article in the *Daily Chronicle* on 1 January 1914 as saying that the level of defence expenditure required reconsideration.[16] Several Ministers then demanded that only two new battleships be laid down in the coming year rather than the four proposed by Churchill in accordance with the programme agreed in 1912. As Sir Francis Hopwood, whom we met in the first chapter at the Colonial Office but who had since become a Civil Lord at the Admiralty, explained to the King's Secretary, Lord Stamfordham:

How is the Canadian Prime Minister to go on when he has staked his existence on giving us 3 battleships *in the name of urgency* when we say we can safely reduce the number of ships *without those three!* It ought to break him.[17]

There then ensued a fierce struggle between Churchill and the Chancellor that took all of Asquith's considerable powers of mediation and persuasion to resolve. Churchill had already made clear to the Prime Minister that if the 1914-15 quota of four battleships were to be reduced 'there is no chance whatever of my being able to go on.'[18] The King, to whom Churchill had sent all the relevant papers, endorsed the First Lord's position and with this support Churchill refused to give way. Finally, after much rumour of impending resignations Lloyd George agreed to Churchill's demands in return for some reductions in the 1915-16 programme. On 11 February, therefore, the Prime Minister was able to advise the King that the crisis had been resolved and Churchill announced the Government's proposals in the Naval Estimates laid before the House on 12 March.

Despite Churchill's vehement defence of the 1912 decisions, there is, nevertheless, some evidence that he remained unconvinced of the need for a dreadnought battle squadron at Malta. For example, in his letter of 18 December 1913 to the Prime Minister in which he warned that he might not be able to go on he also wrote:

The Meditn decision was the foundation of the Canadian policy. All the argument for Borden stands on that . . . If he succeeds, the Cabinet policy in the Meditn can be carried out. If he fails—then 6 months from now I can develop an argument abt submarines in that sea wh will obviate a further constrn of battleships for this 2ary theatre.[19]

This and other remarks in the same vein reflected Churchill's growing belief, prompted no doubt by Admiral Fisher, that the rapid development of submarine warfare posed a worrying threat to the invincibility of the dreadnought battleship. As has been seen in the previous chapter, he had unsuccessfully argued in 1912 that Malta could be adequately defended by the torpedo and naval developments since then appear to have confirmed this view.

While these policy decisions were being hammered out, the discussions with the French naval authorities, which the Cabinet had authorised in August 1912, had resulted in the signing of an agreement on 10 February 1913. This covered arrangements in the Mediterranean, as well as in the North Sea and the Channel, but they were all subject to any future decision to support France in a war with Germany. Much secrecy surrounded these talks but on 5 March the First Sea Lord, Admiral Prince Louis of Battenberg, who had led the discussions with the French Admiralty, advised Churchill that 'we have reached perfect agreement on the Mediterranean arrangement.' As we shall see in the next chapter, the faulty implementation of this 'perfect arrangement' was to add to the difficulty of dealing with the German battle-cruiser *Goeben*.[20]

One further Churchillian initiative in the years before the Great War was to have profound consequences for Malta's security in a later war. This was his decision to establish a naval air station at Malta. Churchill's perception of the potential military value of the aeroplane pre-dated his appointment to the Admiralty. As early as 1909 as a member of the Committee of Imperial Defence (CID) he had become familiar with the work of the Aerial Navigation sub-committee of the CID and when, two years later, he went to the Admiralty he pressed ahead with the development of a naval air capability despite the opposition of the War Office and the Treasury. Characteristically, his enthusiasm for this new instrument of war led to his taking flying lessons ignoring the all too evident dangers of flying at that time. Although he never gained a pilot's licence his logbook recorded over 140 flights before he yielded to the growing pleas of his wife and friends to stop. During the Second World War, as we shall see later, Churchill was awarded honorary Royal Air Force wings and referred then to the work he had done to promote flying in the Royal Navy in 1912.

By the outbreak of war the Royal Naval Air Service (RNAS), as it became known in 1914, had almost 100 aeroplanes and seaplanes (a word coined by Churchill) and 120 trained pilots.[21] It was trained not just for reconnaissance, its original conception, but for bombing and aerial combat. Moreover, in 1913 Lt. Longmore, whom we shall meet again in a later chapter as Air Chief Marshal Sir Arthur Longmore, dropped the first torpedo from an aircraft and the notion of an aircraft carrier was being explored. Fully immersed in these possibilities Churchill wrote on 14 January 1914 to General Sir Ian Hamilton, a former C-in-C at Malta and the future Army commander at Gallipoli, to tell him that he intended to make provision in the 1914 Naval Estimates for the establishment of air bases at Malta and Gibraltar. He hoped to have a flight of aircraft at Malta by the end of that year.[22] He then went on to write:

> The question of establishing an airship base is also being examined. The radius of action of such a vessel would enable her to reconnoitre the Mouth of the Adriatic, the Gulf of Otranto, and the Straits of Messina effectually.

Hamilton welcomed these proposals and replied on 7 March:

> My experience as Commander-in-Chief in the Mediterranean has convinced me that the strategical and tactical advantages to be gained from a well thought out system of reconnaissance from a central place like Malta cannot be exaggerated.

Churchill's plans for aircraft at Malta in 1914 were frustrated by the outbreak of war in August and it was not until 1915 that construction of a seaplane base at Kalafrana at the southern tip of Malta began. The perception that Malta would make an ideal base for aerial reconnaissance in the central Mediterranean was to be fully vindicated during the Second World War. In the summer of 1940, however, Malta possessed virtually no aerial reconnaissance capability and we shall examine in a later chapter the effect this had on operations.

On this third visit to Malta in May 1913 Churchill was striving to meet the demands of the Cabinet that the security of the island and of the Mediterranean required a modern force of dreadnought capital ships based at Malta. He was no doubt reassured to see the new battle-cruisers in the Grand Harbour often reinforced by visiting battleships from Home waters. In addition he had made plans to ensure that the new Royal Naval Air Service would in due course provide additional security against seaborne attack. However, the provision of a separate battle squadron for Malta was still years away and within fifteen months Britain was at war.

## Notes

[1] Churchill, *The World Crisis 1911-1914,* p. 28. The poem is No. XXX in *The Shropshire Lad.*

[2] Ibid., p. 119.

[3] *Churchill, Vol. II,* p. 600.

[4] *Companion, Vol. II, Part 3,* WSC Memorandum, 6 July 1912, p. 1589.

[5] Ibid., Minutes of the 118th CID Meeting, 11 July 1912, p. 1604.

[6] *Churchill, Vol. II,* p. 596.

[7] Esher, *Journals, Vol. III,* Esher to Balfour, 1 July 1912, p. 97.

[8] *Companion, Vol. II, Part 3,* WSC to Grey, 23 August 1912, pp. 1638-9.

[9] Hough, *The Great War,* p. 42.

[10] Halpern, *Naval History,* p. 15.

[11] The story of this ship is told by S. Roskill in *H.M.S. Warspite* (William Collins & Sons, London, 1957). Captain Roskill, the naval historian, was her Gunnery Officer and then her Commander just before the Second World War.

[12] Churchill, *World Crisis 1911-1914,* p. 131.

[13] *Companion, Vol. II, Part 3,* WSC to Lloyd George, 12 July 1912, pp. 1613-14.

[14] Ibid., Admiralty Memorandum, 6 July 1912, p. 1589.

[15] Ibid., Minutes of 118th CID Meeting, 11 July 1912, pp. 1595-1607.

[16] *Churchill, Vol. II,* p. 666.

[17] *Companion, Vol. II, Part 3,* Hopwood to Stamfordham, 5 January 1914, p. 1843.

[18] *Companion, Vol. II, Part 3,* WSC to Asquith, 18 December 1913, p. 1834.

[19] Ibid p. 1835.

[20] Ibid., Battenberg to WSC, 5 March 1913, pp. 1715-6.

[21] *Churchill, Vol. II,* p. 697.

[22] *Companion, Vol. II, Part 3,* WSC to Hamilton, 14 January 1914, p. 1907.

# CHAPTER IV

# *The Pursuit of the* Goeben

Goeben *must be shadowed by two battle-cruisers. Approaches to the Adriatic must be watched by cruisers and destroyers. Remain near Malta yourself.*
Churchill signal to Admiral Sir Berkeley Milne, 2 August 1914

On 28 June 1914 the Austrian Archduke Franz-Ferdinand was assassinated in Sarajevo. For several weeks this seemed no more than a further bloody chapter in the Balkan wars that had brought the Third Battle Squadron to Malta in 1913. But a month later on 24 July the Austrian Government delivered a stark ultimatum to Serbia. Churchill has described the scene in the Cabinet when, at the end of yet another discussion about Ulster, the Foreign Secretary, Sir Edward Grey, quietly read out the terms of the Austrian note.

> As the reading proceeded it seemed absolutely impossible that any State in the world could accept it, or that any acceptance, however abject, would satisfy the aggressor. The parishes of Fermanagh and Tyrone faded back into the mists and squalls of Ireland, and a strange light began immediately, but by perceptible gradations, to fall and grow upon the map of Europe.[1]

The Cabinet's initial disinclination to support France in a European war that now seemed inevitable was swept aside by the German violation of Belgian neutrality. On Monday 3 August Grey told the House of Commons of the Government's intention to deliver an ultimatum to Germany requiring her withdrawal from Belgian territory. This ultimatum, set to expire at midnight on 4 August, was ignored and at that moment the Admiralty signalled to its commands and fleets, 'Commence hostilities against Germany.'

Churchill continued to hold the position of First Lord of the Admiralty from that day until 20 May 1915 when, in the mounting crisis that enveloped the attack on the Dardanelles, he was removed by Asquith. The Conservative Party insisted on Churchill's dismissal from the Admiralty as a condition for their joining a new coalition government. This chapter will not seek to re-tell the story of that campaign or Churchill's part in it since Malta's only role was that of a staging area and later an improvised hospital for the growing casualties. However, right at the outset of the war the waters around Malta were the scene of a naval episode that had a significant bearing on the subsequent campaign and it was an episode in which Churchill was closely involved. This was the failure of the attempt to intercept and sink the German battle-cruiser *Goeben* and her subsequent escape to Constantinople.[2] It was a failure that was remembered with shame in the Royal Navy until in December 1939 in the estuary of the River Plate the German pocket battleship *Graf Spee*, mounting, like *Goeben*, 11-inch guns was hounded to self-destruction by one 8-inch and two 6-inch cruisers of the Royal Navy and the Royal New Zealand Navy. *Goeben*'s escape was the subject of a Court of Enquiry and the subsequent court-martial of Admiral Troubridge. The decisions and actions of all the parties concerned in this affair, including those of Churchill, were subjected to minute examination in these enquiries and will not be repeated here in detail. Rather, attention will be focused on the part that Churchill and Malta played in these events.

As the consequences of Austria's ultimatum to Serbia began to unfold long-prepared war plans were put into operation. War Plans for the Mediterranean, issued in August 1913, stated that if Britain found herself at war with Italy and Austria as well as Germany the Mediterranean Fleet would leave Malta and concentrate at Gibraltar. In all other circumstances, however, the fleet would be concentrated at Malta.[3] In Malta itself, when the implementation of 'precautionary measures' was ordered on 29 July a partial manning of the coastal defences took place and this was completed when the British ultimatum to Germany expired at midnight on 4 August. On the following day two battalions of the King's Own Malta Regiment of Militia (KOMR) were embodied and were then deployed to their war stations in Malta and Gozo.[4]

The initial danger appeared to be the possibility of a surprise bombardment by *Goeben* or *Breslau* since these ships had already in the early hours of 4 August shelled Bône and Philippeville on the Algerian coast. There was even the risk of attack by the new dreadnought battleships of the Italian fleet since Italy's declaration of neutrality was not made until 4 August and not known in Malta until late that evening. The tension was such that within two weeks the first four anti-aircraft guns were established around the Grand Harbour although it is not clear whence an air attack might come. In the event, although there was a moment of alarm when unexpected ships suddenly emerged from the mid-summer haze, no shots were fired by the Malta garrison.[5]

In London Churchill's first concern was for the safe passage of the Grand Fleet from Portland Harbour to its war stations at Scapa Flow and Rosyth. The whole Fleet had been exercising in the Channel in July and was about to disperse when orders not to do so were issued by the First Sea Lord, Admiral Prince Louis of Battenberg, and quickly confirmed by Churchill. On 29 July as war edged closer the Fleet was ordered to leave

Portland and steam through the Straits of Dover at night with lights extinguished. Churchill has left us a vivid account of this passage.

> We may picture them again as darkness fell, eighteen miles of warships running at high speed and in absolute blackness through the narrow Straits, bearing with them into the broad waters of the North the safeguard of considerable affairs.[6]

This accomplished, his attention turned to the Mediterranean where it was vital for France that her XIXth Corps, the Army of Africa, should be transferred to France as quickly as possible. Churchill has described the scene at the Admiralty when, on 4 August, a French naval delegation called to co-ordinate operations in the Mediterranean.

> They spoke of basing the French Fleet at Malta—that same Malta for which we had fought Napoleon for so many years, which was indeed the very pretext for the renewal of the war in 1803. *'Malte ou la guerre!'* Little did the Napoleon of St. Helena dream that in her most desperate need France would have at her disposal the great Mediterranean base which his strategic instinct had deemed vital. I said to the Admirals, 'Use Malta as if it were Toulon.'[7]

Unfortunately, this admirable declaration of allied purpose failed for various reasons, not surprising in the early days of war, to achieve the co-ordination of plans and ship movements that was intended. This was to be one of the many factors that made its contribution to *Goeben's* escape.

A week before this, on 27 July, the Admiralty had telegraphed to the Mediterranean C-in-C, Admiral Sir Archibald Berkeley Milne, who was then at Alexandria with most of his command, warning him of the possibility of war with the Triple Alliance Powers. 'Be prepared to shadow possible hostile men-of-war . . . Return to Malta as arranged at ordinary speed and remain there with all your ships completing with coal and stores'[8] It will be clear from the previous chapters that there was no possibility that Churchill would be content to allow the Sea Lords to take control of events. This would have been quite alien to his nature and to his concept of his responsibilities. This, as we shall see, was to be even more clearly demonstrated when he became Prime Minister in 1940. In this case, therefore, it is not surprising to find that many of the signals sent to Milne in the following two weeks were either drafted or approved by him. Milne commanded the interim force established in 1912 pending the completion of the new battleship squadron ordered by the CID. In July 1914 it comprised three 12-inch gunned dreadnought battle-cruisers, HMS *Inflexible, Indefatigable* and *Indomitable,* four heavy cruisers with 9.2-inch guns, four light cruisers, and sixteen destroyers. Churchill had earlier suggested that the battle-cruiser *New Zealand* be sent to reinforce this fleet but the First Sea Lord was opposed to this and Churchill, to his subsequent regret, did not insist.[9] Despite the earlier decision to switch to oil all these ships were coal-fired and the continual need to re-coal—a dirty, time-consuming business—was at times to complicate Milne's dispositions.

At the end of July these ships were widely dispersed. Milne himself with the bulk of the fleet was at Alexandria while Rear-Admiral Troubridge, his second-in-command, was at Durrazzo in Albania with a detached squadron. By 29-30 July, however, the fleet had assembled at Malta and was hurriedly completing with coal, stores and ammunition. Late on the evening of 30 July Churchill and Battenberg sent Milne a signal, drafted by Churchill, setting out his objectives and general instructions. The key sentences in this read:

> The attitude of Italy is uncertain, and it is especially important that your squadron should not be seriously engaged with Austrian ships before we know what Italy will do. Your first task should be to aid the French in the transportation of their African army by covering and, if possible, bringing to action individual fast German ships, particularly *Goeben*, which may interfere with that transportation. You will be notified by telegraph when you may consult with the French Admiral. Except in combination with the French as part of a general battle, do not at this stage be brought to action against superior forces.[10]

Some naval historians have criticised what they saw as ambiguities in this signal, especially the lack of clarity about the meaning of 'superior forces'. Churchill's own subsequent view was that the context made it clear that 'superior forces' referred to the Austrian fleet, and later wrote, 'so far as the English language may serve as a vehicle of thought, the words employed appear to express the intentions we had formed.' Certainly, Milne did not seek clarification at the time, replying on the following day that he was keeping his fleet concentrated at Malta. At the subsequent Court of Enquiry he stated that he understood that 'superior forces' meant the Austrian fleet.[11]

Early on Sunday 2 August, news was received that *Goeben* and *Breslau* had arrived at Brindisi on the heel of Italy to take on coal and later that day Churchill signalled Milne: '*Goeben* must be shadowed by two battle-cruisers. Approach to Adriatic must be watched by cruisers and destroyers. Remain near Malta yourself.' A further signal in the early hours of 3 August confirmed that 'Watch on mouth of Adriatic should be maintained, but *Goeben* is your objective. Follow her and shadow her wherever she goes and be ready to act on declaration of war, which appears probable and imminent.' Milne, consequently, ordered the light cruiser *Chatham* to watch the southern exit of the Messina strait while Troubridge took most of the fleet, including two of the battle-cruisers, *Indomitable* and *Indefatigable,* to guard the approach to the Adriatic and to shadow *Goeben* when she could be found. Milne himself remained near Malta with his flagship, *Inflexible.* Plans to co-ordinate operations with the much larger French naval forces in the western Mediterranean went awry. On the evening of 2 August all C-in-Cs were instructed by the Admiralty to establish communications with the relevant French senior officer, using code books established for this purpose. However, although Milne sent a signal to the French Admiral De Lapeyrère he received no reply and then had to send a cruiser to Bizerta to carry a written message. In the following critical days there was no effective co-ordination between the two naval forces.

Admiral Souchon's arrival in the Mediterranean to command the *Mittelmeerdivision,* comprising the battle-cruiser *Goeben* and the light cruiser *Breslau,* has been related in the preceding chapter. When he was advised by the German Admiralty of impending hostilities he was with *Goeben* at Trieste. He immediately steamed south ordering *Breslau,* which was then at Durrazzo, to join him at Brindisi. Both ships then sailed around the toe of Italy to Messina. He had hoped that Italian and Austrian ships might join him there, as planned in the Triple Alliance Naval Convention, but Italy was preparing to declare her neutrality and the Austrian fleet refused to leave the Adriatic. At Messina on 2 August both German ships hurriedly took on more coal before, at midnight, they steamed north and then headed west along the north coast of Sicily. In the early hours of Sunday 4 August *Goeben* bombarded the French port of Philippeville while *Breslau* shelled Bône. In neither port was much damage inflicted before both ships withdrew. The Admiralty in London then expected both ships to continue west in an attempt to break out into the Atlantic. However, even while he was approaching Philippeville Souchon had received a signal from Berlin advising him that a treaty had been concluded with Turkey and that he should sail east to Constantinople. Accordingly, after initially leaving the Algerian coast on a north-westerly course, Souchon turned east intending to replenish his depleted coal bunkers at Messina.

Meanwhile *Chatham,* at dawn on 3 August, had sailed right through the Messina strait and reported that the German ships were no longer there. Upon this information Milne ordered *Chatham* to follow the German ships westwards along the north coast of Sicily and signalled Troubridge to sail his heavy ships along the south coast. Later that day, however, he ordered the two battle-cruisers to steam westward at 14 knots to a position north of Valletta, leaving the slower heavy cruisers to resume their guard at the mouth of the Adriatic. In the evening the Admiralty fearing an attempt by Souchon to reach the Atlantic ordered Milne to send both battle-cruisers 'to Straits of Gibraltar at high speed ready to prevent *Goeben* leaving Mediterranean.'[12] It is possible that on the evening of 3 August observers in Malta and any fishing vessels in the Malta channel would have seen these two battle-cruisers, their funnels belching black smoke as they headed west at full speed. It was certainly what the lookouts on *Goeben* saw dead ahead at about 9.40 a.m. on 4 August as she headed east. The two squadrons then passed each other on opposite courses at a range of not more than 10,000 yards. *Indomitable* at once signalled the discovery of the German squadron to Milne and both British ships, later joined by the light cruiser HMS *Dublin*, then turned 180° to shadow *Goeben*.

Milne immediately signalled this dramatic news to the Admiralty although he omitted to advise that *Goeben* was sailing *east*. Churchill jubilantly replied, 'Very Good. Hold her. War imminent.'[13] However, although Germany was now at war with France the British ultimatum to Germany was not due to expire until midnight that night. Churchill gave conditional instructions that *Goeben* should be engaged if she attempted to interfere with French convoys but the Cabinet refused to endorse this. Churchill was later to comment on this decision. 'I cannot impeach the decision. It is right the world should know of it. But little did we imagine how much this spirit of honourable restraint was to cost us and all the world.'[14] Churchill and Milne, therefore, could only wait and hope for a decisive engagement on the following day. Unfortunately, although *Goeben* had previously suffered repeated problems with her boilers she gradually managed to draw away from her pursuers and in the evening dusk contact was lost. At midnight on 4 August Milne received the signal, 'Commence hostilities at once against Germany.'[15] *Goeben* and *Breslau*, almost out of fuel, eventually reached Messina again in the early morning of 5 August.

Both German warships immediately began to coal from a number of German ships including the German liner SS *General*. Van Der Vat has described the scene.

> Souchon did not stand on ceremony in his determination to get all the coal available as fast as he could. Rails were torn out and holes cut in the decks of the merchant ships to speed up the plundering process. The sailors were given copious drinks, extra rations, music by the ship's band and endless encouragement from the officers working alongside them. As men keeled over from exhaustion, they were given a few hours sleep in the comfortable bunks of the *General* and the chance to take a bath. Then it was back to work, if they could.[16]

Eventually a halt was called a few hours before dawn on 5 August by which time 2,100 tons of coal had been loaded, two-thirds of capacity.

It was at this point that the fog of war, perhaps always densest at the dawn of a new conflict, began to thicken. Souchon's instruction to head for Constantinople was neither known nor suspected by Milne or by the Admiralty in London where it was still believed that Souchon would attempt to leave the Mediterranean through the Straits of Gibraltar. Milne, therefore, still focusing on his main task of protecting the French convoys from Algeria, the movements of which he had been unable to learn from his French counterpart, decided to concentrate his three battle-cruisers between the western end of Sicily and Cape Bon in Tunisia. Moreover, since one of them, *Indomitable*, was short of coal he sent her into Bizerta to re-fuel rather than to Malta. Churchill was later critical of this decision arguing that had *Indomitable* coaled at Malta she would have been well placed to guard the southern exit from the Messina Strait.[17] Milne's room for manoeuvre was further restricted by a signal received from the Admiralty on the afternoon of 4 August. This advised him that 'The Italian Government have declared neutrality. You are to respect this neutrality rigidly and should not allow any of H.M. ships to come within 6 miles of the Italian coast.'[18] This meant that he could no longer chase through the Messina strait, which is in places only 2 miles wide.

Early on 5 August Milne learned from another British light cruiser, HMS *Gloucester*, which had been detached from Troubridge's squadron in the Adriatic to watch the southern exit of the Messina Strait, that *Goeben* and *Breslau* were again at Messina. Nevertheless, having received no further information or instructions from London and still convinced that the German squadron would sail west again, leaving Messina by the northern exit, he cruised throughout 5 August with his two remaining battle-cruisers to the west and north of Sicily. On the afternoon of 6 August, however, he decided to steam east along the north shore of Sicily in order to block the northern exit of the Messina strait. When, therefore, at 5.10 p.m. on 6 August he received the electrifying signal from *Gloucester* stating that the German ships had left Messina by the southern exit and were heading east, he was powerless to help. A chase through the Messina strait having been ruled out he had no alternative but to reverse course and sail around the western end of Sicily to Malta where he arrived at noon on 7 August. Churchill later wrote that both he and the Admiralty were at fault in not having authorised Milne to chase the escaping German ships though the Messina strait. By the time this prohibition was lifted it was too late.[19]

Only Troubridge with his four 9.2-inch heavy cruisers and supporting light ships, sixteen warships in all, could now save the situation. He steamed to intercept but then decided not to risk an engagement when he was in a position to do so. This resulted from his judgement that the 11-inch gunned, 25-knot *Goeben* was a 'superior force', which he had been instructed not to engage. He, therefore, broke off the chase and the two German warships sailed on to the east. Since this final act of *Goeben*'s escape took place in waters well to the east of Malta we need not follow it in detail. Suffice to say that Battenberg, incensed by the failure to catch and sink the German ships, at once ordered a Court of Enquiry. This exonerated Milne but ordered a court-martial for Troubridge. However, he in turn was cleared, the Court accepting his defence that *Goeben* constituted a 'superior force' which he had been ordered not to engage. On the relevant papers Churchill minuted: 'The explanation is satisfactory, the result unsatisfactory.'[20]

Naval historians since that day have examined the events briefly related here to apportion responsibility and censure and inevitably Churchill has not escaped criticism. In the first place he has been judged to have erred in appointing Milne to the Mediterranean command. Admiral Fisher, in particular, had been violently opposed to this appointment at the time. Later, it is alleged, Churchill interfered too much in tactical matters best left to the 'men on the spot', and the signal of 30 July drafted by him has attracted particular criticism. Indeed it was the failure to make clear that 'superior force' signified the Austrian fleet, not the *Goeben* by herself, that led to the acquittal of Admiral Troubridge. Nevertheless, Troubridge and Milne were thought, then and later, to have been culpable. Van der Vat who has devoted a book to this episode has concluded that Troubridge 'should have had a go.'[21] Many years later Churchill's own judgement of this episode was set out in the relevant pages of *The World Crisis*. After reflecting on the 'influence of sinister fatality' he wrote:

> The terrible 'Ifs' accumulate. If my first thoughts on July 27 of sending the *New Zealand* to the Mediterranean had materialized; if we could have opened fire on the *Goeben* during the afternoon of August 4; if we had been less solicitous for Italian neutrality; if Sir Berkeley Milne had sent the *Indomitable* to coal at Malta instead of Biserta; if the Admiralty had sent him direct instructions when on the night of the 5th they learned where the *Goeben* was; if Admiral Troubridge in the small hours of August 7 had not changed his mind . . . the story of *Goeben* would have ended here.[22]

We may briefly take the story of the *Goeben* to its conclusion. The two German ships arrived off the entrance to the Dardanelles on 10 August and after an initial delay were allowed through the minefields to Constantinople. Several days later, after demands from Britain and France that the ships be seized and their crews interned, the Turkish government purchased them from Germany, renaming them *Sultan Yavuz Selim* and *Midilli*. However, despite British protests the German crews remained on board, even being issued with red Turkish fezzes! The Admiralty at once ordered that if either ship left the Dardanelles, under whatever flag, they were to be sunk. Prolonged diplomatic efforts were then made to maintain Turkey's neutrality but on 29 October the Turkish fleet, under the command of Admiral Souchon and including the two former German warships, entered the Black Sea and bombarded Russian ports. Great Britain and France declared war on the Ottoman Empire on 31 October and two days later British and French warships bombarded the outer forts guarding the entrance to the Dardanelles, the first of many shells that were in the following year to fall on the Gallipoli peninsula.

Churchill later expressed the view in his *World Crisis* that Turkey's entry into the war as Germany's ally and the tragic course of events in the Middle East that led after much suffering and destruction to the collapse of the Ottoman Empire owed much to the escape of the *Goeben,* a ship 'carrying with her for the peoples of the East and Middle East more slaughter, more misery and more ruin than has ever before been borne within the compass of a ship.'[23]

Following news of the arrival of Admiral Souchon's squadron at Constantinople Milne took his fleet to the eastern Mediterranean. However, on 13 August he was ordered to return to England in his flagship, HMS *Inflexible,* and to hand over his command to Troubridge. A week earlier the Admiralty had agreed with the French Ministry of Marine that the French would assume command of the allied fleets in the Mediterranean and have full use of the facilities at Malta and Gibraltar. In Malta itself the initial state of readiness was relaxed and before many weeks had passed the garrison was reduced. Later, in early 1915, the King's Own Malta Regiment volunteered for overseas service and on 14 January the first battalion of the regiment sailed for Cyprus.[24]

Well before then events elsewhere had claimed Churchill's attention and it was not until the spring of 1915 that the growing crisis at the Dardanelles led Asquith, when forming a new coalition government, to remove Churchill from the Admiralty. Churchill then accepted Asquith's offer of the Chancellorship of the Duchy of Lancaster, a non-departmental position but with a seat on the War Council. Five months later, however, on 11 November, Churchill resigned from the government, once again donned his army uniform and made his way to the western front. On 5 January 1916 not far behind the front line in Flanders he assumed command of the 6th Battalion of the Royal Scots Fusiliers.

## *Notes*

[1] Churchill, *World Crisis 1911-1914*, p. 193.

[2] A full account is in D. Van der Vat, *The Ship That Changed The World: The Escape of the Goeben to the Dardanelles in 1914* (Grafton Books, London, 1986); for shorter accounts see Churchill, *World Crisis 1911-1914*, pp. 221-9, 247-56; R. Massie, *Castles of Steel: Britain, Germany and the Winning of the Great War at Sea* (Pimlico, London, 2005), pp. 26-55; P. Halpern, *Naval History*, pp. 51-7; R. Hough, *Great War*, pp. 69-86. All of the relevant documents and signals are presented in E. Lumby, *Policy and Operations in the Mediterranean 1912-14* (Navy Records Society, London, 1970).

[3] Churchill, *World Crisis 1911-1914*, p. 222.

[4] A. Laferla, *British Malta* (Aquilina & Co., Malta, 1947), p. 196.

[5] D. Rollo, *The Guns and Gunners of Malta* (Mondial Publishers, Valletta, 1999), pp. 149-51.

[6] Churchill, *World Crisis 1911-1914*, p. 212.

[7] Ibid., p. 229.

[8] Lumby, *Policy and Operations*, Signal No. 58, p. 145.

[9] Churchill, *World Crisis 1911-1914*, pp. 207, 255.

[10] Ibid., pp. 222-3.

[11] Lumby, *Policy and Operations*, Document No. 388, para. 169, p. 294.

[12] Ibid., Signal No. 93, p. 153.

[13] Churchill, *World Crisis 1911-1914*, p. 224.

[14] Ibid., p. 225.

[15] Lumby, *Policy and Operations*, Signal No. 166, p. 165.

[16] Van der Vat, *The Ship*, p. 133.

[17] Churchill, *World Crisis 1911-1914*, p. 248.

[18] Lumby, *Policy and Operations*, Signal No. 119, p. 157.

[19] Churchill, *World Crisis 1911-1914*, p. 250.

[20] Ibid., pp. 252, 255.

[21] Van der Vat, *The Ship*, p. 236.

[22] Churchill, *World Crisis 1911-1914*, p. 255.

[23] Ibid., p. 252.

[24] Laferla, *British Malta*, p. 197.

## CHAPTER V

# Colonial Secretary and
# a New Malta Constitution

*In Malta a novel experiment has been tried by my predecessor, and we hope it will succeed.*

Churchill's statement to the Imperial Conference, London, June 1921

On 14 February 1921 Churchill returned to the Colonial Office, this time as Secretary of State. Much had happened since 1915 when, disillusioned and angry, he had resigned from the government and left London to take his place on the Western Front in Flanders. Denied by Asquith the command of a brigade he was appointed as Colonel of the 6th Battalion of the Royal Scots Fusiliers in the early days of 1916. First, however, he spent several weeks in training with the 2nd Grenadier Guards to learn the techniques of a kind of warfare wholly different from his previous military experience. The story of his eventful and often dangerous six months with the Royal Scots lies outside the scope of this study; suffice to say that he was often under fire and quite unafraid even when patrolling in no-man's-land. Evidence of the risks he ran can be seen on the windowsill of his Study at Chartwell. Placed there is a large piece of a German shell and on it his cousin, the Duke of Marlborough, inscribed the words: 'This fragment of shell fell between us and might have separated us forever, but is now a token of union.'[1] Despite their initial and understandable misgivings about the presence of a former First Lord of the Admiralty the Grenadiers and his Scottish regiment soon came to admire his courage and concern for their well being. At his funeral fifty years later eight Grenadier Guardsmen bore his coffin into St. Paul's Cathedral and Scots Fusiliers were among those who lined the streets of London.

What surely most astonished his officers and men was his habit of setting up his easel during quiet periods and painting the scenes around him. He had discovered the enjoyment and solace of oil painting a year earlier after his dismissal from the Admiralty and in the course of his busy life Churchill completed over 500 paintings, many of considerable merit for one who painted solely for his own relaxation and enjoyment.[2] One of the earliest and most evocative is known as 'Plugstreet', a painting of the ruined Belgian village of Ploegsteert close to where the battalion headquarters had been established. The painting shows the village under an artillery bombardment with white and black shell bursts overhead and a house in flames. It hangs today at Chartwell, as does the French infantryman's helmet which he habitually wore in the trenches.

The merger of the depleted ranks of the 6th Scots Fusiliers with another regiment in May 1916 brought Churchill's active military life to an end and, still a Liberal MP, he returned to Westminster. In July 1917 the Prime Minister, Lloyd George, despite considerable Conservative opposition, brought him back into the Cabinet as Minister of Munitions and in early 1919, after the Coalition government was re-elected, he became Secretary of State for War and Air. Two years later he accepted Lloyd George's proposal that he move to the Colonial Office with a wide-ranging responsibility for the re-organisation and supervision of British interests in the Middle East which had been much enlarged by the collapse of the Turkish Ottoman empire. In March 1921 he sailed for Egypt, accompanied by his wife and by T. E. Lawrence, better known to the public then and since as 'Lawrence of Arabia', as an adviser. After his arrival he chaired a conference in Cairo and then travelled on to Jerusalem.

Among those he and Clementine met and got to know in the Middle East were General Sir Walter and Lady Congreve. As a young Captain Congreve had won the Victoria Cross in South Africa during the Boer War and his son had also won the Victoria Cross in fighting on the Somme in 1916. In 1921 he was General Officer Commanding the British troops in Egypt and Palestine. In the following two years Churchill often wrote and spoke highly of Congreve's difficult task of trying to maintain peace in Palestine when Arab-Jewish tension was rising. After Churchill had had a meeting in April 1921 with Field Marshal Sir Henry Wilson, who was at the time Chief of the Imperial General Staff, Wilson wrote to Congreve to tell him 'How much pleasure it gave me to hear him praise you in the most generous and unstinted fashion.'[3] During the Cairo conference Clementine stayed with the Congreves and they all became good friends. As will be seen in the next chapter Churchill was to meet him again six years later when he was Governor of Malta.

When Churchill for a second time entered the Colonial Office it was to find that the affairs of Malta had been transformed from the condition in which he had found them when he first visited the island as Under-Secretary in 1907. We have seen in the first chapter that his early attempts to restore a measure of self-government to Malta had failed after his transfer to the Board of Trade. During the war years the constitutional structure had remained frozen but peace brought throughout the world a more insistent demand for self-determination and self-government. In Malta frustration sharpened by many factors, of which rising unemployment, high food prices and genuine hardship were not the least, led to riots and four deaths on 7 June 1919—the day known as *Sette Giugno* in Maltese history.

It was fortunate that on the following day a new Governor of Malta arrived. This was General Sir Herbert Plumer. During the war he had commanded the Fifth and Second Armies on the western front and, after the Armistice, had been appointed to command the British Army of Occupation on the Rhine. This had given him some experience of handling civil unrest. Captain Laferla has provided a fine description of Plumer's way of dealing with the situation.

> At the time of his arrival, the streets were guarded by troops, the general atmosphere was tense and the attitude of the people one of surly hostility. Plumer grasped the situation immediately. He told his chauffeur to drive slowly and walked unconcernedly though a crowd of thousands of people on the main square. He found a large body of blue-jackets in the palace courtyard.
>
> 'What is this?' he asked. 'Your guard, Sir' was the reply. 'How many are there?' 'Three hundred, Sir,' said the G.O.C. 'March out all but twenty within ten minutes,' ordered the Governor.
>
> Plumer had landed at 9.30 a.m.; by noon he had received a deputation, listened sympathetically to what they had to say and impressed them with his personality. They left feeling confident and calm.[4]

A month later the Governor was promoted to Field Marshal and raised to the peerage as Lord Plumer of Messines. Normal conditions were slowly re-established in the days after his arrival but the disturbances served to confirm the realisation in Whitehall that the demand for domestic self-government must be met. Although the principal decisions about Malta were taken by Churchill's predecessor, Lord Milner, and by his Under-Secretary, Leo Amery, a brief review of these developments will help to show the changed position of Malta that Churchill discovered as he took up the Seals of the Colonial Office.

It is to Dr. (later Sir) Filippo Sciberras that the credit must be given for seizing the moment. He was a respected senior political figure in Malta who as early as 1888 had been elected to the Council of Government to represent the graduates of the University of Malta. It was he who in the early months of 1919 invited representatives from all parties and interests to a Maltese National Assembly which, at its first meeting on 25 February, passed a resolution calling for full local self-government. The Assembly then appointed a Commission to draft a new Constitution.[5] After the *Sette Giugno* riots, and the arrival of General Plumer as the new Governor, Amery visited the island to assess the situation for himself. In his memoirs he wrote:

> Long-standing resentment against autocratic Crown Colony government had been worked up by a small disloyal pro-Italian faction into

a general anti-British agitation. The people were over-taxed and the local government bankrupt.[6]

He went on to record his belief that for the desperate financial situation 'the Imperial government was directly to blame' and that, as regards the constitutional position, 'it was necessary to make a completely fresh start.' He found that Lord Plumer shared these views.

Upon his return to London his report led Milner to accelerate his proposals to grant a new Constitution. Milner also persuaded the Cabinet to make a grant of £250,000 to the Maltese government, a sum equal then to one third of the Maltese annual budget. The British government's decision to grant a new Constitution was announced by Amery to the House of Commons on 20 November in the following terms:

His Majesty's Government has decided that the time has come to entrust the people of Malta with full responsible control of their purely local affairs, the control of the naval and military services and functions of Government as are connected with the position of Malta as an Imperial fortress and harbour remaining vested in the Imperial Authorities.[7]

On the same day Plumer at a special meeting of the Council of Government made a similar announcement in Valletta. Two weeks later Milner himself visited the island. Speaking there he said: 'We are giving you the engine; you are to find the engineers.'[8] It was not until 12 June 1920, however, that Field Marshal Plumer was able to present the draft Letters Patent relating to the proposed Constitution.

These envisaged a dyarchy under which local Maltese matters were to be the concern of a Maltese Parliament and Ministry while the Governor, representing the Crown, retained responsibility for specified 'reserved matters'. There then followed a lengthy period of discussion and representations, which revealed strong differences only with respect to religion and language. In these lay the seeds of future difficulties but for the moment compromises were accepted.

Consequently, when Churchill became Colonial Secretary in February 1921 he found the constitutional work virtually complete and only the final details required his attention. On 9 April Churchill was able to send the Governor the new Letters Patent establishing the Constitution and on 30 April the Governor promulgated these at an impressive ceremony at the Palace in Valletta. He wrote to Churchill to say that over 700 people had been present at the ceremonies, that the reading of the Letters Patent had 'evoked enthusiastic cheering' and that their provisions 'have been received with great satisfaction.'[9] At the Imperial Conference that opened in London in June Churchill was able to make the following statement:

In Malta a novel experiment has been tried by my predecessor, and we hope it will succeed. Everybody knows the argument against giving Malta a Constitution. It was said you might as well give a Constitution to a battleship. We have arrived at a dyarchical system—two Governments in the island, one elective dealing with Maltese affairs, and the other dealing with purely military and naval interests.[10]

It is worth noting that the principle of separating debate and decision on local Maltese issues from matters of a wider 'imperial' character was one that Churchill had sought, but failed, to establish in 1908.

The first elections to the Legislative Assembly and to the Senate took place in October, and on 1 November 1921 the Prince of Wales, who was later to become King Edward VIII, inaugurated the new Parliament. Churchill had earlier thought of attending this ceremony. He wrote to his wife in February that 'the new Malta Constitution is to come into operation in early April, and I may take advantage of my presence in the Mediterranean to go and inaugurate it myself.'[11] In the event, and perhaps more fittingly, Leo Amery represented the British government and afterwards sent Churchill a telegram about the ceremonies. In this he wrote of the 'brilliant success' of the Prince's visit and added: 'Visit had undoubtedly come just at the right moment to fuse into enthusiastic affection for Crown and Empire.'[12] After the Prince of Wales had delivered an address and declared the new Parliament open he conferred on Dr. Filippo Sciberras the accolade of knighthood that had been granted by the King.

In the following twelve months before Churchill left the Colonial Office upon the collapse of Lloyd George's Liberal-Conservative Coalition government the affairs of Malta rarely required his close attention. The Colonial Office records reveal few minutes by the Secretary of State on the papers passing through the Malta department. These were the months when the first elected Maltese government led by Mr. Joseph Howard took up the challenge of local self-government in very difficult times.

An exception to this was a dispute, not with the new Maltese administration but with the War Office, about a military matter affecting the island. The government in London, under great pressure from the report of the Geddes Committee to slash government expenditure, demanded large reductions in the naval and military estimates. As part of this process Field Marshal Plumer had reluctantly accepted that the King's Own Malta Regiment of Militia should be disbanded but on the condition that it be replaced by a smaller volunteer force. He had, on the strength of this understanding, made several promises about this force in various speeches in Malta. When, therefore, the War Office proposed in December 1921 to cancel the proposed funding for the new unit Plumer wrote to Churchill saying that if the War Office decision were to be upheld by the Cabinet he would be compelled to resign.[13]

The Colonial Office officials, including the Under-Secretary, Mr Edward Wood, later to become Lord Halifax, were inclined to accept the War Office decision but Churchill would have none of it. He gave instructions that the War Office be advised that the matter was to be referred to the Cabinet and a Cabinet Paper was duly circulated.[14] Faced, however, with this determined opposition the War Office gave way before the issue came before the Cabinet. On 13 April 1922 Churchill cabled to Plumer: 'I am delighted to hear that an expenditure of £25,000 on local force has been agreed to by the Army Council.'[15]

There are no other private letters or correspondence that describe Churchill's reactions to the new Maltese Constitution. His statement to the Imperial Conference has been noted above and there is no reason to doubt the sincerity of his hopes for the success of this 'novel experiment'. As has been narrated in Chapter I he had tried hard in 1907-08 to find a formula that would reconcile the British government's wish to retain the naval and military bases on the island—the value of which, as will be seen later, was to be fully demonstrated in the Second World War— with the legitimate wish of the Maltese people for the management of their domestic affairs and the expenditure of their tax revenues. It has also been conjectured there that had Churchill remained longer at the Colonial Office in 1908 some measure of self-government might have come earlier. In the event it was only after the passage of a further fifteen years that, as Colonial Secretary, he presided over the establishment of a new Constitution that promised so much.

Such a development, although the basic decisions were those of Milner and Amery, was fully consistent with Churchill's wish to see the spread of self-government throughout the empire. His early work on the new constitutions for the Transvaal and the Orange River Colony has been noted but perhaps the best illustration of his view about the changing structure of the empire is his tireless efforts to secure the establishment of the Irish Free State. Churchill was one of those appointed in October 1921 to negotiate the Irish Treaty with the Irish representatives and it was this work, involving daily meetings often conducted under conditions of great strain, that engaged most of his attention while the finishing touches were being put to the Maltese Constitution. Shortly before his assassination on 22 August 1922 Michael Collins, the Irish leader, sent a message to London: 'Tell Winston we could never have done anything without him.'[16]

That is not to say that there were not misgivings in some quarters about the prospects for continued development in Malta. Writing in 1937 after the revocation of the 1921 Constitution Professor Hancock expressed the view that this 'had proved itself to be a fraud', although, he added, 'in all probability an unconscious fraud. Nobody in 1921 could have predicted the strains to which the constitution was to be subjected, and nobody perhaps suspected the jerry-building which its elaborate façade concealed'[17]

But even at the time there were reservations. When Amery's report about the 'brilliant success' of the inauguration ceremony in November 1921 was received at the Colonial Office Mr. Ellis, a member of the Malta department, warned of the religious issue still to be resolved. 'It promises a stubborn and acrimonious struggle' he minuted. The Governor too wondered how the rather vague proposals regarding the teaching of English and Italian were to be implemented. He reported his belief that 'a certain section were trying to establish Italian as the official language.' At the time, however, Churchill took the view that 'the safeguards provided for the English language go as far as convenient.'[18] When Amery, who was Colonial Secretary from 1924 to 1929, came to publish his memoirs in 1952 he wrote:

> For a few years the new Constitution worked happily enough . . .
> It was the vehemence of Maltese internal quarrels that caused the
> 'Amery' Constitution to be temporarily suspended more than once
> from 1930 onwards and finally revoked in 1936.[19]

The fall of Lloyd George's coalition government in October 1922 led to a general election in which the Conservative Party, led by Andrew Bonar Law, was returned to office with an overwhelming majority. Churchill himself, standing as a Liberal, defended his seat at Dundee but his campaign was hampered by his slow recovery from an appendicitis operation a few weeks earlier. Clementine, his wife, was among several who spoke in the constituency on his behalf. All to no avail. When the results were declared on 16 November Churchill came fourth in a field of six candidates and was thus out of Parliament for the first time in twenty-two years. As he later wrote: 'In the twinkling of an eye I found myself without an office, without a seat, without a party and without an appendix.'[20]

During these years his personal life also suffered several heavy blows. In June 1921 his mother, Lady Randolph Churchill, who as Mrs Cornwallis-West had accompanied him on his visit to Malta in 1913, died at the age of 67 after a fall. In the following August he and his wife, to their great grief, lost their youngest daughter, Marigold, at the age of 2½ years following a sudden illness. A year later, however, in September 1922, Clementine gave birth to their fifth child, Mary. In the same month Churchill bought the 80-acre estate of Chartwell Manor in Kent and this was to be his much loved home for the rest of his life.

Churchill's second period at the Colonial Office, during which he did not visit the island, was the last occasion when he held direct departmental responsibility for Malta's civil administration. It would be wrong to suggest that the island's affairs made great claims upon his time and attention during these years. The work on the new Constitution had been largely completed by his predecessors, Milner and Amery, and although Churchill saw this to completion he was more heavily engaged in the search for peace and stability in the Middle East and Ireland. Henceforth it was the island's strategic value as a vital naval and air base that was to command his attention as it had done during his earlier years at the Admiralty. Nevertheless, his Colonial Office experience before and after the First World War gave him an understanding of Malta and its people and he was, consequently, able to see the naval and military problems that arose in the context of an island people who had sought and gained the right to resolve through their elected representatives the issues affecting their daily lives.

## Notes

[1] *Chartwell*, The National Trust, p. 61.

[2] See Winston Churchill, *Painting as a Pastime* (Odhams Press and Ernest Benn, London, 1948). This was a book version of two articles that had originally been published in the *Strand* magazine in 1922.

[3] *Companion, Vol. IV, Part 3*, Wilson to Congreve, 13 April 1921, p. 1437.

[4] Laferla, *British Malta*, pp. 224-5.

[5] For details see Laferla, *British Malta*, p. 220; J. Cremona, *The Maltese Constitution and Constitutional History Since 1813* (Publishers Enterprise Group, Valletta, 1994), pp. 23-37.

[6] L. Amery, *My Political Life, Vol. II, War and Peace 1914-1929* (Hutchinson, London, 1953), p.188.

[7] Quoted in Laferla, *British Malta*, p. 226.

[8] Laferla, *British Malta*, p. 226.

[9] NA CO 158/424/22782, Plumer to WSC, 4 May 1921.

[10] Cmd. 1474, *Imperial Conference 1921: Summary of Proceedings and Documents*, p. 37.

[11] *Companion, Vol. IV, Part 2*, WSC to Clementine Churchill, (hereafter CSC), 21 February 1921, p. 1368.

[12] NA CO 158/428, Amery to WSC, 3 November 1921.

[13] NA CO 158/431/CO 9815, Plumer to WSC, 30 December 1921.

[14] NA CAB 24, CP 3906, WSC Memorandum, 'Maintenance of Maltese Local Force: Lord Plumer's Proposal', 29 March 1922.

[15] NA CO 158/431/CO 17104, WSC to Plumer, 13 April 1922.

[16] *Churchill, Vol. IV*, p. 894.

[17] Hancock, W. *Survey of British Commonwealth Affairs, Vol. I, Problems of Nationality* (Oxford University Press, London, 1937), p. 411.

[18] NA CO 158/428/22782, WSC to Plumer, 8 September 1921.

[19] Amery, *Political Life, Vol. II*, p. 196.

[20] Winston Churchill, *Thoughts and Adventures* (Odhams Press, London, 1947), p. 162.

## CHAPTER VI

# *The 1927 Visit and a Meeting with Mussolini*

*We dined last night with the Congreves and they lit up that splendid palace and armoury.*

Churchill letter to Clementine Churchill, 10 January 1927

On Saturday 8 January 1927 Churchill, at the age of 52, once again set foot in Malta, and on this occasion he was Chancellor of the Exchequer. In the five years since he had had responsibility for Malta as Colonial Secretary the roller coaster pattern of his political life had seen another plunge to be followed by a rise to even greater heights. After losing his Dundee seat in the House of Commons in November 1922 he had fought and lost elections at Leicester and the Abbey division of Westminster before being returned in the election of October 1924 as Member of Parliament for Epping. He was to hold this seat, later to be renamed as Woodford, for the next forty years. Moreover, he was now once again a Conservative although he had stood at Epping as a 'Constitutionalist' with Conservative support. After the election to his considerable surprise, and to even greater astonishment and no little resentment among the Tory diehards, Stanley Baldwin offered him the Chancellorship of the Exchequer, second in rank only to the Prime Minister himself. This was the high office that his father, Lord Randolph, had held almost 40 years earlier and on his first official engagement as Chancellor Churchill wore his father's robes.

His private life had also reached calmer waters. After the anguish of the death of their daughter, Marigold, in August 1921 Clementine gave birth on 15 September 1922 to their fifth child, Mary. Several weeks later on the strength of an unexpected inheritance and the anticipated royalties from sales of *The World Crisis*, he bought Chartwell Manor in Kent. Although modernisation and rebuilding work took another eighteen months to complete, this house, high on the greensand hills near Westerham with its far-reaching views over the Weald, was to be the home for his growing family and his haven from the turmoil and pressures of political life.

It was personal reasons rather than affairs of state that occasioned Churchill's fourth visit to Malta. After the tense weeks of May 1926 when the TUC called a General Strike in support of the coal miners, and the subsequent unsuccessful attempts to find a negotiated settlement, Churchill felt in need of a winter holiday in warmer latitudes. The Mediterranean beckoned and Malta seemed an attractive destination since on old friend, Admiral Sir Roger Keyes, was at that time C-in-C of the Mediterranean Fleet based at Malta.

Roger Keyes had first earned Churchill's admiration by his conduct at the Dardanelles in 1915. There, as Chief of Staff to the C-in-C, Admiral de Robeck, he had repeatedly urged further naval efforts to force the Narrows. Later in the war he was responsible for the raid on Zeebrugge. There, in the space of a few hours early on St. George's Day 1918, eleven VCs and more than 200 other medals for gallantry were won in an attempt to block the German submarine exit to the North Sea. He and Lady Keyes were firm friends of the Churchills and, with a house in Epping, had helped to secure this safe Tory seat for the former First Lord of the Admiralty. He and Lady Keyes were frequent visitors to Chartwell and the Admiral's bold signature appears in several places in the Visitors' Book kept there. Widely, but not universally, admired in the service he had in June 1925 been appointed as C-in-C of the Mediterranean Fleet, the finest seagoing command the Admiralty had to offer and the normal step to an eventual appointment as First Sea Lord.

In the previous chapter the transformation of Malta's constitutional and political condition brought about by the grant of the 1921 Constitution has been described. In the same period, however, there was an equally important transformation in Malta's importance as an imperial naval base, and this will require a brief digression.[1] Italy's decision in August 1914 to remain neutral and, later, to join the Allies removed any possibility that the Mediterranean would become a major war theatre in the First World War. Consequently, after the withdrawal from Gallipoli the Admiralty maintained only a small force at Malta. After the war had ended the inevitable reduction of the Royal Navy's fleets, reinforced by the Washington Naval Treaty of 1922 which limited the number of Britain's battleships to fifteen, forced the Admiralty to review the geographical distribution of its diminished resources. The protection of imperial interests in the Mediterranean area, emphasised by the Chanak crisis of 1922, and of the direct passage through the Suez Canal to the east would of themselves have necessitated some naval force at Malta. However, the Admiralty had for the first time to recognise a new strategic development that had arisen from a major political decision. For the British government had decided not to renew the Anglo-Japanese Treaty when it expired in 1922. Moreover, since under the terms of the Washington Treaty Japan was permitted to maintain a battleship force equal to 60% of Britain's, the Cabinet had also decided to construct a major new naval base at Singapore.

The reasons for all this lie beyond the scope of this study but the effect was to make Malta the Royal Navy's principal base outside Home waters. For in the event of a Japanese attack on Britain's Far East interests before the new Singapore base was completed the Mediterranean Fleet, reinforced from the UK, would sail to the relief under the initial command of its C-in-C. Admiral Keyes carried out numerous exercises in Mediterranean waters to test plans for a passage to the east. To prepare for this possibility the naval docking, repair and provisioning facilities at Malta were substantially expanded to accommodate and service as many as sixty warships. A captured German floating dock was also towed out to Malta to accommodate the battleships. As a member of the Cabinet Churchill had participated in these decisions and their consequences for Malta. He was also eager to see the new 15-inch gun battleships that he had helped to build in the anxious days before the war and which were still the mainstay of the Mediterranean Fleet.

On 16 September 1926 Churchill sent Keyes for comment several draft chapters for the third volume of *The World Crisis* which dealt with the Battle of Jutland. He concluded his letter by writing:

> If at any time I should find myself in Rome, which is not an impossibility next month, I may telegraph to you on the chance of proposing a flying visit . . . I should very much like to see the Fleet. It is more than eleven years since I stood on the deck of the unfinished *Queen Elizabeth,* and I have never been on board a battleship since.[2]

Keyes at once replied inviting Churchill to stay with him for a few days in Valletta and then to join the fleet on a winter cruise to Athens.

Churchill gladly accepted this invitation and on 4 January 1927 he left London accompanied by his brother, Jack, and by his 15-year-old son, Randolph. Throughout his life Churchill had a close and warm relationship with his younger brother but the relationship with his only son was more uneven. At that time Randolph's stubborn and argumentative nature had attracted adverse reports from his schoolmasters at Eton. In thanking his son for his recent birthday present Churchill added: 'It would give me much more pleasure to hear something creditable about you from your masters.' Nevertheless, he later wrote to his wife that Randolph was a 'very good travelling companion.'[3]

The small party travelled via Paris to Genoa where Churchill made the final corrections to the proofs of the third volume of *The World Crisis* and mailed them to London. Before sailing from Genoa on the *Hesperia* Churchill wrote to his wife to tell her how much had changed since they were last in Italy six years earlier. 'The Fascists have been saluting in their impressive manner all over the place.'[4] On their way south they went ashore at Naples where they witnessed an eruption of Mount Vesuvius and visited Pompeii. Randolph later complained that he was not allowed to see some of the frescoes at Herculaneum and 'had to remain above ground, kicking my heels'.[5] The party finally reached Syracuse where they transferred to the destroyer HMS *Witch* and disembarked at Valletta on the morning of Saturday 8 January 1927. Churchill and his son stayed with

Admiral and Lady Keyes at Admiralty House in Valletta while a room for Jack was found at the Palace. Admiralty House on South Street in Valletta is a large rambling building with a central courtyard. It has a fine staircase on the walls of which there are marble tablets which record the names of all the Mediterranean C-in-Cs. Among these now appears Keyes's name with those of Admirals Chatfield, Pound, Cunningham (twice) and Mountbatten. It is now Malta's National Museum of Fine Arts.

Roger Keyes was a keen polo player and when he had invited Churchill to Malta he suggested that during his visit he might wish to join him in a game of polo, an invitation that Churchill could not resist. Although, he told Keyes, he had not played that year, 'I will bring a couple of sticks and do my best. If I expire on the ground it will at any rate be a worthy end!'[6] Churchill had ridden since he was a boy and in *My Early Life* he wrote that 'No hour of life is lost that is spent in the saddle.'[7] He continued to hunt into his seventies. But it was as a cadet at the Royal Military College at Sandhurst that his enthusiasm for polo developed. In India as a subaltern with the 4th Hussars polo became a passion of his, as it was throughout the British regiments in India. Although Churchill was compelled to play with his right shoulder strapped as a result of an earlier dislocation, he was a member of the regimental team that in 1899 won the Inter-Regimental Tournament.[8] He had continued to play throughout his life, but now, in his fifty-third year, the game with Keyes at the Marsa polo grounds on the Saturday afternoon was his last. Afterwards he wrote to Clementine: 'I got through the polo without shame or distinction & enjoyed it so much.'[9]

Before he arrived Churchill had been concerned that the Governor, Lt.-General Sir Walter Congreve, should not feel in any way slighted. The Congreves, as mentioned earlier, were personal friends of the Churchills. Consequently, Churchill had written to Keyes in November:

> One other point. Congreve and his lady are old friends of mine. Perhaps you could explain to him that I am coming out only to see you and the Fleet and in a purely private capacity, and I hope he will let me come and dine with him one night. I shall write to him myself when everything is settled, but perhaps you will prepare the way and see that there is no offence given.[10]

After leaving Egypt, where he had first met Churchill, General Congreve held an appointment in England before succeeding Field Marshal Lord Plumer as Governor of Malta in 1924. Sadly, he died in Malta a month after Churchill's visit. All was suitably arranged by Admiral Keyes who had written to Churchill before his arrival: 'The Congreves and I have often talked over this visit of yours and they'll come here and we'll go there.'[11] Writing to his wife from Admiralty House on Monday 10 January Churchill told her of his activities:

We dined last night with the Congreves and they lit up that splen-did palace and armoury. The night before the Keyes's gave a dance to the fleet and garrison . . . This afternoon we go afloat in the *Warspite*. It is blowing half a gale, but they say the great ships do not move unpleasantly.[12]

Before leaving Malta Churchill also wrote to Baldwin to tell him about his visit. 'After 12 years,' he wrote, 'it interests me greatly to revive all those topics in wh I used to dwell—& see the ships we planned in the far off, thrilling pre-war days.'[13]

That afternoon Churchill left Malta aboard Admiral Keyes's flagship HMS *Warspite* leading the whole Mediterranean fleet of sixty ships. As recounted in Chapter III *Warspite* was one of the fast, oil-burning, 15-inch battleships that Churchill had ordered in 1912 and he had been present at her launch on 26 November 1913. After completion and commissioning she had joined the Grand Fleet at Scapa Flow on 13 April 1915. At the Battle of Jutland on 31 May 1916 she and her sister ships formed the Fifth Battle Squadron supporting Beatty's battle-cruisers. While engaging the leading ships of the German High Seas Fleet her helm jammed and she turned two full circles under heavy fire which put all but one turret out of action. After *Warspite* had been hit by thirteen heavy shells Captain E. M. Philpotts managed to disengage and returned to Rosyth. After extensive repairs she rejoined the Grand Fleet, and on 21 May 1926 she hoisted the flag of Admiral Keyes. Churchill stood on the bridge as *Warspite* led the whole fleet out of the Grand Harbour on 10 January 1927. After carrying out exercises in the central Mediterranean the fleet sailed to Athens and Churchill landed at Piraeus on 13 January. In thanking Keyes he later wrote: 'I do not know when I have enjoyed any expedition more . . . Altogether it has been a most happy and bright page in the book of recollections.'[14] We shall meet Keyes again in later chapters.

There is no record of any discussions that Churchill may have had on this visit with the Governor or Keyes. However, since he was a leading member of the government and both a former Colonial Secretary and First Lord of the Admiralty it would be surprising if the three men did not review in detail developments in Malta and the wider international scene. The Governor knew that Churchill intended to see Mussolini and he no doubt told him of Italian support for attempts to develop fascism in Malta. The Colonial Office records contain various reports from the Governor about these developments but they appear at that time to have provoked mild irritation rather than alarm. A Maltese historian of this period has concluded that 'the fanaticism of the small nucleus of Maltese fascists tended to repel rather than attract most of the local population.'[15] Churchill certainly read the *Daily Malta Chronicle* while he was there and he may have seen the third leader in the issue of Friday 7 January. Under the headline 'Italian Ambitions in the Mediterranean: Claims to Malta Revived', the leader criticised Italian claims to sovereignty over Malta which frequently appeared in the fascist-controlled Italian press.[16]

It is time now to introduce a person who will appear more frequently in the coming chapters, a man whose decisions and actions were in the years ahead to establish a deeper bond between Winston Churchill and the people of Malta. On 30 October 1922 Benito Mussolini formed a fascist government in Italy. Initial British reaction to this development was mixed. Six months later a Foreign Office review of Anglo-Italian relations recorded that prior to his coming to power Mussolini had been 'prophesying on public platforms the day when the Italian navy would be capturing Malta and otherwise inconveniencing the ramshackle British Empire.' However, the analysis went on to accept that Mussolini once in power had behaved very much like previous Italian governments. In May 1923 King George V and Queen Mary visited Rome and after bestowing on Mussolini the Order of the Bath the King referred to 'the wise guidance of a strong statesman.'[17]

The Corfu incident in August of that year when Mussolini in a dispute with Greece ordered the bombardment and occupation of Corfu strained relations and gave early notice that Mussolini was likely to become an aggressive and disruptive force in the Mediterranean world. In this connection it is worth recording that Admiral Keyes, who at that time was Deputy Chief of Naval Staff at the Admiralty, referred to Mussolini as a 'mad dog', a phrase that was often to be applied to him in the years ahead.[18] However, the Corfu crisis passed and Mussolini's signature of the Locarno Agreements in October 1925 and the warm personal relationship established between him and the British Foreign Secretary, Sir Austen Chamberlain, seemed to herald a new era of friendship and cooperation between the two countries.

Churchill, as Chancellor of the Exchequer, was only directly concerned with Italy in relation to the settlement of her war debts to Britain. However, in the discussions that took place in early 1926 he persuaded the Cabinet, against the advice of his officials, to offer Italy generous terms and this was warmly received in Italy. He had not previously met Mussolini, although in an earlier letter to Clementine of 5 September 1923 when referring to the Italian seizure of the port of Fiume he had written: 'What a swine this Mussolini is'.[19] However, in the spring of 1926 Clementine, while staying at the British Embassy in Rome, met Mussolini and wrote effusively to her husband:

He is most impressive—quite simple & natural, very dignified, has a charming smile & the most beautiful golden brown piercing eyes which you see but can't look at . . . He sent you friendly messages & said he would like to meet you. I am sure he is a very great person. It is certain that he inspires fanatical devotion in his followers.[20]

A week later Clementine wrote again:

> I have just received a beautiful signed photograph from Mussolini.
> <u>A la Signora Winston Churchill</u>
> <u>Devotamente</u>
> <u>B. Mussolini</u>
> <u>Roma 25 marzo 1926</u>
> is inscribed on it. All the Embassy ladies are dying of jealousy![21]

To all this Churchill simply replied by quoting a remark of a former Liberal MP and colleague, Augustine Birrell, that, 'It is better to read about a world figure than to live under his rule.'[22] Nevertheless, for a time the signed photograph of Mussolini stood in the drawing room at Chartwell but, as her daughter, Lady Soames, later observed, 'it was removed to obscurity within a short period of time.'[23]

When he was planning his winter trip to the Mediterranean Churchill decided that it would be useful to meet Mussolini to form a judgement for himself about this new force in world politics. As he told Keyes, 'On leaving you I am going to stay in Rome for a few days to see Mussolini (while he lasts).'[24] The parenthetical conclusion was a reference to the fact that Mussolini had survived three attempts on his life in 1926. Consequently, after completing his visit to Athens Churchill and his small party returned to Brindisi by destroyer and then caught an overnight train to Rome where he arrived on Friday, 14 January 1927. He stayed at the British Embassy as the guest of the Ambassador, Sir Ronald Graham.

On Saturday the Ambassador took him to meet Mussolini at the Foreign Ministry and later wrote to Austen Chamberlain at the Foreign Office:

> Churchill's visit has been a great success, at any rate from the Italian point of view. I took him to see Mussolini and left him alone there once the ball was going . . . They had another good talk at the Embassy the next night. There was much mutual appreciation.[25]

Churchill wished to preserve the private character of his visit but, under pressure from the press, he prepared and issued a lengthy press statement at the end of his visit to Rome. This took the form of Churchill's replies to a number of assumed questions and was widely reported in Italy and in Britain. Churchill commented on Mussolini's 'calm, detached poise in spite of so many burdens and dangers', and accepted that his government rested 'on the practical assent of the great masses'. He declined to pass judgement on fascism as such, saying merely that 'different countries have different ways of doing the same thing'. Nevertheless, he went on:

If I had been an Italian, I am sure I should have been whole-heartedly with you from the start to finish in your triumphant struggle against the bestial appetites and passions of Leninism. But in England we have not yet had to face this danger in the same deadly form. We have our own way of doing things. But that we shall succeed in grappling with Communism and choking the life out of it—of that I am absolutely sure.[26]

Baldwin had been advised of Churchill's proposed visit to Mussolini and had written that he 'was looking forward to hearing your account of your talk with Mussolini, tempered only with a natural regret that I shall never hear his impressions. The picture will be vivid but incomplete.'[27] Churchill, in a subsequent letter to the Prime Minister, wrote: 'You will see I had to give an interview in Rome to the journalists, but I daresay it will be found helpful.'[28] Graham for his part told the Foreign Secretary that 'it seemed to me extremely good as well as striking an original note. Mussolini was perfectly delighted with it, but I cannot say the same as regards the Russian press representatives.'[29]

The reports in the London newspapers of his meetings with Mussolini and the comments in the press statement were mixed. *The Times* simply printed a lengthy extract from the press statement. The Labour and Liberal press, as Clementine advised him, were more indignant. On 28 January the *New Leader* wrote: 'We always suspected that Mr. Winston Churchill was a Fascist at heart. Now he has openly avowed it.'[30] This same accusation had been levelled at him during the Westminster by-election in March 1924 when cartoonists had depicted him as 'England's Mussolini'. He also encountered some criticism in France since Mussolini's attacks on that country, including Italian claims for Tunis and Corsica, had caused widespread anger. On his way back to England Churchill attended a lunch in Paris and later wrote to his wife to report that he had been obliged to defend his interview with Mussolini 'with some spirit'.[31]

What Churchill said and wrote publicly about Mussolini at that time was determined by his own loathing of communism and, more importantly, by the overall foreign policy being pursued by the British government in the context of the Locarno Agreements and must be read in this context. What he personally thought about the Dictator after meeting him is not known, since there are no personal letters or diary entries that might give a clue. He doubtless gave his personal impressions to Baldwin and Austen Chamberlain upon his return to London. He must also have discussed his Rome meetings with his wife whom he met in the south of France after leaving Italy. Certainly, when Clementine visited Italy again that October she wrote, 'My culte for Mussolini is somewhat diminished.'[32] One can only assume that if after at last meeting Mussolini Churchill still thought of him as a 'swine' and said as much to his colleagues and to his wife they kept this to themselves. His later views about Mussolini will be considered in subsequent chapters.

We may end this chapter on a lighter and more personal note by posing an intriguing question. Did Churchill paint while he was in Malta? Brief mention has been made in the previous chapter of Churchill's discovery of the pleasures of painting in 1915 after his three previous visits to the island. During his busy life he managed to find time to paint over 500 canvasses but since he painted for his own enjoyment very few of these are dated and the location is rarely noted. In addition he is thought to have given away about 100 of his total output and the present whereabouts of all these is not certainly known. We know that he brought all his painting equipment with him on this 1927 visit since, after he reached Athens, his son Randolph wrote to Professor Lindeman that 'we drove straight to the Acropolis where Papa painted.'[33] Further when he reached Rome a week after leaving Malta *The Times* reported that 'he will devote most of his time in Rome to his artistic activities.'[34] The canvasses he painted in Athens and Rome are among those which hang in his Studio at Chartwell.

Churchill spent only three days in Malta and was busy with official engagements and his polo match. However, his enthusiasm for painting was so keen at that time that he often found an opportunity to fit a painting session into a busy schedule. He was primarily a landscape painter and was particularly struck by the bright colourful scenes he found in the Mediterranean and at Marrakesh, what he once called 'paintatious' scenes. Such scenes were all around him in Valletta and he surely viewed the Grand Harbour and the buildings of Valletta with a painter's eye. Nevertheless, there is no known painting by him of a Malta scene or any documentary evidence of such a painting, and it seems that bad weather may have prevented this. Had Sunday 9 January dawned bright and clear it is surely not too fanciful to suppose that Churchill might have set up his easel in some 'paintatious' spot. Alas! the weather that Sunday was wretched. The north-east gregale was blowing hard and the *Daily Malta Chronicle* carried reports that on the afternoon of that day 'a drizzling rain was falling and the wind was piercingly cold.'[35] On the following morning, as noted above, Churchill told his wife that there was half a gale blowing. Regretfully, we must conclude that if Churchill had wished to paint a Maltese scene during his visit this intention was thwarted by the weather. Had conditions been dry and bright he, and we, might have had a permanent and colourful record of this 1927 visit to the island.

From our point of view it is fortunate that Clementine did not accompany her husband on this trip since his frequent and detailed letters to her enable us to see how much he enjoyed this further visit to Malta. In one of them he told her that 'there were many requests we return next year together.'[36] He was delighted to have the company of his brother and son, and both Keyes and Congreve were old friends. It seems reasonable to assume that these three had wide-ranging discussions about the situation in the Mediterranean and in Malta itself although we have no record of this. Churchill was clearly pleased to have the opportunity, at last, to sail on the ship that he had ordered in 1912 and to witness the manoeuvres of Britain's Main Fleet. However, since this was an unofficial visit he had no reason to become involved in Maltese domestic affairs other than, as a senior member of the Cabinet and a former Colonial Secretary, to listen to what the Governor had to say.

## *Notes*

[1] For details see the author's *Malta and British Strategic Policy 1925-1943* (Frank Cass, London, 2004), pp. 6-19.

[2] P. Halpern (ed.), *The Keyes Papers, Vol. II, 1919-1938* (George Allen & Unwin for the Navy Records Society, London, 1980), WSC to Keyes, 16 September 1926, p. 190.

[3] *Churchill, Vol. V*, pp. 222, 224.

[4] Ibid., p. 224.

[5] Randolph S. Churchill, *Twenty-One Years* (Weidenfeld and Nicolson, London, 1964), pp. 48-9.

[6] Halpern, *Keyes Papers, Vol. II*, WSC to Keyes, 15 November 1926, p. 191.

[7] Winston Churchill, *My Early Life: A Roving Commission* (Thornton Butterworth, London, 1930), p. 59.

[8] Ibid., pp. 221-5.

[9] M. Soames (ed.), *Speaking for Themselves: The Personal Letters of Winston and Clementine Churchill* (Black Swan, London, 1999), p. 305.

[10] Halpern, *Keyes Papers, Vol. II*, WSC to Keyes, 15 November 1926, p. 191.

[11] *Companion, Vol. V, Part 1*, Keyes to WSC, 23 November 1926, p. 886.

[12] Ibid., pp. 910-11.

[13] *Churchill, Vol. V*, WSC to Baldwin, 10 January 1927, p. 224.

[14] *Companion, Vol. V, Part 1*, WSC to Keyes, 16 January 1927, p. 913.

[15] Frendo, *Party Politics*, p. 196.

[16] *Daily Malta Chronicle*, 7 January 1927.

[17] R. Lamb, *Mussolini and the British* (John Murray, London, 1997), p. 39.

[18] Halpern, *Keyes Papers, Vol. II*, p. 95.

[19] *Churchill, Vol. V*, WSC to CSC, 5 September 1923, p. 13.

[20] Soames, *Letters*, CSC to WSC, 20 March 1926, p. 295.

[21] Ibid., CSC to WSC, 25 March 1926, p. 297.

[22] Ibid., WSC to CSC, 28 March 1926, p. 298.

[23] Ibid., Note 1 to CSC to WSC, 25 March 1926. p. 297.

[24] Halpern, *Keyes Papers, Vol. II*, p. 191.

[25] *Companion, Vol. V, Part 1*, Graham to Foreign Secretary, 21 January 1927 pp. 916-7.

[26] *Churchill, Vol. V*, p. 226.

[27] *Companion, Vol. V, Part 1*, Baldwin to WSC, 18 January 1927, pp. 914-5.

[28] Ibid., WSC to Baldwin, 22 January 1927, p. 917.

[29] Ibid., Graham to Austen Chamberlain, 21 January 1927, pp. 916-7.

[30] *Churchill, Vol. V*, p. 226.

[31] Ibid., p. 228.

[32] Soames, *Letters*, CSC to WSC, 28 September 1927, pp. 310-11.

[33] *Companion, Vol. V, Part 1*, Footnote 1, p. 912.

[34] *The Times*, 17 January 1927.

[35] *Daily Malta Chronicle*, 12 January 1927.

[36] *Companion, Vol. V, Part 1*, WSC to CSC, 10 January 1927, pp. 910-11.

## CHAPTER VII

# The 1930s and the Abyssinian Crisis

*It is wise for the Fleet to quit Malta which, I understand, is totally unprovided with anti-aircraft defence.*

Churchill to Sir Samuel Hoare, 25 August 1935

Between May 1929 when the Conservative Party lost the election and the outbreak of the Second World War Winston Churchill, although he continued to be an active Member of Parliament, held no ministerial appointment. During these 'Wilderness Years' he alienated himself from the Tory leadership by his determined opposition to the plan to give Dominion status to India. His exclusion from government gave him time to develop his estate at Chartwell, to write the biography of his ancestor, the first Duke of Marlborough, and to paint. With increasing skill and enjoyment he completed 200 of his paintings in the 1930s, many of them while on holiday in the south of France. A journalist since his youth he also wrote many newspaper articles, which were widely syndicated throughout Europe, to generate the income to support his growing family and to repair the losses he suffered in the Wall Street 'crash' of 1929.

During this decade he did not visit Malta and he was not involved in the political crisis on the island that led in 1930 and again in 1933 to the suspension of the Constitution that he had helped to establish in 1921. It was not until 1935-6 that events once again directed his attention to Malta. These were the years when Mussolini's invasion of Abyssinia in October 1935 marked a fateful step towards the Second World War. It was then that the British government became alarmed about the possibility of Italian air attack on Malta in which poison gas might be used. To the surprise of Churchill and many others outside government it then became clear that Malta, which since the re-distribution of the Fleet in 1923, had become Britain's major overseas naval base, had virtually no defence against air attack.

To understand why this was so we will first need to review the steps that the government's military advisers had taken, and not taken, in the early 1930s to modernise Malta's defences.[1] As has been narrated in the preceding chapter Churchill's 1927 visit to Malta and the subsequent cruise with the Mediterranean Fleet gave him first hand confirmation of the strategic value of the island. Until 1929 while he remained a member of the CID he will have been aware of the plans being worked out to modernise the island's defences, especially against the new and growing threat of air attack. In 1928 a special sub-committee of the CID, known as the Defence of Ports Committee (DOP), studied Malta's requirements. It recommended that Malta be defended by a garrison of four infantry battalions supported by the KOMR and the Royal Malta Artillery (RMA), five squadrons of modern aircraft and the installation of twenty-four AA guns.

Unfortunately, the implementation of these plans was delayed for more than three years by two technical problems. Firstly, bombardment trials at Malta in 1928 revealed that the heavy coastal artillery, all installed before 1914, needed considerable modernisation and it took a further three years to decide how this was to be done and to make the necessary changes. Secondly, there was a dispute, which became known as the 'Gun v. Air' controversy, between the RAF and the other two services over the Air Ministry's claim that its aircraft would provide a better and more economical defence against naval attack than heavy coastal artillery. It was only in May 1932 that the Coast Defence Inquiry, chaired by Baldwin, was established to decide the matter.

In the course of this investigation the Chief of the Air Staff (CAS), Sir John Salmond, was forced to concede that he could not guarantee that the aircraft necessary to defend Malta would be deployed there at the critical moment. The disposition of British forces in war, he admitted, lay ultimately with the War Cabinet, or other controlling authority, and not with the Air Staff. The Committee was more influenced by a statement attributed to the American naval historian, Admiral Mahan, that 'permanent works . . . have the advantage that they cannot be shifted under the influence of panic.' The Committee, therefore, ruled that coastal artillery should be the primary means of anti-ship defence.[2]

It was not, therefore, until 1932 that another sub-committee of the CID, the Joint Defence Committee (JDC), resumed discussions about Malta's defence requirements. It is of some interest to note that the RAF member of the JDC in 1932 was Group Captain Charles Portal and he was succeeded several years later by Group Captain Arthur Harris. The recommendations of the JDC followed the general lines of the earlier DOP enquiry although only two squadrons of aircraft were now envisaged. However, when in 1933 this report came before the Chiefs of Staff (COS) its implementation was once again postponed. This was due initially to their growing concern about the Japanese threat in the Far East, which led them to accelerate the completion of the Singapore naval base. However, as the British government struggled to deal with the economic and social consequences of the worldwide depression of the early 1930s overall British defence estimates had been reduced to their lowest inter-war level in 1932. There was simply not enough money to complete Singapore and also to carry out the Malta proposals.

Later that same year worries about Japanese intentions took second place to concern about Hitler who, having become German Chancellor, immediately embarked on a major rearmament programme. This finally prompted a reluctant British government to authorise a modest increase in defence expenditures. Crucially for Malta, however, the CID at a meeting in November 1933 ruled that no expenditure be undertaken to guard against possible attack by Italy. The result was that the report about Malta's defences which was finally submitted in October 1934 contained no provision for any modern aircraft to be stationed on the island. In addition, there were then only two under-strength battalions in the island, the coastal artillery was still being modernised and only eight of the twenty-four AA guns that had been recommended had been installed. Moreover, these were obsolescent 3-inch guns unable to reach high-flying aircraft.

This was Malta's condition when the British government's belief that Italy would continue to be aligned with Britain and France in opposing a resurgent Germany began to crumble in 1935 as it became increasingly clear that Mussolini intended to attack Abyssinia, another member of the League of Nations. It is now known that as early as 1933 Mussolini had resolved to acquire Abyssinia to add to Italy's existing colonies of Eritrea and Italian Somaliland in north-east Africa. He, therefore, took advantage of a clash at Wal Wal on the border between Abyssinia and Italian Somaliland in December 1934 as a pretext to send additional troops to the area. In March 1935 Abyssinia formally protested to the League of Nations about Italian aggression in the disputed border area. Nevertheless, at the Stresa Conference that met in April to reaffirm support for Austrian independence and opposition to Germany's violation of treaty obligations, Ramsay MacDonald, the British Prime Minister, and Sir John Simon, the Foreign Secretary, deliberately refrained from warning Mussolini against an attack on Abyssinia. Inevitably, therefore, Mussolini took the view that he had been given a free hand with regard to Abyssinia and the Italian military build-up in Italian Somaliland and Eritrea continued.

Throughout the early months of 1935 the British Embassy in Rome passed back to the Foreign Office mounting evidence of Italian preparations. The Italian press, under Mussolini's personal control, carried numerous articles about Italy's determination to resist, by force if necessary, any attempt to frustrate her claims in Abyssinia. At the same time the Foreign Office began to receive reports that Malta might be attacked. An Egyptian source reported comments made by two Italian officials to the effect that 'the Italians would have no difficulty in demolishing Malta in twenty-four hours'. A little later a British visitor to Rome reported to the Director of Naval Intelligence (DNI) that he had been told that 'the Italians are ready to bomb Malta and would do it without thinking twice'. In August Mussolini himself told the French Ambassador in Rome that if the Suez Canal were closed to prevent the passage of Italian troopships, 'out of desperation I would not hesitate, if necessary, to make war on [the British]'.[3]

In this deteriorating atmosphere Baldwin, who had in the previous month succeeded Ramsay MacDonald as Prime Minister, asked the COS in July to consider the military implications of a possible imposition of League of Nations sanctions against Italy. A month later, just before Parliament rose for the summer recess, the Chiefs were again asked to examine what steps should be taken 'if Italy took the bit between her teeth'.[4] By that time it was widely believed that Mussolini intended to invade Abyssinia as soon as the rainy season ended in October unless he were given effective control of the country without fighting. Moreover, there was now a very strong conviction in Whitehall that, if he were thwarted, the dictator might make a 'mad dog' pre-emptive attack on the Mediterranean fleet at Valletta. In August Sir Samuel Hoare, who had succeeded Simon as Foreign Secretary, wrote to Cunliffe-Lister, the Secretary of State for Air:

> We are dealing with a monomaniac and no one can tell what he may or may not do. My fear is not that we shall drift into a war with Italy but rather that Mussolini and some of his wilder Fascists may commit some mad dog act against us.[5]

As we have previously noted, the 'mad dog' description had been applied to Mussolini a dozen years earlier by Admiral Keyes. The upshot of these discussions was a decision to move the Mediterranean fleet from Malta to Alexandria in late August and to send substantial reinforcements to the area. Signals flashed from the Admiralty around the world and naval ships steamed to the eastern Mediterranean from every direction.[6]

As regards Malta itself, dangerously close to Italian airfields in Sicily, the Cabinet decided, on the strength of the advice of the COS, that every effort should be made to defend the island and air force and army reinforcements, including additional AA guns, began to arrive in September. Such was the condition of the RAF at this time, however, that only two squadrons could be made available at such short notice. One was a fighter squadron equipped with Hawker Demons and the other a torpedo-bomber squadron of Vickers Vildebeests. Both of these types were bi-planes with appearance and performance similar to aircraft of the First World War and they had to be crated up for a passage by sea to Malta. Opposing these obsolescent aircraft was the *Regia Aeronautica*, thought by the early 1930s to possess up to 1,000 modern aircraft. RAF Intelligence considered that the Italian air force would have no difficulty in deploying 100 bombers against Malta.[7]

There was widespread anxiety in Malta about the possible use of poison gas, which both sides had used in the First World War and the

Italians were to employ in Abyssinia. After some delay respirators and anti-gas materials were sent to the island and other precautions taken. Another concern was that after the Fleet had left for Alexandria about 5,000 naval wives and children had been left on the island.[8] The Cabinet discussed whether these should be immediately returned to England but decided that this would make a bad impression. The degree of alarm about conditions in Malta was starkly expressed in a letter that the Governor, Sir David Campbell, then recovering in London from a serious operation, sent on 20 August to Sir John Shuckburgh at the Colonial Office:

> . . . the Secretary of State should know that, in my opinion, if by any unfortunate chance we were to go to War with Italy in the near future, Malta would be utterly defenceless against such an air attack as Italy could launch against it. In a short space of time it would be a veritable shambles.[9]

When considering this letter and other comments that will be quoted in the following pages the reader should bear in mind the inordinate fear of bombing that was prevalent in these inter-war years.[10] Ministers shared this fear and Baldwin, if for nothing else, is remembered for his saying in the House of Commons on 10 November 1932:

> I think it is as well also for the man in the street to realise that there is no power on earth that can protect him from being bombed. Whatever people may tell him, the bomber will always get through. The only defence is in offence, which means that you have to kill more women and children more quickly than the enemy if you want to save yourselves.[11]

It was fortunate for the British people that there were those, as we shall see later, who were determined to make every effort to see that the bomber did *not* get through.

How did Churchill react to this growing possibility of war with Italy and the danger of an air attack on Malta? Not being a member of the government he did not automatically have access to all of the information that came before the Cabinet and its advisers. Nevertheless, his contacts in government and official circles were extensive. Moreover, his forthright opposition to German rearmament, to which the government had in his view made an inadequate response, had persuaded a number of officials to pass secret information to him. Several of these are known to have made visits to Chartwell to advise him of developments, but it is believed that other visitors declined to sign the Visitors' Book kept there. Much of the information that Churchill received has now been documented but it seems possible that Churchill was made aware of other matters in private conversations or by telephone, especially as he remained at Chartwell during July and August.

At an early stage of the crisis he and several of his friends considered a visit to Mussolini but this was not pursued. In the House of Commons on 11 July he endorsed the proposal of Sir Samuel Hoare that the government would support whatever recommendations the League might make but without taking the lead. He rejected the notion that 'we were ourselves coming forward as a sort of bell-wether or fugleman to lead opinion in Europe against Italy's Abyssinian designs.' He then went on:

> It was even suggested that we would act individually and independently. I am glad to hear from the Foreign Secretary that there is no foundation for that. We must do our duty, but we must do it only in conjunction with other nations and in accordance with obligations that others recognize as well. We are not strong enough—I say it advisedly—to be the lawgiver and spokesman of the world. We will do our part, but we cannot be asked, and we ought not to put ourselves in a position of being supposed, to do more than our part in these matters.[12]

A month later Hoare, who had been left in charge while Baldwin and most of the Cabinet were on holiday, obviously felt rather isolated. As he wrote to Neville Chamberlain, 'I have received little or no help from other quarters. Stanley [Baldwin] would think about nothing but his holiday and the necessity of keeping out of the whole business almost at any cost.'[13] He, therefore, decided to consult a number of leading figures outside the government. Accordingly, on 24 August Churchill called at the Foreign Office where he met Hoare and Anthony Eden, at that time Minister for League of Nations Affairs. Hoare's note of the discussion recorded that Churchill was 'deeply incensed at the Italian action,' and thought this was mainly the result of British naval weakness in the Mediterranean. Hoare had been led to believe by Lloyd George that Churchill had at one stage favoured unilateral British action against Italy but Churchill made clear, as he had in his July speech, that he supported a collective response. His view, moreover, was that the British government should only go as far as it could carry France. He did not, however, expect France to go very far and the government should not put undue pressure on her.[14] Despite Hoare's blandly worded note, Churchill seems to have expressed his views with characteristic force, for Harold Nicolson later noted in his diary that Eden had told him that 'Winston was all out for blood and thunder.'[15]

A day later Churchill, after reading that the Mediterranean fleet was leaving Malta, wrote to Hoare that 'certainly it is wise for the Fleet to quit Malta, which, I understand, is totally unprovided with anti-aircraft defence.'[16] Churchill spent the first two weeks of September on holiday in the south of France. There he read of Hoare's speech at Geneva on 11 September which, to Hoare's subsequent surprise, was taken to mean that Britain would give a firm lead in opposing Italian aggression in Abyssinia. He also read of the arrival at Gibraltar on the following day of substantial naval reinforcements including the battle-cruisers *Hood* and *Renown*. On 5 September his wife had written to him, 'Wow! I really think Mussolini must be mad. He clearly wants War for the sake of War!' Churchill replied, writing: 'I do feel that if the League of Nations pull this off and stop the Abyssinian subjugation, we should all be stronger and safer for many a long day.'[17]

On his return to London he had a lengthy meeting with the First Sea Lord, Admiral Sir Ernle Chatfield. Chatfield had been Captain of the new battle-cruiser, HMS *Lion*, at Jutland where she had been the flagship of Admiral Beatty's Battle-Cruiser Squadron. In 1930 he became C-in-C of the Mediterranean Fleet and in January 1933 was appointed First Sea Lord, a post he held until early 1938 when he was raised to the peerage. He was then appointed Minister for the Coordination of Defence. It is reasonable to assume that Chatfield gave the former First Lord of the Admiralty a full account of the plans that had now been worked out by the COS. After an initial disagreement between the Admiralty and the Air Ministry about the disposition of aircraft the COS had agreed their overall strategy at a meeting on 7 September. In the event of war the navy would blockade Italy and seek to engage the Italian fleet, should it put to sea, by using an anchorage in Navarino Bay on the west coast of the Peloponnese. Every effort would be made to defend Malta, to which air and army reinforcements were being sent, but if the island were temporarily lost this would not be fatal to overall strategy. Chatfield may well have told Churchill what he had already written to Admiral Sir William Fisher, C-in-C of the Mediterranean Fleet: 'If Italy is mad enough to challenge us, it is at the ends of the Mediterranean she will be defeated . . . and Malta, even if it is demolished, will come back again.'[18]

Churchill was clearly reassured by what he heard since he subsequently wrote to Admiral Keyes that 'I had a good talk with Chatfield and I have a feeling that the Navy is quite capable of looking after itself in view of the precautions so rightly taken . . . Chatfield strikes me as a very fine fellow . . . he gives me a good feeling to talk to.'[19] Against this sentence in the letter Keyes wrote, 'Yes, talk', and Churchill was later to change his mind about Chatfield. By that time Keyes, although an Admiral of the Fleet, was no longer on active service and had entered politics in February 1934 as Conservative MP for Portsmouth North. The subject of the dangers facing Malta came up again on 20 September when Churchill received at Chartwell a delegation from his Epping constituency. Among them was former naval Commander Maitland whom Churchill asked how Malta could stand up to naval or aerial bombardment. Maitland reminded him of the fact that 'the houses there have small windows and two feet thick walls', but this could hardly have provided much reassurance.[20]

Fearing that the unexpected reception given to Hoare's speech in Geneva and British naval moves might provoke the 'mad dog' attack they were designed to deter the Cabinet instructed the British Ambassador in Rome, Sir Eric Drummond, to see Signor Suvich, the Italian Under-Secretary for Foreign Affairs, which he did on 21 September. Drummond then told him that British actions were purely precautionary in light of Italian press articles that spoke among other matters about the weakness of Malta and how easily it could be bombed. Britain had no intention of attacking Italy or of closing the Suez Canal. This was all made public in a *communiqué* that the Foreign Office released on 23 September. With Italian invasion of Abyssinia now highly probable Churchill made one last appeal for a negotiated settlement at a speech to the City Carlton Club on 26 September. He concluded by warning Mussolini that 'to cast an army of nearly a quarter of a million of men . . . upon a barren shore two thousand miles from home . . . is to give hostages to fortune unparalleled in all history.'[21] He, nevertheless, confided to Austen Chamberlain a few days later that 'I am very unhappy. It would be a terrible deed to smash up Italy, and it will cost us dear. I do not think we ought to have taken the lead in such a vehement way'[22] But it was too late; the Italian invasion was launched on 4 October.

Was there any danger that Malta might have been attacked? We now know that as early as May 1935 Mussolini instructed the Italian Chiefs of Staff to draw up plans for a war with Britain including an attack on Malta. In response to this General Valle, the air force chief, stated in August that his forces could drop 100 tons of bombs a day on the island and Italian air force units were transferred to Sicily. However, Admiral Cavagnari, the naval Chief of Staff, thought that such an attack would serve no strategic purpose since the Royal Navy would concentrate at Gibraltar and Alexandria. He added that Italian forces could only give the *impression* of action in order to make the British hesitate. This is the key to an understanding of Mussolini's tactics. He played on and fed, through rumours and threats, British fears that he might act irrationally causing, even in defeat, losses that the British could ill afford in face of German rearmament. How effective these threats were can be judged by a remark that Baldwin made in December 1935. 'If Mussolini broke out,' he warned, 'there would be more killed in Valletta in one night than in all the Abyssinian campaign up to date.'[23] Critically, too, Mussolini knew through intercepts of messages between the Foreign Office and the British Ambassador in Rome that the British government was determined not to go to war with Italy over Abyssinia. On 21 December 1937 Ciano, who by then had become Italian Foreign Minister, wrote in his diary about Mussolini:

I remember his wanting to make a surprise attack on the Home Fleet [sic] at Alexandria and Malta in August 1935. He said to me then, 'In one night the course of history can be changed.' However, he didn't do it, because we had no precise information about the efficiency of the English fleet and because our navy put on the brakes.[24]

As Churchill later wrote, 'Mussolini's bluff succeeded and an important spectator drew far-reaching conclusions . . . In Japan, too, there were pensive spectators.'[25]

The evidence examined in this chapter suggests that Churchill fully shared the British government's anxiety about the safety of Malta and its civilian population in the summer and autumn of 1935. Since he remained out of government it would be wrong to suggest that he had much influence on the decisions that were taken. When he was later criticised by Lord Cranborne he replied by saying that the responsibility lay with the Government, 'not with private persons at all, even though they have from time to time tried to give the Government as much support as possible.'[26] Nevertheless, he took pains to inform himself of the relevant facts and to express his views when invited to do so. It may well be that his most useful discussion was with Admiral Chatfield although there are no records of what was said at this meeting. He clearly endorsed Chatfield's decision to move the Mediterranean fleet to Alexandria, a decision that, as Admiral Cavagnari appreciated, made an attack on Malta less likely.

Nevertheless, for Churchill in a broader perspective the whole crisis was a most unfortunate distraction. Speaking in the House of Commons on 24 October 1935 he declared that the Italian attack on Abyssinia was 'a very small matter' compared to the German danger. '*There* is the dominant factor; *there* is the factor that dwarfs all others', he told the House.[27] The rights and wrongs of the policy pursued by the British government during the Abyssinian crisis have been much discussed and a full analysis lies outside the scope of this narrative. When he came to write the first volume of his memoirs of the Second World War in 1948 Churchill had this to say about the Abyssinian crisis: 'If ever there was an opportunity of striking a decisive blow in a generous cause with the minimum of risk, it was here and now.' But, he went on to write, 'the nerve of the British Government was not equal to the occasion.'[28]

It has to be said, however, that, as has been shown in this chapter, Churchill did not favour a strong British stance against Italy. Indeed in his speech in the House of Commons on 11 July and at his private meeting in August with Hoare and Eden he clearly favoured a low-key response similar to that adopted by France, and was later critical of the government for giving too strong a lead at Geneva. After making due allowance for his being out of office and not, therefore, being fully aware of all the relevant facts and arguments it is difficult to acquit Churchill of the charge he subsequently levelled at Baldwin. He, like Baldwin and the rest of the Cabinet, failed to see at the time that it was not possible both to maintain the strength and authority of the League of Nations, which required the frustration of Italian aggression, and to retain Italian support against Germany. Once Mussolini had decided to pursue his attack on Abyssinia the better defence against Hitler's still early rearmament was not the dubious support of Italy but a resolute and effective League of Nations. But Churchill at the time did not advocate strong measures against Italy such as the closing of the Suez Canal to Italian shipping or the imposition of oil sanctions and he seems to have shared the government's hope that the Italian campaign in Abyssinia might fail. In December 1935 the publication of the Hoare-Laval proposals, which proposed the cession to Italy of roughly two-thirds of Abyssinia, caused a political crisis that led to Hoare's resignation. Churchill who was abroad on holiday decided, after some reflection and strong advice from his son, Randolph, not to return to London. In April 1936 Italian troops entered the Abyssinian capital, Addis Ababa, and on 9 May Mussolini proclaimed the country's annexation.

In the event the faint-hearted policy pursued by the British government, and generally supported at the time by Churchill, fatally undermined the League of Nations. Even worse, Italy was alienated and in October 1936 the Rome-Berlin Axis was proclaimed. The result for Malta, as for Britain, was only a temporary reprieve. The island was spared bombing attack in 1935, only to suffer five years later much greater death, injury and destruction. We shall see in a later chapter the reply Mussolini gave to Churchill when the latter, having become Prime Minister, appealed in May 1940 for continued Italian neutrality.

## Notes

[1] For a more detailed account see the author's *Malta and British Strategic Policy*, pp. 20-34.

[2] The Report of the Coast Defence Enquiry, 24 May 1932, is in NA CAB 16/105.

[3] G. Baer, *The Coming of the Italian-Ethiopian War* (Harvard University Press, Cambridge, Mass., 1967), p. 255.

[4] NA CAB 53/5, 146th COS Meeting, 5 July 1935; CAB 23/82, CP 159 (35), 6 August 1935.

[5] NA FO 371/19197, J3861, Hoare to Cunliffe-Lister, 17 August 1935.

[6] The author's father and two of his uncles, all then serving on different ships of the Royal Navy, met that autumn in Alexandria.

[7] NA CAB 53/22, COS Memorandum 274, 'The Air Threat to Our Sea Communications in the Mediterranean', 8 July 1931.

[8] The author, his mother, and his brother, Peter, were three of those left behind.

[9] NA CO 158/484/89001/3, Campbell to Shuckburgh, 20 August 1935.

[10] This subject is analysed in U. Bialer, *The Shadow of the Bomber* (Royal Historical Society, London, 1980).

[11] K. Middlemas and J. Barnes, *Baldwin: A Biography* (Weidenfeld and Nicolson, London, 1969), p. 735.

[12] R. Rhodes James, *Churchill Speaks: Winston Churchill in Peace and War. Collected Speeches, 1897-1963* (Windward, London, 1981), p. 608.

[13] Viscount Templewood (Sir Samuel Hoare), *Nine Troubled Years* (Collins, London, 1954), p. 164.

[14] *Companion, Vol. V, Part 2*, Note of conversation between Churchill, Hoare and Eden, 21 August 1935, pp. 1239-40.

[15] N. Nicolson (ed.), *Harold Nicolson: Diaries and Letters 1930-1939* (Collins, London, 1966), p. 211.

[16] *Companion, Vol. V, Part 2*, WSC to Hoare, 25 August 1935, pp. 1248-9.

[17] Ibid., CSC to WSC and WSC to CSC, 5 and 11 September 1935, pp. 1256-8.

[18] National Maritime Museum, Chatfield Papers, CHT/4/5, Chatfield to Fisher, 25 August 1925.

[19] Halpern, *Keyes Papers, Vol. II*, WSC to Keyes, 24 September 1935, pp. 344-5, 435.

[20] *Companion, Vol. V, Part 2*, Colin Thornton-Kernsley Diary, 20 September 1935, pp. 1262-3.

[21] Rhodes James, *Speeches*, pp. 610-12.

[22] *Companion, Vol. V, Part 2*, WSC to Austen Chamberlain, 1 October 1935, p. 1279.

[23] NA PREM 1/177, Note of Meeting, 13 December 1935.

[24] G. Ciano, *Ciano's Diary 1937-1938* (Methuen, London, 1952), p. 47.

[25] Winston Churchill, *The Second World War, Vol. I* (Cassell, London, 1948), p. 138.

[26] *Companion, Vol. V, Part 3*, WSC to Cranborne, 8 April 1936, p. 92.

[27] Rhodes James, *Speeches*, p. 613.

[28] Churchill, *Second World War, Vol. I*, p. 138.

# CHAPTER VIII

# *Return to the Admiralty 1939*

*Assuming Italy is hostile, which we may perhaps hope will not be the case, England's first battlefield is the Mediterranean.*
Churchill: 'Memorandum on Sea Power', 1939

On the late afternoon of 3 September 1939 Winston Churchill, accompanied by his secretary, Kathleen Hill, strode into the First Lord's room at the Admiralty. He went up to a cupboard in the panelling and, as Kathleen Hill described it, 'He flung the door open with a dramatic gesture—there behind the panelling was a large map showing the disposition of all German ships on the day he had left the Admiralty in 1915.'[1] Much though Churchill himself, and his growing number of supporters, had hoped for a return to office in the 1930s he and they had to wait until the outbreak of war with Germany before this happened. On that day, for the second time, Churchill at the age of 64 became a wartime First Lord of the Admiralty.

Before we move on to the second part of this study it may be useful to ask what sort of man Winston Churchill had become in 1939. For upon his shoulders was soon to fall, among his many other burdens, the responsibility for the lives of the 250,000 inhabitants of Malta. We may take the answer given by one close observer as typical of many others. Colonel Ian Jacob, as a Military Assistant in the War Cabinet Office, was not alone in wondering whether Churchill, not far short of his sixty-fifth birthday and out of office for ten years, would be able to cope with his new responsibilities. These doubts were soon dispelled. It was Jacob's duty to attend the meetings of the Military Co-ordination Committee to take notes for the subsequent Minutes. At one such meeting at which Churchill was present a RAF bombing plan was under consideration. Jacob has described the scene:

> What struck me as some time later I sat listening to the committee discussing the plan was that though Churchill was not then the chairman of it, or nominally senior to the others, he somehow contrived to dominate it. He seated himself in the middle with everybody else around him, as though the committee has assembled for *his* convenience . . . Three things struck me: that he had dominated the proceedings by sheer personality and personal record; that his experience

showed him the faults in the plan that others didn't see; and that, in spite of ten years or so in virtual isolation immediately prior to the war, he had not gone to seed.[2]

Jacob's view of Churchill's unrivalled experience of government and his undiminished energy was to become widely shared in the months and years ahead.[3]

Let us suppose now that, after dealing with immediate naval dispositions in Home waters, Churchill had turned his attention to the Mediterranean and called for the files about Malta, the navy's principal base there. What would he have found in them? He would undoubtedly have read about constitutional and political development with disappointment. The Constitution which he had introduced in 1921 and about which he had expressed such high hopes at the Imperial Conference had proved a failure. It had been suspended in 1930, re-established in 1932, after the implementation of the recommendations of a Royal Commission, and then suspended and revoked in 1933. The reasons for this major setback to hopes of self-government lie outside the scope of this study but Amery's judgement has been noted in Chapter V above. The island had then reverted to direct rule from London through the Governor, General Sir Charles Bonham-Carter.[4] He had introduced several measures designed to promote the Maltese language at the expense of Italian, and to reduce the Italian influences in Malta which had disconcerted the British government at the time of the Abyssinian crisis. After prolonged discussion a limited new Constitution was introduced in February 1939 and all political parties put up candidates for ten elected members of the Executive Council. The fact that Lord Strickland's pro-British Constitutional Party won six of these seats and other Colonial Office reports in the files would have suggested to Churchill general Maltese acquiescence in these arrangements although they fell far short of the provisions of the 1921 Constitution.

Of more immediate concern to Churchill as First Lord of the Admiralty was whether the navy could rely upon the support of the Maltese people, and in particular, the dockyard workers, should Britain become involved in war with Italy. Here the files would have been more encouraging. The Governor had set up a civil defence organisation on lines established in Britain and considerable numbers of Maltese had joined this organisation. Others had volunteered for the Home Guard and, more importantly, a recruitment campaign for the Royal Malta Artillery had been a considerable success. It was planned to increase its strength by forty-three officers and 1,000 men and 1,000 applied when the first 200 recruits were sought. Later, when 400 volunteers were requested from the dockyard's workforce to man an AA battery there, 5,000 offered their services. When Italy entered the war in June 1940 General Dobbie, the island's Acting

Governor, was able to report to London that Maltese citizens provided no less that 44% of the garrison.

Despite this Churchill would have read with some dismay that Malta's defences, especially against air attack, were so weak that, as in 1935 and during several later periods of tension, the Mediterranean fleet had been forced to leave Malta and concentrate at Alexandria. Churchill had been concerned about this during the Abyssinian crisis, as we saw in the previous chapter, and in October 1937 he wrote to Sir Maurice Hankey, the Secretary of the CID. 'Is it true', he enquired, 'that there are under twenty AA guns at Malta and these only of an old pattern?'[5] Hankey was forced to admit that there were at that time only twelve obsolescent 3-inch AA guns at Malta.

Why this was so will require an examination of the development of Britain's relations with Italy after Mussolini's conquest of Abyssinia. By the end of 1936 the British government was faced with the appalling prospect of a three-front war with Germany, Italy and Japan. Since it would never be in a position to meet such a danger, even with the support of France, the government sought to reduce the number of its potential enemies by renewed attempts to restore friendly relations with Italy. The COS wrote in their 1937 Review of Imperial Defence: 'Our military situation in the Middle East will remain unsatisfactory until friendly relations with Italy have been permanently restored.'[6] Sir Maurice Hankey, had earlier urged that, 'We should grasp the hand of friendship held out by Signor Mussolini, however repugnant it may be.'[7] Neville Chamberlain, who had succeeded Baldwin as Prime Minister in May 1937, was particularly keen to attempt this, forcing in February 1938 the resignation of Anthony Eden who as Foreign Secretary had favoured a tougher approach to Mussolini. Although Churchill after the Abyssinian crisis retained a lingering hope that friendly relations with Italy might be restored he supported the position adopted by the Foreign Secretary. News of Eden's resignation reached Churchill at Chartwell and plunged him into gloom. A well-known passage in his war memoirs recalls that he was unable to sleep that night, and, he wrote, 'I watched the daylight slowly creep in through the windows, and saw before me in mental gaze the vision of Death.'[8] During the subsequent debate in the House of Commons on 22 February Churchill, after praising Eden's resignation speech, went on:

This has been a good week for Dictators. It is one of the best they have ever had. The German Dictator has laid his heavy hand upon a small but historic country [Austria], and the Italian Dictator has carried his vendetta to a victorious conclusion against my right Hon friend the late Foreign Secretary ... Signor Mussolini has got his scalp.[9]

Mussolini's acquiescence a month later in Germany's seizure of Austria and the 1939 Italian invasion of Albania further dimmed Churchill's hopes for Italian friendship.

Churchill's focus on the German threat made him less responsive to events in the Far East. The Cabinet could not, however, ignore the growing anxiety expressed by the Australian and New Zealand governments about Japan's intentions, to counter which they urged the rapid completion of the Singapore base and sought a reassurance that a sufficiently strong British fleet would be sent there if danger threatened. As a result the British government at the Imperial Conference in June 1937 declared that 'no anxieties or risks connected with our interests in the Mediterranean can be allowed to interfere with the despatch of a fleet to the Far East.'[10] On this occasion there was no public outcry that the Mediterranean was 'being abandoned' as there was in 1912. Two years later, however, as European dangers grew and the threat from Japan appeared to have receded, the British government changed its priorities. Mediterranean interests would not necessarily be subordinated to Far East concerns and favourable consideration was given to an Admiralty proposal that, in the event of a European war, the Allies' first objective would be to 'knock out Italy'.

Churchill contributed to this debate in March by sending a 'Memorandum on Sea Power, 1939' to Chamberlain and Lord Halifax, the Foreign Secretary.[11] This began by stating: 'Assuming Italy is hostile, which we may perhaps hope will not be the case, England's first battle-field is the Mediterranean.' He then argued for an all-out attack on the Italian fleet in order to secure command of the Mediterranean and thought that this might be achieved within about two months. 'On no account,' he went on, 'must anything which threatens in the Far East divert us from this prime objective.' However, further consideration of strategic options and of the awkward question of whether to initiate an attack on Italy if she declared her neutrality—the possibility raised in Churchill's memorandum—led the COS to revise their position in August 1939. They then advised the Cabinet that Britain's interests would best be served by Italian neutrality and that nothing should be done to provoke her. The Cabinet accepted this advice and this, therefore, was the policy that Churchill inherited when he arrived at the Admiralty the following month.

We should now describe the defences of Malta as Churchill found them in September 1939, particularly since a misunderstanding of the situation has gained wide currency.[12] It has been stated by some writers that the Chiefs of Staff had 'written off Malta as indefensible', and that the RAF, in particular, had abandoned any hope of defending the island. The British government records held at the National Archives at Kew tell quite a different story. Ever since the Abyssinian crisis had led to the cancellation of the 1933 injunction that no defences be prepared against Italy the island's defensive needs, particularly against air attack, had been under continual review. The problem lay, however, not in making sensible plans but in carrying them out. The pace of British rearmament continued to be painfully slow and Churchill's calls for a Ministry of Supply—he himself had been Minister of Munitions in 1917—to co-ordinate and accelerate arms production were routinely rejected by Chamberlain until April 1939. One consequence was that production of modern AA guns was quite inadequate to meet the demand. The first of the new 3.7-inch guns only entered service in mid-1938 and in the previous November the Cabinet had ruled that Home Defence should have absolute priority. This was not relaxed until January 1939 in order to allow the installation at Malta of the first twenty-four of an agreed forty-eight-gun programme.

Modern fighter aircraft were no more plentiful and the needs of Fighter Command paramount. The first of the new eight-gun monoplane fighters, the Hawker Hurricane, had only entered squadron service in December 1937, and the Supermarine Spitfire followed eight months later. Nevertheless, the Air Staff made plans to station a first squadron of Hurricanes at Malta as soon as circumstances at home allowed. In the meantime in order to accommodate additional squadrons they had completed the airfield at Takali on level ground below the ramparts of the old capital of Mdina, and begun an all-weather airfield at Luqa, the site of the present international airport. However, the best evidence of the Air Staff's determination to play a full part in the air defence of Malta was their decision to send to the island in January 1939 the first radar equipment sent out of England. The development of radar, then known as RDF, after the experiments conducted by Robert Watson-Watt in 1935, was well known to Churchill. The day before Watson-Watt's trials Churchill had been invited by Baldwin to join the Air Defence Research Committee and he was, therefore, able to follow the further development of the radar chain across southern England that was just completed before war broke out. Watson-Watt attended a JDC meeting in April 1938 when Malta's air defences were under discussion and the Air Staff then agreed to send to the island an experimental mobile radar set. This first unit was established in January 1939 on the high ground at Dingli Cliffs and other sets followed.

These decisions of the Air Staff and a careful reading of official documents makes clear that the reservations expressed by the Air Staff did not indicate a belief on their part that Malta could not be defended against invasion or air attack. Rather they were doubtful whether the RAF could *guarantee* the safety of the naval base from air attack and thus permit its use by the Mediterranean fleet. It was this problem that was considered at a meeting of the CID on 27 July 1939.[13] Since the technical experts could not agree the CID was invited to choose between two alternative levels of defence against air attack. Scale A comprised sixty-four AA guns and one fighter squadron and Scale B 172 AA guns and four fighter squadrons. After a lengthy discussion the Committee ordered Scale B. While recognising that it would take time to achieve this, Ministers insisted that for political as well as strategic reasons every effort should be made to defend Malta. The evidence makes abundantly clear that the incomplete structure of Malta's defences in 1939 was the result not of a lack of resolve but of inadequate resources. Further decisions about Malta taken by the COS are considered below.

As Churchill took up his duties at the Admiralty the weight of his responsibilities was to some extent lightened by Mussolini's decision to remain 'non-belligerent'. Ciano, Mussolini's Foreign Secretary and son-in-law, recorded in his diary Mussolini's attitude:

> The Duce is convinced of the necessity of remaining neutral, but he is not at all happy. Whenever he can he reverts to the possibility of action. The Italian people, however, are happy about the decisions taken.[14]

Churchill was initially, therefore, more anxious about the weak air and AA defences at Scapa Flow, the Home Fleet's war station in the Orkney Islands, than at Malta. At the first meeting of the Anglo-French Supreme War Council on 12 September Chamberlain and Daladier, the French Premier, quickly agreed to avoid any action that might antagonise Italy[15] and in subsequent speeches and broadcasts while he was at the Admiralty Churchill carefully followed this line. Throughout 1939 he and other Ministers even retained the hope that Italy, as she had done in 1915, might eventually join Britain and France. Nevertheless, Admiral Pound, who had become First Sea Lord in July 1939, and had been succeeded as C-in-C of the Mediterranean fleet by Admiral Cunningham, with Churchill's concurrence, at once put into operation the Admiralty's Mediterranean plans. The Mediterranean Fleet had already left Malta for its war stations in the eastern Mediterranean leaving only a few submarines and motor torpedo boats (MTBs) for the sea defence of Malta. Shipping through the Mediterranean was at first halted but as Mussolini's intention to remain uncommitted became clearer convoys were started under naval escort. At the same time there was some relaxation of the precautions taken by the Governor in Malta when war was declared.

In the following months, as an uneasy peace prevailed in the Mediterranean, Cunningham's force was steadily reduced and at the end of October his flagship, HMS *Warspite,* returned to Home waters. On 1 November he returned to Malta with only a few light cruisers and destroyers still under his command. In December the COS explained to the War Cabinet that their broad policy in the Middle East envisaged only 'administrative development', and they warned, in particular, that no aircraft reinforcements could be sent to the area. The Chief of the Air Staff, Air Chief Marshall Sir Cyril Newall, added that: 'Italy was slowly moving towards the Allied camp, and precipitate action on our part might drive her in the opposite direction.'[16] This policy of avoiding any action that might provoke Mussolini was endorsed by a newly established Military Co-ordination Committee (MCC) of which Churchill was a member. In the same month Churchill followed at the Admiralty the chase and destruction of the *Graf Spee* by three cruisers commanded by Commodore Harwood. Describing this action to the War Cabinet on 14 December 'he contrasted the offensive spirit shown by Commodore Harwood with the lack of enterprise shown . . . at the beginning of the last war when the *Goeben* was allowed to escape.'[17]

The period of what became known as the 'Phoney War' allowed some increase in Malta's defences. The garrison was raised to four battalions and the strength of the Royal Malta Artillery (RMA) and the King's Own Malta Regiment (KOMR) significantly increased by recruitment. The most pressing need, however, was for more of the AA guns authorised by the CID in July 1939. Since the demand for these far outstripped supply the Deputy Chiefs of Staff (DCOS) were charged with the distribution of new guns as they became available and a number of these were allocated to Malta. However, in February 1940 the Treasury pointed out to the MCC that the continued ordering of AA guns for Malta required to meet Scale B would delay production of urgently needed 25-pounder field guns for the army. In light of this it was Churchill who proposed at the MCC meeting on 8 February that Scale A (i.e. 48 heavy guns) be the immediate aim with Scale B 'a very low priority' and the Committee accepted this.[18] When in April twenty-four more guns became available these were, after strong pressure from Admiral Pound, sent to Alexandria, the war station of the Mediterranean Fleet, which was then almost defenceless. Nevertheless, Malta in the period between September 1939 and June 1940 received a further ten heavy guns, including eight of the more powerful 4.5-inch guns, and eight Bofors light guns. The total of thirty-four heavy and eight light guns operational in June 1940, although still well short of Scale A, compared favourably with the forty heavy guns each at Scapa Flow and Portsmouth, both major naval bases vulnerable to German air attack. Malta, which was not then the Mediterranean fleet's main base, cannot be considered to have been unfairly treated.

These gradual improvements in Malta's military strength were not matched in the air. The Air Ministry still hoped to establish the first Hurricane squadron there in April-May 1940, and some consideration was given to accelerating this, but the re-equipment of Fighter Command and the German invasion of Norway in April prevented this. However, the local air commander, Air Commodore Maynard, persuaded Admiral Cunningham to let him have six naval Sea Gladiator fighters held in crates in Malta and from these he formed a flight of four aircraft flown by RAF staff then in Malta on other duties. Efforts to complete the Luqa airfield were re-doubled and this became operational at the end of June.

Doubts about continued Italian neutrality grew in the early months of 1940. On a visit to Cunningham in Malta in December 1939 Sir Percy Loraine, the British Ambassador in Rome, told him of Mussolini's increasing anger at the effects of British contraband control measures and warned him of the growing possibility of Italian attack.[19] In February 1940 Churchill opposed suggestions for further easing of precautions at Malta saying that he was 'not convinced that [Italian] neutrality can be relied upon'. On 6 March, before leaving for a visit to the Home Fleet on the Clyde, he instructed Pound to work out plans with the French for naval reinforcement in the Mediterranean 'which would be appropriate to a hostile or menacing Italian attitude'.[20] Publicly, however, he repeated previous government assurances. In a broadcast on 30 March he said: 'We have no quarrel with the Italian or Japanese peoples. We have tried, and shall try, our best to live on good terms with them.'[21]

The German invasion of Norway on 8 April caused a postponement of the plans to reinforce the Mediterranean; indeed, the aircraft carrier *Glorious* was sent from Malta to Norwegian waters where she was sunk on 8 June by the German battle-cruisers, *Scharnhorst* and *Gneisenau*. However, by the end of April the Supreme War Council agreed on the need to strengthen the naval forces in the Mediterranean and the Admiralty began gathering together a fleet at Alexandria. On 30 April the War Cabinet authorised precautionary measures to be taken including the manning of Malta's defences. Despite Churchill's concentration on events in the north he found time to read all the naval signals and despatches. In April he criticised the prolonged repair of the battle cruiser *Hood* in the Malta dockyard and a month later questioned the large number of naval ships still under repair at Malta. 'I am not quite sure,' he minuted to Pound, 'that C-in-C, Med., is in fact preparing himself for a possible Italian attack. He may be convinced there will be none, and he may well be right, but our position is that precaution should be taken.'[22] Almost his last action as First Lord was to control the passage through the Sicilian narrows of three British battleships. These included *Warspite*, which on 13 April had entered Narvik fjord to engage a force of German destroyers but which was now urgently required at Alexandria. Churchill reported the safe passage of these reinforcements to the War Cabinet on 9 May.[23] By the middle of May the Mediterranean fleet had been re-established at Alexandria and once again *Warspite* hoisted Cunningham's flag

While this was happening the COS had been prompted once more to review the condition of Malta by a recommendation from the Foreign Office that the defences of both Gibraltar and Malta be strengthened to deter Italy. This led them on 28 April to recommend that an additional battalion of infantry be sent to Gibraltar but they concluded that 'there is nothing practicable we can do to *increase* the power of resistance of Malta'.[24] Several writers have misquoted this statement to read 'Nothing can be done to defend Malta' to support their contention that the COS had 'written off Malta'.[25] However, two weeks later the COS changed their minds. In response to a warning from the new Acting Governor of Malta, General Sir William Dobbie, about the possibility of an airborne attack, the War Cabinet's Defence Committee ordered an additional infantry battalion to Malta and this reached the island on 21 May.[26]

Throughout this second period at the Admiralty the neutrality of Italy and events elsewhere ensured that Malta was only occasionally at the forefront of Churchill's concerns. Nevertheless, the enormous number of his minutes and memoranda show that his capacity for work and attention to detail had not diminished during his period out of office. Moreover, the wide view he took of his responsibilities ensured that he was always aware of important developments and intervened when he thought necessary. However, the period of uneasy peace that Malta had experienced was about to end. On 10 May 1940 German forces attacked France, Belgium and Holland. Later that day Churchill became Prime Minister and assumed full responsibility for the conduct of the war. In the months and years that followed the Mediterranean and Malta, in particular, were to make larger claims on his attention.

## Notes

[1] M. Gilbert, *Churchill: A Life* (Heinemann, London, 1991), p. 624. Gilbert prints a slightly different version of this comment in *Churchill, Vol. VI*, p. 4.

[2] Sir Ian Jacob, *Churchill By His Contemporaries: An "Observer" Appreciation* (Hodder and Stoughton, London, 1965), pp. 65-6.

[3] For other assessments of Churchill see Sir J. Wheeler-Bennett (ed.), *Action This Day: Working With Churchill* (Macmillan, London, 1968).

[4] See J. Manduca, (ed.), *The Bonham-Carter Diaries: 1936-1940* (Publishers Enterprise Group, San Gwann, Malta, 2004).

[5] *Companion, Vol. V, Part 3*, WSC to Hankey, 16 October 1937, p. 799.

[6] NA CAB 53/30, COS Draft Memorandum 553(JP), "Review of Imperial Defence", 26 January 1937, para. 71.

[7] NA CAB 63/51, Hankey to Baldwin, 8 June 1936.

[8] Churchill, *Second World War, Vol. I*, p. 201.

[9] *Churchill, Vol. V*. p. 905.

[10] NA CAB 53/30, COS Memorandum 560, 'Review of Imperial Defence', 22 February 1937.

[11] NA PREM 1/345, WSC to Chamberlain, 27 March 1939.

[12] For details see the author's *Malta and British Strategic Policy*, pp. 49-63.

[13] NA CAB 2/9,CID 370th Meeting, 27 July 1939.

[14] M. Muggeridge (ed.), *Ciano's Diary: 1939-1943* (Heinemann, London, 1947), p. 143.

[15] NA CAB 99/3, Supreme War Council, 1st Meeting, 12 September 1939.

[16] NA CAB 65/2, War Cabinet (39) 107th Meeting, 7 December 1939.

[17] M. Gilbert, *The Churchill War Papers, Vol. I, At the Admiralty: September 1939-May 1940,* p. 508. (Hereafter, *War Papers*).

[18] NA CAB 83/8, MCC (40) 9th Meeting, 8 February 1940.

[19] Admiral Viscount Cunningham, *A Sailor's Odyssey* (Hutchinson, London, 1951), p. 221.

[20] Gilbert, *War Papers, Vol. I.* p. 853.

[21] Ibid., p. 938.

[22] Ibid., p. 1188.

[23] Ibid., p. 1257.

[24] NA CAB 66/7, COS Memorandum, (40) 312, 28 April 1940.

[25] See, for example, I. Cameron, *Red Duster, White Ensign: The Story Of Malta and the Malta Convoys* (Bantam Books, London, 1983), p. 1.

[26] NA CAB 69/1, Defence Committee (Operations), (40) 3rd Meeting, 16 May 1940.

# CHAPTER IX

# *The Italian Attack on Malta, June 1940*

*Whenever the Fleet is moving from Alexandria to the central Mediterranean reinforcements should be carried in to Malta, which I consider to be in grievous danger at the present time.*

Churchill Minute to the Chiefs of Staff, 6 October 1940

Within days of Churchill's appointment as Prime Minister the French and British armies in France and Belgium were in full retreat and the complete defeat of France now loomed. To add to this mounting crisis there was growing concern in Paris and London that Mussolini would seize the opportunity to declare war on the Allies. Such concern was fully justified. Mussolini's ambitions in the Mediterranean were well known and of long standing.[1] In February 1939 he had spoken of Italy's imprisonment in the Mediterranean. 'The bars of this prison are Corsica, Tunis, Malta, Cyprus . . . The task of Italian policy is to first of all break the bars of this prison.' As the winter of 1939-40 came to an end Mussolini resolved on action. German and Italian records reveal that Hitler and Mussolini met at the Brenner Pass on 18 March 1940 and that Mussolini promised to enter the war on Germany's side within 'three to four months'. On 31 March he issued a strategic directive to his Chiefs of Staff ordering preparations for war. They, having been led to believe by the dictator that Italy would not be involved in war before 1943, reacted with alarm. General Badoglio, the Head of the Armed Services, reminded Mussolini of all the deficiencies and warned him that Italian intervention would be 'suicide'. Mussolini brushed all objections aside; the war would be such a short one that Italian weakness would not matter. As he put it to Badoglio, 'I assure you the war will be over in September and that I need a few thousand dead so as to be able to attend the peace conference as a belligerent.'[2] Whatever their misgivings the Italian Chiefs offered no further objection and on 10 June Italy declared war on France and Britain.

Since March British government suspicions about Italian intentions had been growing, as we have seen. On 15 May Churchill signalled President Roosevelt, in his first message to him as Prime Minister, that Mussolini was expected to 'hurry in to share the loot of civilisation'.[3] On the following day, in a last attempt to retain Italian neutrality, Churchill wrote to Mussolini.

Now that I have taken up my office as Prime Minister and Minister of Defence I look back to our meetings in Rome and feel a desire to speak words of goodwill to you as Chief of the Italian nation across what seems to be a swiftly-widening gulf. Is it too late to stop a river of blood from flowing between the British and Italian peoples?[4]

He made no offers of any kind and warned the Dictator that 'whatever may happen on the Continent England will go on to the end, even quite alone, as we have done before.'

Two days later Mussolini rejected this appeal writing: 'I remind you of the initiative taken in 1935 by your Government to organise at Geneva sanctions against Italy.' He went on: 'I remind you also of the real and actual state of servitude in which Italy finds herself in her own sea.'[5] Of this reply Churchill later observed 'The response was hard. It had at least the merit of candour.' This left only the date of his intervention in doubt.

We must now deal with a matter affecting Malta that has caused some confusion. This is the allegation that Lord Halifax, the Foreign Secretary, and Neville Chamberlain, both members of Churchill's War Cabinet, had developed detailed plans that involved the offer to Mussolini of Malta and other British territories if he would keep out of the war and also persuade Hitler to offer the Allies reasonable peace terms.[6] These allegations are derived from four long and incompletely recorded meetings of the War Cabinet between 26 and 28 May while the British Expeditionary Force under General Lord Gort was fighting its way to Dunkirk with little hope of escape. As noted above, Churchill's 16 May letter to Mussolini made no offers of any kind but ten days later the French government determined to make specific territorial offers. With the French armies in full retreat, and a mood of defeatism growing in his Cabinet, the French Premier, Paul Reynaud, hastened to London on 26 May. In an attempt to secure Mussolini's continued neutrality and intercession with Hitler he was authorised to offer certain French territories and he urged the British government to support such a plan with a similar offer. He thought Mussolini would require, at least, the 'demilitarisation of Malta' and he stressed that 'geographical precision' was essential.

Halifax was not in favour of offering specific territories but was tempted to support the French in general terms. 'If we found', he said, 'that we could obtain terms which did not postulate the destruction of our independence we should be foolish if we did not accept them.' Chamberlain initially supported this suggestion although largely to reduce the risk that France might negotiate a separate peace. Throughout their lengthy discussions it was assumed by all six members of the War Cabinet that if Mussolini showed any interest in such a proposal he would demand Malta. Attlee and Greenwood, the two Labour Party members of the War Cabinet, firmly opposed Halifax's proposal. Sinclair, the Liberal party leader, thought that 'the suggestion that we were prepared to barter away pieces of British territory would have a deplorable effect.'

Churchill, already convinced by intelligence reports and their recent correspondence that Mussolini was intent on war, was nevertheless anxious not to cause an irrevocable split in the War Cabinet at such a critical time. Churchill was conscious that a majority of the Conservative MPs in the House of Commons had favoured Halifax's claim to the Premiership and they remained loyal to Chamberlain as Leader of the Conservative Party. He, therefore, argued that not only was it most unlikely that acceptable terms would be offered but also that British determination to resist would be fatally undermined should it become known that an approach to Mussolini had been made. He added that such an approach,

. . . implied that if we were prepared to give Germany back her colonies and to make certain concessions in the Mediterranean, it was possible for us to get out of our present difficulties. He thought no such option was open to us.

In the middle of these discussions Churchill left to attend a meeting of the full Cabinet and returned to report that he had received overwhelming support for his declaration that 'Whatever happens at Dunkirk, we shall fight on'. In his memoirs Churchill gave a vivid description of the reaction of the Cabinet to this simple statement. 'Quite a number seemed to jump up from the table and come running to my chair, shouting and patting me on the back. There is no doubt that had I at this juncture faltered at all in the leading of the nation I should have been hurled out of office.'[7] Halifax, increasingly isolated, threatened resignation but later thought better of it.

The upshot was that Churchill on 28 May sent a telegram to Reynaud declining to join the French in their approach to Mussolini. In the event the subsequent French offer of specific territories was simply ignored by the Italian dictator. Ciano later told the French Ambassador: 'Mussolini was not interested in recovering any French territories by peaceful negotiation. He had decided to make war on France.'[8] There is no evidence in these records to support the allegations referred to above. Even Halifax was opposed to naming specific territories and it can only be a matter of speculation whether he would have favoured the cession of Malta had Mussolini demanded it. But it is clear that neither Churchill nor any other member of the War Cabinet would have accepted this.

While the War Cabinet debated and decided this supreme question the Chiefs of Staff, on instructions from the Prime Minister, considered the military implications of French surrender and a possible Italian declaration of war. On 25 May they responded by advising that any attempted invasion of the British Isles could be defeated so long as the RAF maintained its strength. With regard to a possible Italian attack on Malta they wrote:

> Malta has six months' food reserve for the population and garrison, but AA guns and ammunition are short, and the island is not likely to withstand more than one serious sea-borne assault, nor could it be used as a naval base.[9]

It is worth digressing at this point to state that, despite some speculation to the contrary, the Italians had no intention of attempting an invasion of Malta in 1940. Not only was this considered unnecessary given their expectation of a short war which would deliver Malta to Italy at the peace conference, but such an amphibious, tri-service assault against defended positions was beyond Italian military capabilities.[10] Had it been attempted Malta might have taken its place in history alongside Gallipoli and Dieppe.

The British Joint Intelligence Committee (JIC) continued to monitor Italian preparations and predicted on 29 May that Italian involvement was imminent. With regard to Malta their opinion was that 'sudden attack by airborne troops is highly probable',[11] a view perhaps influenced by the successful German airborne attacks in the Low Countries. On the same day the Deputy Chiefs of Staff (DCOS) reviewed a further request from General Dobbie in Malta for additional troops and AA guns but concluded that, in view of the invasion threat to Britain, no further help could be given.[12] On 7 June intercepted signals revealed the arrival of strong Italian bomber units in Sicily and the Admiralty warned Cunningham at Alexandria that Italy was likely to declare war at any time between 10 and 20 June. On the afternoon of 10 June Churchill was woken from his afternoon nap to be told of Mussolini's declaration of war against France and Britain. His only comment then, as the RAF prepared to bomb Italy, was: 'People who go to Italy to look at ruins won't have to go as far as Naples and Pompeii in future.'[13]

Early on the morning of 11 June the *Regia Aeronautica* carried out the first air raid on Malta and there were several more during that first day. Among those who lost their lives on that day of infamy were six members of the Royal Malta Artillery when a stick of three bombs fell on Fort St. Elmo.[14] On that day the air defences of the island comprised 42 AA guns, supported by a number of naval AA guns, a flight of three Sea Gladiator fighters, soon to be known as *Faith, Hope,* and *Charity,* and one Hurricane. Despite his earlier refusal to send modern fighters to the Middle East Air Chief Marshal Newall had in early June ordered six Hurricanes to Alexandria via France, Tunis and Malta. The Middle East Air Commander, Air Chief Marshal Sir Arthur Longmore, whom we met

**1** Portrait of the young statesman in the George Grantham Bain Collection, Library of Congress. The photograph is undated but was probably taken around 1900.

*Above:* **2** Grand Harbour, Valletta, *c.* 1927.

*Below:* **3** Churchill and Marsh at the Grand Master's Palace, Valletta, 1907. With them are General Barron, the Acting Governor, Sir Edward Merewether, the Lt-Governor, and two officers of the garrison.

*Above:* **4** The Admiralty Yacht, HMS *Enchantress,* which took Churchill to Malta in 1912 and 1913.

*Below:* **5** Churchill and Asquith in the Mediterranean, together with Admiral Beatty (left), Violet Asquith and Admiral Prince Louis of Battenberg (centre), 1912.

**6** Churchill and Admiral Battenberg inspecting the guard of honour, 1912, Grand Harbour, Valletta; HMS *Enchantress* is in the background.

**7** Clementine Ogilvy Spencer-Churchill in formal pose. Rear-Admiral Beatty, present at the 1912 Malta Conference as the First Lord's Naval Secretary, described her as 'a perfect fool'. Beatty, on this evidence at least, was clearly not a good judge of character.

**8** HMS *Invincible* leaving the Grand Harbour, 1913, one of four battle-cruisers sent to Malta in 1912.

**9** The Mediterranean Fleet moored in the Grand Harbour, 1913.

**10** Staircase of the former Admiralty House, Valletta, where Churchill stayed as the guest of Admiral Sir Roger Keyes in 1927.

**11** HMS *Warspite*, the flagship of the Mediterranean Fleet, entering the Grand Harbour, Valletta, 1938.

**12** The bombing of HMS *Illustrious* in the Grand Harbour, Valletta, January 1941.

**13** Attack on SS *Talabot* moored in the Grand Harbour, March 1942.

**14** Digging a shelter in Malta in the soft limestone.

**15** Bomb damage in Valletta, 1942. Clearly visible are the limestone blocks from which Maltese houses are built.

**16** Bofors position facing Senglea. The Malta barrage became a formidable deterrent to enemy bombers in 1942.

**17** Submarine base on Manoel Island from which the 10th Flotilla launched many devastating attacks on enemy convoys to North Africa.

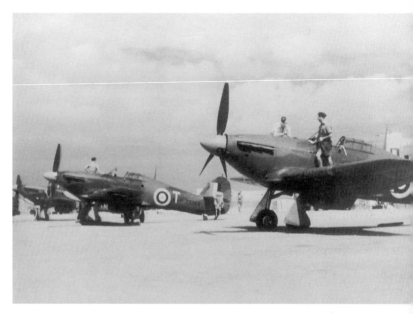

**18** Hurricanes at Hal Far airfield. Hurricanes were the only modern fighters in Malta until the arrival of Spitfires in 1942.

**19** Faery Albacore torpedo bomber flown in to reinforce the older Swordfish squadrons. The torpedo weighed 730 kg.

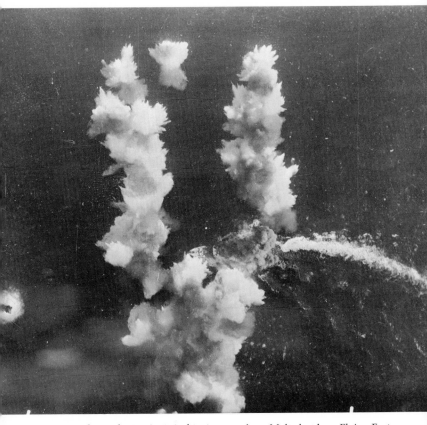

**20** A direct hit in the Med, 1943, this time not from Malta but by a Flying Fortress of the Northwest African Strategic Air Force. The target was an Italian liner converted to a troop carrier.

**21** General Dobbie with Monckton and Tedder, April 1942. The Governor's gaunt appearance contrasts with that of this well-fed visitors from Cairo.

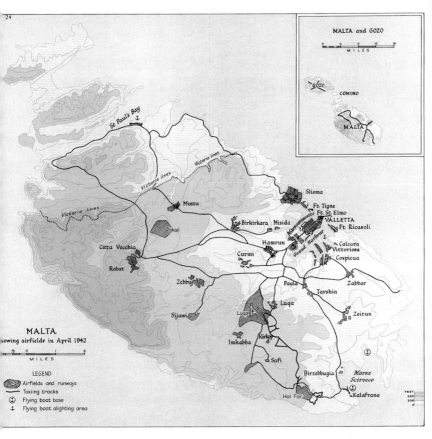

MALTA and GOZO

0        5        10        15
MILES

GOZO

COMINO

MALTA

St Paul's Bay

Victoria lines

Victoria lines

Victoria lines

Musta

Ta Kali

Sliema

Ft. Tigne
Ft. St. Elmo
VALLETTA
Ft. Ricasoli

Birkirkara   Misida
Marsamuscetto
Grand Harbour

Citta Vecchia

Hamrun
Curmi

Calcara
Vittoriosa
Cospicua

Rabat

Zebbuj

Sijuwi

Luqa

Paula
Tarshin

Zabbar

Zeitun

Luqa

Imkabba    Kirkop

Safi

Birzebbugia

Marsa
Scirocco

Hal Far

Kalafrana

FEET
500
200
0

MALTA
showing airfields in April 1942

½       0                    1                    2
MILES

LEGEND
Airfields and runways
Taxiing tracks
Flying boat base
Flying boat alighting area

22 Malta airfields and runways, April 1942. The air attack on Malta reached its climax in the following month.

**23** SS *Ohio* entering the Grand Harbour, August 1942, the last, vital survivor of the 'Pedestal' convoy.

BUCKINGHAM PALACE

The Governor
    Malta.

        To honour her brave people
I award the George Cross to the
Island Fortress of Malta to bear
witness to a heroism and devotion
that will long be famous in history.

                George R.I.

April 15th 1942.

**24** The George Cross and the letter from King George VI, April 1942

25 General Lord Gort presenting the George Cross, September 1942.

**27** Churchill touring the Malta dockyard, November 1943. Churchill was suffering from a heavy, feverish cold, but insisted on making this tour of inspection.

*Opposite:* **26** A famous photograph at the Russian Embassy during the Teheran conference of 28 November to 1 December 1943. Churchill had left Malta nine days earlier. His punishing workload would see him suffer pneumonia and a mild heart attack on 11 December.

**29** Churchill and President Roosevelt in the Grand Harbour, January 1945. With them are Churchill's daughter, Sarah, in the WAAF uniform, and Roosevelt's daughter, Anna Boetigger.

*Opposite:* **28** Churchill on the balcony of the Palace in Valletta, November 1943.

**30** The Malta Shield at Chartwell. This was made by Antonio Attard and presented to Churchill in July 1946 by Edward Ceravolo.

# Churchill's gift

From Fr George Aquilina, OFM
I FOLLOWED with interest the letters by Mr Michael Refalo, A&CE (The *Sunday Times,* October 17) and the reply from Dr Douglas Austin (October 24) about a gift which was offered to Sir Winston Churchill by Edward Ceravolo in 1946.

My particular interest arises from the fact that Mr Ceravolo happened to be the maternal uncle of the late Fr Remigio Vella, OFM, from whom I had heard a lot about his uncle, who was of a good-humoured character, like Fr Vella.

But more interesting to the subject is that when I was reorganising our Franciscan archives in 1970, Fr Vella gave me a photo of Churchill, signed and dated 1946, exactly as described by Dr Austin, "framed in walnut" to be kept in our Franciscan archives.

Fr Vella knew well about the silver gift offered to Sir Winston, and I remember that he told me to keep the photo in a safe place. Mr Ceravolo wanted this photo, so dear to him, to be kept by his Franciscan priest nephew as a sign of affection. Knowing now all

**THE WALNUT-FRAMED autographed portrait which Sir Winston Churchill gave to Edward Ceravolo**

this written information, we Franciscans appreciate and treasure this photo more than ever.

G. AQUILINA
Valletta.

31 Letter about the Churchill photograph given by him to Edward Ceravolo.

**32** The three meet again, this time on the brink of victory in Europe at the Yalta, or Crimea, Conference, February 1945. Churchill seems little changed since the Teheran picture, but President Roosevelt has clearly deteriorated. Both had been on Malta immediately prior to the momentous Conference. Roosevelt died on 12 April 1945.

**33 & 34** Presentation to Churchill of portrait bust, August 1955 *(above)*. The bust was the work of Mr. Vincent Apap, and was presented by Judge Montanaro-Gauci. Governor Sir Robert Laycock unveils the bust in the Upper Barrakka Gardens in May 1956 *(below)*.

**35** Valletta today; Fortress Malta. In the words attributed to Sir Walter Scott, 'The city built by gentlemen for gentlemen'. Though this attribution is unsure, Scott certainly did write, 'This town is really quite like a dream'.

**36** Fort St. Angelo from which Grand Master Jean de la Valette conducted the resistance to the Turkish attack in 1565.

**37** The Grand Harbour, Valletta where Churchill landed on his first visit in 1907. His bust now stands in the Upper Barrakka Gardens above on the right.

**38** Bust in the Upper Barrakka Gardens. 'TO THE RT. HONOURABLE SIR
WINSTON SPENCER CHURCHILL, K.G. THE PEOPLE OF MALTA AND GOZO MCMLV'.

in Chapter III, wanted to retain all these aircraft at Malta. He was, however, overruled by the Air Ministry; these aircraft had been released for the defence of the Mediterranean fleet at Alexandria. Nevertheless, one of these aircraft, delayed for repairs at Tunis, was held at Malta.

Churchill, his ministerial colleagues and his military advisers were now confronted with the second of the three enemies the government had feared in the 1930s. Moreover, the collapse of France was only days away. Nevertheless, plans had been made, such forces as could be spared for a war with Italy were assembled and Churchill had made it quite clear that Britain would fight on whatever the French government might decide. Churchill was above all determined that British forces, wherever possible, should take the offensive. Thus on 28 May, the day on which he had declined to join the French approach to Mussolini, he minuted to the COS that it was 'extremely desirable' that if Italy declared war the Allied fleets in the Mediterranean 'should pursue an active offensive against Italy'. He criticised what he considered the 'purely defensive strategy' proposed by Admiral Cunningham in a signal of 23 May and wrote: 'It will be much better that the Fleet at Alexandria should sally forth and run some risks than that it should remain in a posture so markedly defensive.'[15]

In the following pages various exchanges between Churchill and Admiral Cunningham will be quoted and they make clear that the relationship between the two men was never an easy one. In his own post-war memoirs, published on the same day as the third volume of Churchill's history, Cunningham referred to the Prime Minister's often 'ungracious and hasty prodding messages' and went on to write:

> We realized, of course, the terrible mental and physical strain under which he was labouring: but so were we. Such messages to those who were doing their utmost with straitened resources were not an encouragement, merely an annoyance.[16]

Any doubts that Churchill may have had about Cunningham's aggressive spirit were removed, at least temporarily, when in a naval engagement off the Calabrian coast of Italy in early July a 15-inch shell from Cunningham's flagship, HMS *Warspite*, hit the Italian flagship, *Giulio Cesare*, at a range of 13 miles. The Italian fleet promptly withdrew behind a smoke screen.

On 17 June, as Petain succeeded Reynaud as Head of the French Government and sought armistice terms, Admiral Pound circulated a rather surprising memorandum to his fellow Chiefs. This proposed the withdrawal of the Mediterranean fleet from Alexandria to Gibraltar. Cunningham, who had been advised of this proposal, responded by warning that such a move would probably mean the loss of Malta and perhaps of Egypt too. Churchill was adamantly opposed to this and at once sent a minute to the First Lord, A. V. Alexander which stated:

It is of the utmost importance that the Fleet at Alexandria should remain to cover Egypt from an Italian invasion, which would otherwise destroy prematurely all our position in the East.[17]

The COS referred the matter to the JPC who agreed with Churchill's position. He later justified this veto by saying that such a move would have jeopardised the entire British position in the Middle East and 'also seemed to spell the doom of Malta'.[18]

Despite the continued threat of a cross-Channel invasion Churchill was determined to respond to Italian attacks on Malta and elsewhere. His overall strategic priorities in the Mediterranean were to strengthen the British and Commonwealth forces in Egypt against the anticipated Italian attack from Cyrenaica, to eliminate the Italian position in Abyssinia and north-east Africa, and then to clear the north African shore of all Italian forces. What was Malta expected to contribute to the achievement of these tasks? The posing of this question then revealed that despite all the pre-war attention given to the *defence* of Malta its offensive role had been examined in only the most general terms. The island's principal strategic task, it was generally assumed, was to sever the sea supply lines from Italy to her wholly dependent possessions in North Africa. But how this was to be done under air attack from Italian bases only 60 miles away had been given little thought.

The study of this problem was belatedly set in motion by a series of Prime Minister's minutes, two of which were sent in July. The first was addressed to the COS:

It also seems most desirable that the Fleet should be able to use Malta more freely. A plan should be prepared to reinforce the air defences of Malta in the strongest manner with AA guns of various types and with aeroplanes . . . If we could get a stronger air force there we might obtain considerable immunity from annoyance by retaliation. Let a plan for the speediest anti-aircraft reinforcement of Malta be prepared forthwith, and let me have it in three days, with estimates in time.[19]

The second, directed to the Admiralty, suggested that the new aircraft carrier, *Illustrious*, 'take a good lot of Hurricanes to Malta', where they could be flown by the Gladiator pilots.[20] This suggestion was to lead to the use of the old aircraft carrier, HMS *Argus*, to fly off the first dozen Hurricanes to Malta on 2 August. Many hundreds of Hurricanes and Spitfires were subsequently to be delivered to Malta in this way.

More importantly, Churchill established a special committee, under Eden's chairmanship, to 'consult together upon the conduct of the war in the Middle East'. At a meeting of this committee on 12 August Lord

Lloyd, the Colonial Secretary, asked 'if it was contemplated that Malta would be developed as a base for offensive operations'. On his copy of this enquiry Churchill wrote: 'Yes, it is most important!'[21] There then followed a period of intense discussion and debate about the action to be taken concerning Malta. General Wavell, summoned back from Cairo, favoured an early bombing offensive from Malta to ease the expected Italian invasion of Egypt. Air Chief Marshal Newall rejected this partly because Bomber Command could not spare the necessary aircraft, but also because this might provoke Italian retaliation on Malta. This might put out of action the newly completed runway at Luqa that was essential to the urgent flow of aircraft through the island to the Middle East. For their part the Admiralty argued strongly that before a naval force could safely operate from Malta against the Italian supply convoys the island's AA and fighter defences, as planned under Scale B in 1939, should be completed. The Admiralty also stressed that air and naval forces at Malta could achieve nothing unless there was an effective air reconnaissance capability. The Italian navy had recently changed their cyphers and at that stage it was not even known which routes the Italian convoys were using. It was finally agreed that the AA guns required under Scale B would be established no later than April 1941, that the fighter force be built up as quickly as home needs allowed, that some Maryland reconnaissance aircraft be sent to the island and that a naval force be established at Valletta as soon as the defences were complete. In the meantime offensive operation against Italy or Sicily would be avoided.[22]

There are many accounts of Churchill's energy and determination in the dark days of 1940. Lord Bridges who, during the war, was Cabinet Secretary later recalled:

Within a very few days of his becoming Prime Minister the whole machinery of government was working at a pace, and with an intensity of purpose, quite unlike anything that had gone before.

To this John Colville, who had been Chamberlain's Private Secretary and then had held the same position under Churchill, added that 'respectable civil servants were actually be seen to be running along the corridors.'[23] Churchill's enormous energy was such that despite the growing threat of an attempted invasion of England Churchill made time to keep a close eye on developments at Malta. On 23 June he sent the first of many signals to the Acting Governor, General Dobbie, which read:

The Cabinet watch with constant attention the resolute defence which your garrison and the people of Malta are making of that famous fortress and Island. I have the conviction that you will make that defence glorious in British military history, and also in the history of

Malta itself. You are well fitted to rouse and sustain the spirit of all in enduring severe and prolonged ordeals for a righteous cause.[24]

General Sir William Dobbie had been sent to Malta in April 1940 to replace General Sir Charles Bonham-Carter, whom serious illness had compelled to return to London. However, he was not formally appointed as Governor of Malta until March 1941 when it became clear that Bonham-Carter would not be fit enough to return. In the succeeding chapters General Dobbie will be frequently mentioned but here it may be appropriate to quote the tribute that Churchill subsequently paid to him.

In General Dobbie Malta found a Governor of outstanding character who inspired all ranks and classes, military and civil, with his own determination. He was a soldier who in fighting leadership and religious zeal recalled memories of General Gordon, and, looking further back, of the Ironsides and Covenanters of the past.[25]

Churchill's constant concern for Malta was reflected in a stream of minutes and memoranda of which only the most important can be summarised here.[26] In July he urged that additional AA guns be sent directly to Malta on fast merchant ships. 'The immense delay involved in passing these ships around the Cape cannot be accepted', he minuted. He also thought that the subsequent passage from Alexandria to Malta would be more dangerous than the route from Gibraltar. However, when Admiral Pound, after consulting Cunningham, replied that the risks to merchant ships from air attack in the Sicilian Narrows were too great, Churchill, with the greatest reluctance, bowed to this advice, grumbling that 'the Admiralty appeared to be taking an unduly pessimistic view of the risks involved.'[27] Nevertheless, later that month naval reinforcements for Cunningham while *en route* to Alexandria in Operation 'Hats' delivered more AA guns, ammunition and stores to the island. Describing all this to the House of Commons on 5 September Churchill added: 'Some of our great ships touched at Malta on the way, and carried a few things that were needed by those valiant islanders and their garrison, who, under a remarkably resolute Governor, General Dobbie, are maintaining themselves with the utmost constancy.'[28]

In the following month Churchill's attention turned to the weakness of Malta's infantry garrison and at a COS meeting on 14 September he suggested that an additional two battalions be sent there. A week later, after reading a signal from General Dobbie which explained how stretched his infantry resources were, he minuted that although four battalions were required 'we must be content with two for the moment. We must find two good ones.' This provoked discussions with the Governor who eventually accepted one new battalion, drafts to strengthen the existing units on the island and a battery of 25-pounder field guns. Several weeks later, however the COS received another minute:

> Whenever the Fleet is moving from Alexandria to the central Mediterranean reinforcements should be carried in to Malta, which I consider to be in grievous danger at the present time . . . Make sure that at least one battalion goes to Malta on the next occasion.

Yet another lengthy minute beginning 'FIRST in urgency is the reinforcement of Malta . . .' asked a series of questions about the progress being made on the defences of the island. The COS studied this on 15 October and the result was that General Dobbie received additional infantry, field and anti-tank guns and a troop of six tanks.

These extracts can only give an impression of the Prime Minister's continual scrutiny of the COS meetings, many of which he chaired, and of his exhortations to them to build up the defences of Malta. Mussolini's unexpected invasion of Greece on 28 October brought forward the plans to use Malta for offensive purposes. The newly-appointed CAS, Air Chief Marshal Sir Charles Portal, agreed to establish at Luqa a temporary Wellington squadron out of the aircraft flying on to the Middle East and in the following two months raids were carried out on targets in Sicily, Italy and in North Africa. Recently arrived Maryland reconnaissance aircraft operating from Malta also provided the aerial photographs that made possible the crippling Fleet Air Arm attack on the Italian fleet at Taranto on 11 November. In this surprise attack, which foreshadowed the later Japanese attack on Pearl Harbor, a force of twenty-one Swordfish aircraft was launched from HMS *Illustrious* and three of the Italian navy's six battleships were sunk at their moorings in Taranto harbour.

While all these military reinforcements were being decided, organised and despatched the War Cabinet, presided over by Churchill, was also considering the critical problem of maintaining Malta's supplies of food and other essential stocks. While Mussolini remained neutral it had been decided to build up Malta's reserve stocks to an 8-month consumption level but only a 6-month level had been reached by June 1940.The reserves of the major items were then as follows: 8-month supply of wheat, flour, and edible oil; 6-month supply of coal and coffee; 5-month supply of soap, sugar, fats, and kerosene. In August Vice-Admiral Sir Wilbraham Ford, the Vice-Admiral Malta, signalled that, since no convoys had arrived since June, stocks had fallen to a 2-month level and the Governor requested shipments of 80,000 tons a month to restore stocks to a safer level. The shipping required to achieve this was, however, in short supply and closely controlled in London. Consequently, the Colonial Secretary, Lord Lloyd, made a special plea to Churchill who then authorised the release of the necessary ships for this task.[29] By the end of the year a 7-month consumption level had been achieved. A rationing system was not initially introduced but this soon led to hoarding and black market sales. However, in February 1941 Marquis Barbaro, who had earlier established an unofficial rationing system in the north of the island, was appointed as Food Distribution Officer. He then organised an island-wide scheme under which the first items to be rationed were sugar, coffee, soap and matches.

At the same time strenuous efforts were being made to provide more underground shelters. Work on this had begun, albeit rather slowly, in 1939 and the Admiralty had provided shelters for over 1,000 of the Malta dockyard workers. Within the civil administration a Shelter Construction Department was established and several senior dockyard engineers were seconded to this department. The soft Malta limestone eased the excavation of new shelters and full use was made of the numerous underground storerooms in the Valletta bastions and a disused railway tunnel. In addition to these public works many families excavated shelters of their own. The result was that by the time the Maltese suffered the worst of the bombing in the spring of 1942 there was some underground shelter for the whole community and to this can be attributed the relatively low level of civilian casualties.

By the end of 1940 despite mounting casualties and bomb damage the Maltese people were beginning to adapt to a diminishing scale of Italian attack. Air raids had fallen from 53 in June to only 18 in December and many of those who had earlier left their homes around Valletta had returned. On 1 December 1940 Churchill asked General Ismay 'What actually we have put into Malta in the past couple of months or so, both in guns and men'. Two days later Colonel Jacob replied that since 15 September Malta had received forty-four more AA guns, twenty-four 25-pounder field guns, six tanks, almost 3,000 infantry, and fourteen Hurricanes.[30] On 20 December Admiral Cunningham judged Malta secure enough to pay a two-day visit to the island aboard his flagship, HMS *Warspite*. Cunningham later described this visit:

It was our first visit since May, and news of our arrival had been spread abroad. As we moved in with our band playing and guard paraded the Barracas and other points of vantage were black with wildly-cheering Maltese. Our reception was touchingly overwhelming. It was good to know that they realized that though the fleet could not use Malta for the time being, we had them well in mind.[31]

In North Africa, too, the tide had turned. On 7 December General Wavell launched his Operation 'Compass' and the initial withdrawal of the Italian forces soon turned into a rout.

Thus in the first six months of the Mediterranean war the Maltese people had withstood the first shock of war and the island's defences had been significantly strengthened. As this chapter has shown the flow of men and material to Malta owed much to Churchill's determination that the island should become strongly defended so that forces based there should contribute as fully as possible to the defeat of Italy. By the end of 1940, however, offensive operations had barely begun and Malta had made virtually no contribution to the interruption of Italian supplies to North Africa. What had seemed in peacetime planning a relatively straightforward task had in reality proved a problem of considerable complexity. Without effective reconnaissance or intelligence Malta's few submarines and Swordfish torpedo bombers rarely sighted an enemy ship and scarcely knew where to look. Consequently, in the last six months of 1940 the Italian navy had escorted almost 300,000 tons of supplies to their North African ports with losses of a mere 2%.

The development of Malta's offensive capability was already being planned for 1941 but in the last month of 1940 Malta was about to enter a darker stage of the war. As Churchill had long feared, Hitler, anxious that the Italian military debacle in North Africa might lead to the collapse of the fascist regime, determined to assist his faltering ally.

## Notes

[1] See M. Knox, *Mussolini Unleashed 1939-1941: Politics and Strategy in Fascist Italy's Last War* (Cambridge University Press, Cambridge, 1988).

[2] P. Badoglio, *Italy in the Second World War: Memories and Documents* (Oxford University Press, London, 1948), p. 15.

[3] Churchill, *Second World War, Vol. II*, pp. 22-3.

[4] NA PREM 4/19/5, FO/s. 699-700, WSC to Mussolini, 16 May 1940.

[5] Mussolini to WSC, 18 May 1940.

[6] See for example, M. Arnold-Forster, *The World at War* (Collins, London, 1975), p. 54. All of the official records of the meetings on this subject are in NA CAB 65/13, War Cabinet Meetings 140th, 142nd, and 145th, 26-28 May 1940.

[7] Churchill, *Second World War, Vol. II*, p. 88.

[8] Ibid., pp. 109-11.

[9] NA CAB 66/7, COS Memorandum (40) 390, "British Strategy in a Certain Eventuality", 25 May 1940, para. 10.

[10] See MacGregor Knox, *Hitler's Italian Allies* (Cambridge University Press, Cambridge, 2000).

[11] NA CAB 80/12, COS Memorandum (40) 407 (JIC), "Possible Courses Open to Italy", 29 May 1940.

[12] NA CAB 82/2, DCOS (40) 24th Meeting, 29 May 1940.

[13] J. Colville, *The Fringes of Power: Downing Street Diaries 1939-1955* (Hodder & Stoughton, London, 1985), p. 152.

[14] P. Vella, *Malta: Blitzed But Not Beaten* (Progress Press, Valletta, 1985), pp. 6-9.

[15] NA CAB 80/12, COS Memorandum (40) 404, "Policy in the Mediterranean", 28 May 1940.

[16] Cunningham,*Odyssey*, p. 231.

[17] Churchill, *Second World War, Vol. II*, p. 563.

[18] Ibid., p. 390.

[19] Ibid., p. 568.

[20] Ibid., pp. 392, 568.

[21] NA PREM 3/266/10A, Fols. 954-5.

[22] NA CAB 79/6, COS (40) 280th Meeting, 26 August 1940.

[23] Sir J. Wheeler-Bennett (ed.), *Action This Day: Working With Churchill* (Macmillan, London, 1968), pp. 220, 50.

[24] Gilbert, *War Papers, Vol. II*, WSC to Dobbie, 23 June 1940, p. 402.

[25] Churchill, *Second World War, Vol. III*, p. 54.

[26] Quotations from NA CAB 80/20 COS Memoranda (40) 805, 814,and 833, October 1940.

[27] Gilbert, *War Papers, Vol. II*, p. 656.

[28] Ibid., p. 778.

[29] NA CAB 65/9, War Cabinet (40) 254th Meeting, 19 September 1940.

[30] NA PREM 3/266/10A, Fols. 897-8.

[31] Cunningham, *Odyssey*, p. 297.

# CHAPTER X

# *The First German Blitz 1941*

*The eyes of all Britain, and indeed of the whole British Empire, are watching Malta in her struggle day by day, and we are sure that success as well as glory will reward your efforts.*
Churchill to General Dobbie, Governor of Malta, 21 January 1941

On 10 December 1940 Hitler ordered *Fliegerkorps X*, a balanced force of 350 aircraft trained in anti-shipping attack, from Norway to southern Italy. Its primary task was to gain air control over the central Mediterranean and to attack British shipping. Its presence and its power were dramatically shown on 10 January 1941 when the aircraft carrier, HMS *Illustrious*, was severely damaged while escorting a convoy through the Sicilian Channel. She was then subjected to further heavy attack while undergoing emergency repairs in the Grand Harbour before she escaped to Alexandria on 23 January. This attack heralded the first German blitz of Malta.

Although we will be concerned in this and the following chapters largely with Churchill's minutes and decisions that affected Malta's military contribution to the war it should not be thought that he ignored or was unaware of the dangers and the hardships that the war brought to the Maltese people. Within the enormous archive of the Prime Minister's Office in the National Archives at Kew the series of files relating to Malta runs to over 1000 pages.[1] They include many of the Governor's signals and despatches to London on a wide range of civilian problems caused by the war. All of them were read by Churchill and bear his initial and date, usually in red ink. Many of them gave rise to a dictated minute addressed through General Ismay to the appropriate department. One example may be quoted here to show Churchill's concern for the welfare of the civilian population of Malta.

On 23 January 1941 after the first heavy German bombing raids on Malta Sir Kingsley Wood, the Chancellor of the Exchequer, received a minute from the Prime Minister to which was affixed a red ACTION THIS DAY label. Churchill had found in his despatch box a Treasury paper that proposed that compensation for bomb damage in Malta be on a lower scale than in the UK. Churchill at once wrote:

23 January 1941
ACTION THIS DAY
<u>Financial Assistance for Air Raid Damage at Malta</u>

Surely they should be allowed to come into our scheme on exactly
the same terms as our own people, and in retrospective effect.
They are under siege.

On the following day he elaborated on this: 'Frankly, I do not think the
conventional phrases about "urgent consideration" and "sympathy and
support" are good enough at this time for these people, who have so
loyally espoused our cause, and are under constant attack.'[2] There could
be no better evidence than these internal minutes of Churchill's concern,
amid all his other anxieties, for the victims of enemy attack, whether
British or Maltese.

To understand the overall context in which decisions relating to Malta
were taken it will be necessary to review briefly the wider development
of the fighting in the Mediterranean in the first half of 1941. The major
British decision in early 1941 was to halt Wavell's advance towards
Tripoli in order to send a large part of the Army of the Nile to Greece.
The extent to which this was a political rather than a military decision is
still disputed but it proved disastrous. By the end of April the Navy had
been compelled to evacuate 53,000 British and Commonwealth troops
but a further 11,000 men and much valuable equipment were lost. Worse
was to follow. Despite accurate British intelligence of German plans Crete
succumbed to a fierce airborne assault and the Navy sustained heavy
losses in a further evacuation.

An equally severe blow to Churchill's hopes was the loss by the end of
May of the whole of Cyrenaica. Anxious that Mussolini might be forced
out of the war if defeated in North Africa Hitler in January ordered a small
armoured force to Libya. He then appointed General Erwin Rommel to
command what was named the *Deutsches Afrika Korps* and Rommel
landed at Tripoli on 14 February. A month later he began to probe the
weakened British defences and capitalising on an initial tactical success
he pushed the British forces back to the Egyptian frontier. Tobruk became
isolated and Wavell's attempt to relieve it in Operation 'Battleaxe' was
decisively defeated in mid-June. The result of these sweeping German
successes was that Malta was further isolated by the loss of supporting
air bases in Cyrenaica and Crete.

All of this lay over the horizon as Churchill and the COS digested the
implications of the attack on the *Illustrious*. As he wrote to the COS on
13 January, 'The effective arrival of German aviation in Sicily may be the
beginning of evil developments in the Central Mediterranean.'[3] Among
these was the possibility that Malta might soon be invaded or at the very least
be subjected to a heavy bombing campaign designed to destroy the island's
naval and air bases. The strengthening of the defences was, consequently,
of the utmost importance and we will first examine Churchill's response to
this problem before considering Malta's offensive role.

In the preceding chapter we noted that, under Churchill's pressure, the COS had decided that Malta's AA defences be completed to the Scale B level by April 1941. Consequently, allocations of modern AA guns had been made to Malta each month and, despite the difficulty of transporting this equipment together with the ammunition and the additional gunners through the western Mediterranean, Scale B was almost complete by April. It is worth remarking that by mid-1941 the Grand Harbour area had stronger AA defences than London possessed at any time during the war. By the end of the war the gunners of the Royal Malta Artillery and the Royal Artillery had shot down a total of 241 enemy aircraft, with a further 48 probably destroyed and many others damaged. But the cost was high. 350 gunners lost their lives while fighting their guns.

In January 1941 Churchill became increasingly concerned about the possibility that Malta might be invaded. Rumours and reports grew about the appearance of German troops, including armoured formations, in southern Italy and Sicily. The destination of this force was in fact Tripoli but this was by no means clear in London or Valletta. The extra battalion of troops planned for Malta in the autumn had been diverted to Crete when Mussolini attacked Greece and the Governor in January sent an urgent request for more infantry. He thought three additional battalions were really required but at least one was essential. This request was reviewed at COS meeting on 6 February. In a Minute dated that day the Prime Minister urged that two battalions should be sent. As he expressed it:

> Considering that in view of the Italian rout there should be no difficulty in sparing this seventh battalion from Egypt, and the trouble is carrying them there by the fleet, one must ask whether it is not as easy to carry two as it is to carry one. It seems a pity to let the baker's cart go with only one loaf, when the journey is so expensive and the loaf available, and that it might as easily carry two. Pray consider this. But no delay.[4]

The two battalions arrived from Alexandria by cruiser on 21 February.

By these bold but difficult measures the military defences of Malta were significantly strengthened in the early months of 1941. However, as more and more *Luftwaffe* squadrons became established in Sicily the weight of air attack steadily grew and the RAF was very hard pressed. On 21 January Churchill sent General Dobbie a message of encouragement:

> I send you, on behalf of the War Cabinet, our heartfelt congratulations upon the magnificent and ever-memorable defence which your heroic garrison and citizens, aided by the Navy and above all by the Royal Air Force, are making against Italian and German attacks. The eyes of all Britain, and indeed of the whole British Empire, are

watching Malta in her struggle day by day, and we are sure that success as well as glory will reward your efforts.[5]

On the same day he minuted: 'The first duty of the AOC-in-C ME is none-theless to sustain the resistance of Malta by a proper flow of fighter rein-forcements.'[6] In response to this directive Air Chief Marshal Longmore in Cairo sent batches of Hurricanes to Malta via airfields in the western desert.

On 6 March, however, Air Commodore Maynard, the AOC in Malta, cabled Portal to report that his dwindling fighter force was unable to cope with raids of as many as sixty German bombers. He also reported that his Mark I Hurricanes were dangerously outclassed by the latest German Bf 109E fighters and urgently requested reinforcements of Hurricane IIs. During February seven squadrons of these new German aircraft had arrived in Sicily and they were commanded by experienced pilots, such as Oberleutnant Joachim Müncheberg, who before his arrival in Sicily had already shot down twenty-three aircraft.[7] Portal read Maynard's signal to the COS on 8 March and on the following day Churchill sent the following Minute to Admiral Pound: 'Air Marshal Longmore has been told that Malta is a first charge on his resources; but in view of all the other strains upon him a resolute effort should be made to put in the Fighter reinforcements from here.'[8] He went on to suggest that the aircraft carrier, HMS *Argus*, which was carrying a batch of Hurricane IIs to Takoradi in West Africa, be diverted into the Mediterranean. 'It would be a very fine thing,' he concluded, 'to reinforce Malta direct.' The Admiralty took the view, however, that the provision of a suitable escort for an aircraft carrier would conflict with their main task of fighting the 'Battle of the Atlantic', a phrase coined by Churchill that month.

After a further two weeks of discussion and delay Churchill lost patience with the Admiralty. At a Defence Committee meeting on 27 March he stated that, despite the Governor's urgent appeals, 'all kinds of objections had been raised' by the Admiralty. Admiral Pound vigorously defended the Admiralty's actions. They had, he said, 'done everything in their power' to find means by which aircraft could be delivered to Malta. Moreover, he insisted that the Admiralty had been told that the Battle of the Atlantic was their first priority. This battle could not be won if 'their forces were liable at any moment to be snatched away for other operations.' Air Chief Marshal Portal, however, while acknowledging that the Admiralty had been very helpful, stressed the urgency of getting some Hurricane IIs into Malta as soon as possible. Both Attlee and Beaverbrook supported the Prime Minister and Operation 'Winch' was ordered to be carried out 'at the earliest opportunity'.[9] In early April *Argus* transferred a batch of aircraft to HMS *Ark Royal* at Gibraltar and a dozen Hurricane IIs reached Malta safely. This set a new operational pattern and in the next three months as many as four aircraft carriers were engaged in flying 224 fighters to Malta. Of these 109, mostly

Hurricane IIs, were retained in Malta and the remainder were flown on to Egypt to strengthen the Middle East air force. The inflow of new aircraft and additional pilots enabled Maynard to re-organise his squadrons.[10]

However, by early May it became clear that as the German air attack reached a new peak the air situation had become critical. On 8 May the Governor first consulted Maynard and then wrote at length to Portal in London expressing his concern about the RAF's difficulties. These were caused, he wrote, by several factors—the shortage of experienced officers on Maynard's staff, the inexperience of many of the pilots faced with *Luftwaffe* veterans, the shortage of Hurricane IIs, and the inadequacy of the ground crews. The Governor added, 'A number of officers and others have been here for a long time and are tired and jaded. They must be relieved by others from home, and by 1st class men.' However, he had nothing but praise for Maynard himself, writing: 'He has done extremely well. He has made bricks without straw, but unless he gets the sort of help I have indicated he will be unable to compete.'[11] Portal responded at once by issuing orders for a substantial strengthening of the Malta Command, adding that 'I regard Malta as the station which, above all others, anywhere should have priority in personnel and material.'[12]

Nevertheless, the situation in the air over Malta continued to worsen as the number of serviceable aircraft fell. Maynard continued to press for better aircraft and more experienced pilots. On 15 May he cabled: 'Disparity in aircraft performance and lack of experienced leadership amongst our fighter pilots continues seriously to affect morale.'[13] On the following day the Governor cabled to Portal.

Since I wrote my letter of 8/5 situation regarding air superiority here has gravely deteriorated. It has completely passed into enemy's hands. Enemy is obviously set on eliminating our fighters and has gone a considerable way towards achieving this end . . . [This has] inevitably affected morale to the extent of almost destroying it in one squadron.[14]

Churchill closely followed this exchange, sending two cables to Maynard in May about additional staff. However, he and Portal decided that Maynard, who had served on the island for more than a year, should be relieved by AVM Lloyd. In communicating this decision to the Governor Churchill assured him that 'everyone here appreciates splendid work Maynard has done working up from the very beginning, but it is felt that a change would be better now. Maynard will be well looked after here.'[15] Upon his return to London he was made a Companion of the Order of the Bath (CB). By the end of May the RAF in Malta had begun to recover air control. Forty-six Hurricanes arrived on 21 May in Operation 'Splice', and forty-three more on 6 June in Operation 'Rocket', although some of these flew on to Egypt where the need for the latest fighters was just as great. Equally important they were flown by pilots with greater combat experience

The air reinforcement of Malta came none too soon since the German capture of Crete in late May strongly suggested that Malta might be the next German objective. Post-war records reveal that this was indeed urged by Admiral Raeder, Chief of the German navy, and by the army's planning staff. However, Hitler ordered that such plans be postponed until the autumn, citing Goering's argument that an air landing on Malta would be made difficult by the close network of stone walls on the island. Unaware of this General Dobbie on 5 June requested additional troops to protect against a possible airborne attack. Churchill at once replied that this was being considered but went on to advise that, partly as a result of the heavy German airborne losses in Crete, an early attempt on Malta seemed less likely. He concluded by telling the Governor:

> You may be sure we regard Malta as one of the master-keys of the British Empire. We are sure that you are the man to hold it and we will do everything in our power to give you the means.[16]

Despite these necessary and urgent measures to strengthen Malta's defences against air attack and possible invasion Churchill never lost sight of the island's main strategic purpose. The principal reason for holding Malta was to provide a base in the central Mediterranean from which naval and air forces could interrupt the flow of men and supplies to the Axis armies in North Africa. This task assumed even greater importance after Rommel had pushed Wavell's British and Commonwealth forces back to the Egyptian border. We must, therefore, retrace our steps to see what measures Churchill and his military advisers took to ensure that Malta-based forces inflicted as much damage as possible on the Italian supply route to North Africa.

The reports and rumours in February of German troops in Italy and Sicily proved quite accurate but their objective was not Valletta but Tripoli and it soon became clear that German reinforcements were crossing the Mediterranean in great strength. How was this to be prevented? The Admiralty's first step was to increase the submarine force at Malta. The first of the small, slow U-class submarines arrived in January to form what later became the 10th Flotilla under Commander Simpson's command. This was based at Manoel Island in Lazaretto Creek on the north side of Valletta. In the following three years this force, under commanders such as Lieutenant-Commander Wanklyn VC, was to achieve a remarkable record of successes but in the first four months of 1941 Malta's submarines only sank ten ships and there were many fruitless patrols.[17] Churchill consequently urged that surface forces be moved to Malta. Cunningham replied that he had long had plans to do this but had delayed their implementation until stronger air defences had been established over Malta and the surrounding waters.

Alarming news forced a decision. Reports in early April of the intended despatch of a full German armoured division to North Africa led to a flurry of signals between London and Alexandria. As a result Cunningham ordered four destroyers of the 14th Flotilla to Malta under the command of Captain Mack and these arrived on 11 April. Two unsuccessful attempts to intercept Italian convoys led to an angry minute from Churchill to Admiral Pound: 'This is a serious NAVAL failure. Another deadly convoy has got through.' Fortunately, several nights later Captain Mack's destroyers caught and sank five enemy merchant ships and their three escorts. When Pound reported this to the Prime Minister he replied, only partly mollified, 'Yes. Brilliantly redeemed. But what about the next?'[18] Admiral Pound responded by sending a further six destroyers of the 5th Flotilla to Malta under the command of Captain Lord Mountbatten while Cunningham sent a cruiser, HMS *Gloucester*, from Alexandria. However, these ships achieved very little against the Italian convoys.

Somewhat earlier Cunningham had complained to Pound that the RAF was not doing enough to attack Axis convoys. When he saw this signal the Prime Minister at once minuted to Pound:

I am distressed at the C-in-C Mediterranean's signal which begins by pointing out vital consequences of stopping German reinforcements via Tripoli and reaches the very easy conclusion that, in spite of the numerous difficulties about Malta, the Air Force must do it . . . We must be prepared to face some losses at sea, instead of the Navy sitting passive and leaving it to the Air. [19]

To make his views quite clear the Prime Minister issued a Directive on 14 April. In this he wrote:

2. It becomes the prime duty of the British Mediterranean Fleet under Admiral Cunningham to stop all sea-borne traffic between Italy and Africa by the fullest use of surface craft, aided so far as possible by aircraft and submarines . . . Every convoy which gets through must be considered a serious naval failure. The reputation of the Royal Navy is engaged in stopping this traffic . . .

5. In order to control the sea communications across the Mediterranean, sufficient suitable naval forces must be based at Malta, and protection must be afforded to these naval forces by the Air Force at Malta, which must be kept at the highest strength in Fighters of the latest and best quality that the Malta Aerodromes can contain. The duty of affording Fighter protection to the naval forces holding Malta should have priority over the use of the Aerodromes by Bombers engaged in attacking Tripoli.[20]

When he came to include this Directive in his post-war memoirs Churchill added, 'All this was easier to say than to do.'

Later in April Cunningham was forced to concentrate his still limited resources to evacuate the British and Commonwealth forces from Greece as noted at the beginning of this chapter. On 1 May Churchill cabled his congratulations 'upon the brilliant and highly successful manner in which the Navy have once again succoured the Army and brought off four-fifths of the entire force.' He then went on to say:

> It is now necessary to fight hard for Crete, which seems soon to be attacked heavily, and also for Malta as a base for flotilla action against the enemy's communications with Libya . . . But above all we look to you to cut off seaborne supplies from the Cyrenaican ports and to beat them up to the utmost. It causes grief here whenever we learn of the arrival of precious aviation spirit in one ship after another.[21]

Cunningham, however, was soon compelled to rescue another Army force from Crete and his losses were severe. They included *Gloucester,* and two of Mountbatten's destroyers, *Kelly* and *Kashmir*. *Warspite*, on which Churchill had sailed with Admiral Keyes in 1927, also suffered extensive bomb damage and after emergency repairs at Alexandria sailed to the USA for major repairs. These losses precluded the stationing of any surface vessels at Malta.

The provision of offensive air forces at Malta proved, if anything, even more difficult. The remaining Wellington bombers sent there at the end of 1940 had been withdrawn after suffering serious losses on the ground and Maynard had only a handful of short-range Swordfish torpedo bombers with which to attack enemy shipping. Moreover, the increasing weight of German attack on Malta's few airfields and the urgent need for fighters left little room for bombers. The most that Portal felt able to do was to order to Malta a flight of six Blenheim light bombers specially trained in low level anti-shipping attack. Nothing more could be accommodated at Malta until the air battle in the skies above the island had been won.

The setbacks in May soon forced a re-ordering of priorities, demonstrating quite clearly that Hitler still retained the strategic initiative. Naval and air resources, as noted above, were initially pre-empted by the urgent need to deliver additional aircraft and tanks to the Middle East and then by the evacuations from Greece and Crete. These pressures compelled Churchill and the COS to acknowledge in mid-May that, for the time being at least, the attack on Axis convoys to North Africa must take second place to operations in the eastern Mediterranean.

The events of the first six months of Mediterranean fighting in 1941 can be read as a story of unrelieved British failure. As Churchill had long feared the advent of strong German air and ground forces into the Mediterranean theatre had proved irresistible. Greece, Crete and Cyrenaica had all been lost to superior German forces and British losses in men, aircraft, ships and material had been severe. Nevertheless, despite these serious defeats Churchill, after absorbing the initial blow of each setback, continued to press the COS, using at times all his formidable powers of persuasion, to transfer additional resources to the area and to urge the local commanders to employ these aggressively against the enemy. As Colonel Jacob, one of his Military Assistants, later wrote: 'He wanted constant action on as wide a scale as possible; the enemy must be made continually to "bleed and burn".'[22]

Throughout this grim period of the war Churchill kept a close eye on civilian developments in Malta. On several occasions he sent messages of praise and encouragement for the Governor to convey to the garrison and civilian population. There can be no doubt about the sincerity of these signals or of his concern for the island's people. For example, in his files is a long signal from the Governor on 14 June 1941 about the progress of the shelter programme. Dobbie reported that deep shelters were being dug as fast as the available force of miners would allow and attributed to these shelters the relatively light casualties suffered during the spring blitz.[23] Somewhat surprisingly, in view of the almost continuous Axis air attacks, a total of 130,000 tons of supplies had reached Malta in the first five months of 1941, nearly all from the east. These enabled the authorities to maintain reserves of essential commodities at the 6-month level.[24]

This chapter has concentrated on Churchill's determination that Malta should play a full part in the Mediterranean war. We have examined the steps he took or instigated to see that the island's defences were strengthened in the face of heavy air attack so that Malta's offensive potential could be enhanced. In the first six months of 1941 much was done to improve the island's defences as additional infantry, AA guns and ammunition, aircraft and food supplies were fought through the Sicilian Narrows. Moreover, offensive operations from Malta were growing in effectiveness. In the first five months of 1941 Malta's forces sank twenty-five enemy cargo ships with a tonnage of 96,000 tons. Fifteen of these ships fell to the submarine force at Manoel Island and six to Captain Mack's destroyers. Despite these successes Italian records show that in the first six months of 1941 only 6% of the supplies sent to North Africa were lost. In May events in Greek waters had compelled even Churchill to accept that, for the time being at least, the attack on the Axis convoys could not be the first priority.

But despite the undoubted setbacks of the early months of 1941 the whole shape of the war was about to change. In his history of the war Churchill has described how, on 17 June, while in the desert Operation 'Battleaxe', of which he had high hopes, was being fought and lost:

I went down to Chartwell, which was shut up, wishing to be alone. Here I got reports of what had happened. I wandered about the valley disconsolately for some hours.[25]

What he does not say is that, despite his bitter disappointment about the defeat in the desert, he also surely pondered the implications of another development that British Intelligence had led him to expect. Five days later when he was spending the weekend at Chequers confirmation came. He was awoken at 8 a.m. on Sunday 22 June to be told that Hitler had invaded Russia.[26]

## Notes

[1] Churchill's Malta files in the National Archives are listed under PREM 3/266/1-10A.

[2] Gilbert, *War Papers, Vol. III,*, p. 126.

[3] Quoted in Churchill, *Second World War, Vol. III,* p. 52.

[4] Ibid., p. 55.

[5] NA PREM 3/266/10A, Fol. 888, WSC to Dobbie, 21 January 1941.

[6] NA CAB 69/2, Defence Committee (Operations) (41) 6th Meeting, 20 January 1941.

[7] For a detailed account of air operations over Malta during this period see C. Shores, B.Cull, and N. Malizia, *Malta: The Hurricane Years: 1940-1941* (Grub Street, London, 1987).

[8] NA ADM 205/10, WSC Minute to Pound, 9 March 1941.

[9] NA CAB 69/2, Defence Committee (Operations) (41) 10th Meeting, 27 March 1941.

[10] One of the new squadrons established was 185 Squadron, the War Diaries of which have been published in A. Rogers, (ed.), *185: The Malta Squadron* (Spellmount, Staplehurst, 2005).

[11] NA AIR 8/500, Governor to Portal, 8 May 1941.

[12] Ibid., Portal to Air Staff, 14 May 1941.

[13] Ibid., Maynard to HQ Middle East, 15 May 1941.

[14] Ibid., Governor to Portal, 16 May 1941.

[15] NA PREM 3/266/10A, Fol. 840, WSC to Dobbie, 18 May 1941.

[16] Ibid., Fol. 844, WSC to Dobbie, 6 June 1941.

[17] The story of the 10th Flotilla has been told by Rear-Admiral G. Simpson in *Periscope View* (Macmillan, London, 1972). See also J. Wingate, *The Fighting Tenth* (Leo Cooper, London, 1991).

[18] NA PREM 3/274/1, Fols. 101-2, WSC to Pound, 14 April 1941.

[19] Ibid., Fol. 106, WSC to Pound, 12 April 1941.

[20] Quoted in Churchill, *Second World War, Vol. III,* pp. 186-8.

[21] Ibid., WSC to Cunningham, 1 May 1941, p.243.

[22] Sir Ian Jacob in Wheeler-Bennett, *Working With Churchill,* p. 198.

[23] NA PREM 3/266/10A, Fols. 812-4, Governor to Colonial Secretary, 14 June 1941.

[24] Details in *The Royal Navy and the Mediterranean: Vol. II, November 1940-December 1941* (Whitehall History Publishing, London, 2002), p. 144.

[25] Churchill, *Second World War, Vol. III,* p. 308.

[26] Ibid., pp. 330-1.

# CHAPTER XI

# Malta Fights Back, Autumn 1941

*Many congratulations on your fine work since you arrived at Malta, and will you please tell all ranks and ratings from me that the two exploits in which they have been engaged, namely, the annihilation of the enemy's convoys on 8th November, and of the two oil ships on Monday last, have played a very definite part in the great battle now raging in Libya.*

Churchill to Captain Agnew, Commander Force K, 27 November 1941

The most immediate consequence for Malta of Hitler's invasion of Russia was the departure of *Fliegerkorps X* to the eastern Mediterranean. To the relief of the hard-pressed defenders they were replaced on the Sicilian airfields by the *Regia Aeronautica* whose raids were less frequent and caused much less damage. Moreover, they were now confronted by a significantly strengthened fighter force of Hurricane IIs under the command of the newly appointed AOC Malta, Air Vice-Marshal Hugh Lloyd. Two weeks earlier Lloyd had been Senior Air Staff Officer (SASO) with No. 2 Group Bomber Command, which flew a force of Blenheim aircraft trained in anti-shipping attack. He was the most senior of those whom Portal rushed out to Malta to meet the May crisis discussed in the previous chapter.[1]

In the last chapter we noted General Dobbie's appeal for substantial troop reinforcements in the aftermath of the German capture of Crete. Although Churchill had sought to reassure the Governor that a German attempt to seize Malta did not appear imminent he nevertheless urged the COS to respond to the Governor's request while the *Luftwaffe* was absent in Russia and the eastern Mediterranean. Since the Admiralty thought it too dangerous to run convoys to Malta from the east they made plans to send from the west a convoy of six merchant ships and a troopship with a powerful escort provided by Force H based at Gibraltar. On 25 June Colonel Hollis advised Churchill that the convoy, code-named Operation 'Substance', would carry sixteen heavy and sixty light AA guns, thirty field guns, two more battalions of infantry and 700 RAF ground crew. The merchant ships would also carry 65,000 tons of ammunition, food and supplies. Unfortunately, the troopship, *Leinster*, a former Irish Sea ferry which carried all the RAF personnel, ran aground while leaving Gibraltar at night and several of the warships carrying army reinforcements were also forced by enemy action to return to Gibraltar. Nevertheless, the merchant ships, despite constant air and Italian MTB attack that seriously damaged the *Sydney Star,* reached Malta on 24 July. A week later a force of cruisers and destroyers brought to Malta the 1,800 army and RAF personnel who had been left behind at Gibraltar. On the night of 25-26 July the Italian navy attempted to destroy the recently arrived merchant ships. A force of small launches packed with explosives and several 'human torpedoes' made its way to the entrance to the Grand Harbour but the approach of these had been picked up by radar and the gunners of the RMA were ready. All of these craft were sunk and none of the merchant ships suffered any damage.[2]

Mention should be made here of the small amounts of vital supplies which were ferried in by submarine. These voyages, which became known as the 'Magic Carpet' service, were undertaken by the larger submarines based at Alexandria or Gibraltar, although some originated in England. They began in early 1941 and continued until the siege of Malta had ended in November 1942. A typical cargo was 24 personnel, 147 bags of mail, 2 tons of medical stores, 62 tons of aviation fuel and 45 tons of kerosene. The cargo on each trip was arranged to meet the most urgent needs and in 1942 food concentrates were often carried.

Encouraged by the success of the July convoy the COS decided to attempt to increase Malta's reserves of food and other essential supplies to a nine-month level by the spring of 1942. Accordingly plans were at once made for Operation 'Halberd', a convoy of no fewer than nine transports. These were loaded with 85,000 tons of supplies and they and the accompanying warships carried a further 2,700 army and RAF personnel. The convoy was heavily attacked as it approached Malta but eight of the transports reached Valletta on 28 September. The result of these two large convoys and supplies delivered by other ships sailing alone was to strengthen considerably Malta's powers of resistance. After the arrival of the 'Substance' convoy Churchill, who had instigated and presided over the arrangements, again cabled the Governor on 3 August:

> Now that the convoys have reached you safely with all their stores and reinforcements, I take this occasion to congratulate you on the firm and steadfast manner in which you and your devoted garrison and citizens have maintained Malta inviolate against all attacks for more than a year, and to express my confidence that with the help of God our cause will continue to prosper, and that the contribution of Malta to the final victory will add a noble chapter to the famous story of the island.[3]

The arrival of the additional AA guns, now more numerous than had been envisaged in Scale B, provided a daunting barrage against Italian air raids, many of which were not pressed home. More dramatic, however, was the recovery of air superiority over Malta. This was made possible not only by the flow of Hurricane IIs and experienced pilots and controllers but also by the arrival of essential maintenance crews, together with spare parts, tools and servicing equipment. Among this necessary equipment were 200 bicycles to enable the ground crews to move more rapidly to aircraft now held in widely dispersed pens. Lloyd had previously warned that with fewer ground staff than was available at a single Bomber Command airfield in England serviceability levels were bound to suffer. RAF records show the steady improvement in these figures in the autumn of 1941. The Governor reported on the beneficial effects of these changes and Air Chief Marshal Sir Edgar Ludlow-Hewitt, the Inspector General of the RAF, after a visit to Malta in July reported to Portal: 'This place I find in much better form than I expected. Lloyd has and is working wonders. Everybody here is singing his praises, and he has certainly got a move on.' He noted the effect of the departure of the *Luftwaffe* by adding as a postscript, 'In the absence of the Germans this island is just a pleasant seaside resort. The Italian air raids are just childish.'[4]

However, although Malta's fighters and AA guns were crucial to its survival Lloyd's instructions from Portal were quite clear. 'Your main task at Malta,' he wrote, 'is to sink Axis shipping sailing from Europe to Africa.'[5] Before we take a closer look at the operations of Malta-based air and naval forces in the second half of 1941, and Churchill's involvement in them, we must step back and consider the wider scene of the Mediterranean war. It was clear to everyone in London and Cairo that the German attack on Russia afforded the opportunity to restore the military position in North Africa by driving Rommel out of Cyrenaica. This was now the task of General Sir Claude Auchinleck who, after the failure of Operation 'Battleaxe' in mid-June, had succeeded General Wavell in command of the Army of the Nile. Inevitably the Prime Minister was soon pressing for a plan to relieve Tobruk and defeat Rommel's German-Italian force. Auchinleck, however, refused to be rushed. Despite being summoned back to London in July and subjected to the Prime Minister's powerful force of argument and persuasion Auchinleck held to the view that preparations for his Operation 'Crusader' could not be complete before November. Churchill complained bitterly about the consequent idleness of the large British forces in Egypt while the Russian army was fighting for its life. The minutes of the Defence Committee, which considered the matter on 1 August recorded that the Prime Minister 'thought it was a frightful prospect that nothing should be done for four and a half months at a time when a small German army was having the greatest difficulty in so much as existing.'[6] He was, nevertheless, forced to acquiesce but he later wrote: 'I must record my conviction that General Auchinleck's four and a half months' delay in engaging the enemy in the desert was alike a mistake and a misfortune.'[7]

The prospect of a long delay before Auchinleck felt ready to launch his offensive worried Churchill because it opened up the possibility that Rommel's force would also be reinforced and might then be able to strike first. To prevent this Churchill saw that it was of paramount importance that the flow of men and supplies from Italy to North Africa be restricted or delayed. This, as we have seen, was Churchill's view of Malta's primary role, employing all the air and naval forces that the island could sustain. The successful deployment of these forces was considerably helped in mid-1941 by two technological developments in both of which Churchill had long been involved.

The first lay in the field of Intelligence where a breakthrough was achieved the significance of which for the Mediterranean war it would be difficult to exaggerate. Reference has already been made in earlier chapters to intercepted enemy signals and many readers will be aware of British success in breaking signals that had been encyphered by the German Enigma machine. Professor Hinsley, the official historian of British Intelligence, has written that 'Churchill was exceptional among British statesmen of his time for his familiarity with intelligence and his consuming interest in it.'[8] This interest went back to the First World War when, as First Lord of the Admiralty, he presided over the decryption work of Room 40 of the Naval Intelligence Department. As soon as he became Prime Minister he insisted on seeing the most important enemy signals. These were delivered to him daily in a special buff-coloured despatch box, the key to which he kept on his watch chain.

The Mediterranean proved to be an ideal area for the development of decryption techniques since not only was it an active war zone but most of the enemy communications were sent by radio. In June 1941 the cryptanalysts at what was known as the Government Code and Cypher School at Bletchley Park (GC&CS) made a momentous advance when they first broke a new Italian machine cypher referred to as C38m. This gave details of all planned convoys from Italy to North Africa. GC&CS at once established a Special Liaison Unit (SLU) at Malta to expedite the delivery of this information and the result was that from the summer of 1941 the naval and air force commanders on the island and in Cairo had detailed advance information of all Axis convoys to North Africa. This 'Special Intelligence' allowed the Malta commanders to deploy aircraft and submarines along the convoy routes, to plan reconnaissance flights to locate enemy ships at sea, and later to direct bombers to ports where ships that had escaped interception were unloading. When he was advised of this development Churchill wrote to Admiral Pound: 'I hope Admiral Cunningham realises the quality of this information. If he cannot intercept on this we do not deserve success.'

The second technological advance was the development of a type of airborne radar known as Air-to-Surface Vessel (ASV) radar, designed to facilitate the location of surface ships at night or in poor visibility. Churchill first became aware of the development of radar when Baldwin in 1935 invited him to join the Air Defence Research Committee of the CID. At the very first meeting of this committee that he attended on 25 July 1935 he listened while Robert Watson-Watt described the successful experiment he had carried out just the day before to locate an aircraft by reflected radio waves. From this beginning radar developed in many directions and one variation was ASV. In mid-1941 a short-range version of this equipment was installed in several of the Malta-based Swordfish enabling them to locate and attack ships at night while in September, on the recommendation of Professor Lindeman (who in June had been raised to the peerage as Lord Cherwell), Malta received a number of Wellington bombers fitted with a long-range model. These Wellingtons could scour the central Mediterranean for as long as twelve hours and direct surface ships and aircraft to any contacts revealed by the ASV.[9]

Aided by these developments Lloyd implemented a three-pronged strategy for the deployment of his growing air force. The night-flying Swordfish and Albacore torpedo bombers operated within about 200 miles of Malta against convoys whose routes had been revealed by C38m and were also used to drop mines outside enemy ports. A force of Wellington medium bombers also operated at night carrying bombs up to 4,000lbs. to targets in North Africa, Sicily and Italy. Tripoli and Benghazi, now out of range of Egyptian-based bombers, were prime targets and Italian records show that capacity at Tripoli was reduced by as much as 50% as a result of bomb damage. Lloyd's third arm was a newly-arrived force of Blenheim light bombers trained to deliver attacks with 250lb bombs at mast-head height. These flew by day as far as 600 miles from Malta but as the Axis convoys became equipped with stronger AA defences Blenheim losses began to cause concern both in Malta and London.

Apart from the damage and disruption caused at the loading and unloading ports by the Wellington raids Lloyd's squadrons in the last seven months of 1941 sank thirty Axis merchant ships with a gross tonnage of 135,000 tons. Many others were damaged, delayed or forced to turn back and this was second in importance only to an outright sinking since Auchinleck and Rommel were effectively in a race to build up supplies for the forthcoming battle. Churchill presided over the COS meetings at which these RAF plans were made and implemented and read the signals between the Air Ministry and Malta but he had few occasions to interfere with Portal's handling of these operations except to recommend that more Blenheims be sent to Malta from the North Sea.

The Admiralty was not let off so lightly perhaps because Churchill had twice been First Lord and felt better informed about naval matters. He had, however, no complaint to make about the Malta-based submarine operations. Admiral Pound sent every available submarine to the Mediterranean and at

Malta Commander Simpson and Vice-Admiral Ford had a growing fleet of U-class submarines reinforced from time to time by other boats arriving at the Manoel Island submarine base from Alexandria to rearm, refuel and rest their crews. With the help provided by C38m and with growing experience of operating in Mediterranean waters the 10th Flotilla achieved a widely acclaimed success, albeit at the cost of several losses including that of Lieutenant-Commander Wanklyn and his crew after the exploits of HMS *Upholder* had previously earned him the VC. In the last seven months of 1941 Malta's submarines accounted for thirteen enemy merchant ships with a total tonnage of 90,000 tons and inflicted damage on several others.

Nevertheless, Churchill believed that in order to exert greater pressure on the Axis supply line to North Africa it was essential to re-establish a surface force at Malta and he urged that this be done with increasing vehemence during the summer and autumn of 1941. Before examining some of the Prime Minister's minutes and arguments on this matter, some of which are highly critical, it should be remembered that Churchill clearly saw it as his paramount duty, endorsed by Parliament and public opinion, to urge the leaders of the country's armed forces to fight the enemy. He was often generous with encouragement and praise, as some of the signals quoted in these chapters demonstrate, but he was at times dismayed by what he regarded as excessive caution.

In October in a private letter to his son, Randolph, who was serving with the army in Cairo he wrote: 'The Admirals, Generals and Air Marshals chant their stately hymn of "Safety First" ... In the midst of this I have to restrain my natural pugnacity by sitting on my own head. How bloody!'[10] He expressed similar criticisms to Harold Macmillan in November 1943. When it was suggested to him that the Chiefs of Staff system worked well he replied:

> Not at all. It leads to weak and faltering decisions—or rather indecisions. Why, you may take the most gallant sailor, the most intrepid airman, or the most audacious soldier, put them at a table together—what do you get? *The sum of their fears!*[11]

He also thought it essential that difficult and contentious problems be fully argued out either in writing or, better still, in a face to face meeting. When asked by a young Brigadier at a meeting whether he could speak freely Churchill at once replied: 'Of course. We are not here to pay each other compliments.'[12] This 'no-holds-barred' approach to discussion and decision-making led on occasion to minutes that were often scathing and at times sarcastic but the circumstances in which these were written should be borne in mind.

There had been no naval surface force at Malta since the 5th Destroyer Flotilla had been withdrawn in May to assist in the evacuation from Crete. On 30 June Churchill, after reading signals about RAF operations from

Malta which revealed large enemy shipping concentrations at Tripoli, minuted to the COS: 'Although we take a heavy toll very large enemy reinforcements are crossing to Africa continually. The Navy seem unable to do anything. The Air Force only stop perhaps a fifth. You are no doubt impressed with the full gravity of the situation.'[13] In his reply Pound emphasised that fifty-two enemy ships had been sunk or damaged in May and June and considered that this was a 'creditable effort on the part of our naval and air forces.' He also argued that without strong fighter cover it was too dangerous to operate warships in the central Mediterranean in the face of German dive-bombers now established in Crete and Cyrenaica. What Churchill thought of this response can no longer be read. In his personal papers the lower part of Pound's memorandum has been removed and there is the notation, 'Torn off by the Prime Minister'. If, as one imagines, his initial comment was critical it appears that he had second thoughts about the matter. In the event nothing was done.

Nevertheless, the Prime Minister continued to read the daily C38m intercepts and six weeks later asked General Ismay to provide details of recent Axis shipments to North Africa. On 22 August Ismay told him that the Axis forces had received 265,000 tons in July and a further 194,000 tons in the first twenty days of August. Although post-war records show that these figures were exaggerated Churchill immediately sent an aggrieved minute to Admiral Pound which began: 'Further to my minute about supplies reaching Tripoli from Italy, will you please consider the sending of a flotilla and, if possible, a cruiser or two to Malta as soon as possible.' He went on to complain:

> We must look back to see how much our purpose has been deflected. There was the plan, considered vital by you, of blocking Tripoli harbour, for which *Barham* was to be sacrificed. There was the alternative desperate proposal by the C-in-C Mediterranean to bombard it, which was afterwards effected without the loss of a man or a single ship being damaged. There was the arrival of Mountbatten's flotilla at Malta. All this took place several months ago. It would be well to get out the dates. How is it that the urgency of this matter has declined? How is it that we are now content to watch what we formerly thought unendurable, although it is going forward on a bigger scale against us? . . . We have thus lost sight of our purpose, on which there was such general agreement, and in which the Admiralty was so forward and strong.[14]

Pound at once signalled Cunningham to ask if he was in a position to establish a surface force at Malta and the latter replied on the following day. Cunningham said that he thought that this should and could be done but that a shortage of fuel oil at Malta and the reduced number of his destroyers and cruisers ruled out the provision of any force from the Mediterranean fleet before the end of September.

While this interchange was taking place Churchill read another C38m intercept that described the passage of several ships including a German tanker to Benghazi. He at once sent a further angry minute to Pound:

What action will the C-in-C Mediterranean take on this information? Surely he cannot put up with this sort of thing . . . Is he going simply to leave these ships to the chance of a submarine, without making any effort by his surface forces to intercept them? Please ask specifically what if anything he is going to do. We are still at war.[15]

In the event the tanker was not intercepted and in early September discharged her cargo of aviation fuel at Benghazi. When he learned of this Churchill minuted to Pound: 'Admiral Cunningham sh'd feel sorry about this. It is a melancholy failure.'[16]

On 24 August Pound sent Churchill a four-page note that incorporated Cunningham's views about the requested surface force at Malta and his own analysis. This was discussed at a COS Committee meeting on the following day when Pound emphasised that 'a force of the kind that Admiral Cunningham could afford to employ at Malta would be faced with an almost impossible task.' He pointed out that the navy was critically short of fleet destroyers and cruisers and endorsed Cunningham's judgement that a small force at Malta could only act as temporary deterrent and might then be attacked by Italian capital ships. He also argued that the attack on the Axis convoy route by air and submarine forces from Malta was proving successful. The minutes of the meeting do not record any objection by the Prime Minister to Pound's analysis and conclusion.[17] Churchill in his memoirs later wrote that the principle of establishing a Malta surface force was agreed but that was certainly not the case in August.

It was not until 5 October that Churchill again pressed for a Malta surface force when he minuted to Admiral Pound: 'Is there no possibility of helping the Air Force on the Tripoli blockade with some surface craft, including a cruiser or two? We seem to leave it all to the Air Force and submarines.' When Pound in reply repeated the arguments he had expressed in August a frustrated Churchill wrote, 'Cunningham seems to be lying low since Crete. Is he going to play any part in "Crusader"?'[18] This was the code name for the offensive being prepared by General Auchinleck. This barbed comment, made more pointed by the fact that Admiral Cunningham's younger brother, General Sir Alan Cunningham, had been appointed to command what had now been renamed the '8th Army', finally achieved its purpose. On 11 October Pound signalled Cunningham to advise that two cruisers, HMS *Aurora* and *Penelope*, and two destroyers, HMS *Lance* and *Lively*, were being sent to him from Home waters to form Force K at Malta. He remained dubious about the results such a force might achieve but told Cunningham: '. . . should "Crusader" fail then I think there would

110

have been lasting criticism because we had not made any attempt to cut the communications to Africa by surface forces.'[19]

Contrary to Pound's and Cunningham's doubts Force K, soon joined by a further two cruisers and as many as six destroyers, achieved remarkable results, sinking on 7 November a complete Axis convoy of seven heavily-escorted merchant ships. Churchill read avidly the C38m intercepts that told the story of these Axis losses. How closely Churchill followed the air and naval attacks launched from Malta can be illustrated by the interception and sinking of two German merchant ships. On 23 November a C38m decrypt revealed that two German supply ships, the *Maritza* of 2910 tons, and the *Procida* of 1842 tons, had left Piraeus and were heading for Benghazi. They carried urgently needed ammunition and aviation fuel. Churchill discussed this with Admiral Pound and the latter at once sent a signal to Malta ordering Force K to raise steam. He then signalled Cunningham recommending that Force K intercept the two supply ships unless Cunningham had already made other plans.[20] Churchill also sent a signal to Cunningham, which read:

> I asked the First Sea Lord to wireless you today about the vital importance of intercepting surface ships bringing reinforcements, supplies, and, above all, fuel to Benghazi. Our information here shows a number of vessels now approaching or starting. Request has been made by enemy for air protection, but this cannot be given owing to absorption in battle of his African air force. All this information has been repeated to you. I shall be glad to hear through Admiralty what action you propose to take. The stopping of these ships may save thousands of lives, apart from aiding a victory of cardinal importance.[21]

On the afternoon of 24 November Force K, directed by an ASV-equipped Wellington from Malta that had been deliberately sent to the area to conceal the fact that the convoy's position had been established by a decyphered signal, intercepted the two supply ships with an escort of two Italian torpedo boats 100 miles north of Benghazi. Within the hour the guns of the four British warships had sunk the *Maritza* and the *Procida* and were returning to Malta at high speed. On the following day Churchill was no doubt delighted to read among the signals in his buff box a *Luftwaffe* signal that confirmed the losses and stated that these had placed operations 'in real danger', and that emergency fuel was consequently being sent by air and by Italian destroyers. This welcome news prompted the signal to Captain Agnew of HMS *Aurora* that is quoted at the beginning of this chapter.[22]

In the month of November Force K sank ten ships of 48,000 tons to which Malta's aircraft and submarines added a further four of 10,000 tons. Others were damaged and forced to return to port. Moreover, the mere presence of Force K compelled the Italian authorities to restrict their convoy programme in the remaining weeks before 'Crusader' was launched on

18 November. The impact of these operations is best seen in the Axis supply figures. In broad terms Rommel required a minimum of 70,000 tons a month to sustain operations. In November, however, only 30,000 tons of the 79,000 tons of supplies sent to North Africa arrived and in December only 39,000 tons of a very restricted programme of 48,000 tons.

Tragically, however, in the early hours of 19 December Force K, composed on this occasion of three cruisers and four destroyers, ran into a minefield while trying to intercept an Axis convoy near Tripoli. The cruiser, HMS *Neptune*, was lost with all but one of her 765-man crew, the two other cruisers, HMS *Aurora* and *Penelope*, were damaged and compelled to return to Malta and the destroyer, HMS *Kandahar*, had to be sunk after suffering extensive damage. On the very same day the battleships HMS *Queen Elizabeth* and *Valiant* were sunk at their moorings in Alexandria by Italian frogmen. The Mediterranean Fleet had already lost in November its other battleship, HMS *Barham*, while in the western Mediterranean a German U-boat had sunk the aircraft carrier, HMS *Ark Royal*. These severe losses effectively brought Malta's naval operations against the Axis convoys to an end and deteriorating weather conditions hampered air operations. The result was that in the following weeks Rommel received substantial supplies, including a large number of armoured vehicles. These enabled him, first, to hold Auchinleck's final attacks and then to launch on 21 January 1942 a counter-attack which pushed the 8th Army well back into Cyrenaica.

From this necessarily abbreviated account of a period of high activity at sea and in the air we may draw two conclusions. There can be little doubt that in the last seven months of 1941 Malta's air and naval forces waged an increasingly powerful campaign to restrict the flow of supplies to Rommel's forces. In this critical period Malta's forces sank no fewer than 56 ships with a total tonnage of 290,000 tons and damaged many others. As a result Rommel's plans to seize Tobruk and then advance into Egypt were continually postponed as he struggled to build up reserves and this delay allowed Auchinleck to attack first. As 'Crusader' turned into a battle of attrition the additional successes of Force K in November and December forced Rommel, unable to make good his battlefield losses, to abandon Cyrenaica and retire into Tripolitania. It was only the crippling of Force K on the night of 19 December that allowed a vital Axis convoy to deliver urgently needed tanks and supplies to the Axis army. As the German naval staff commented:

> The sinking of the *Neptune* may be of decisive importance for holding Tripolitania. Without this the British force would probably have destroyed the Italian convoy. There is no doubt that the loss of these supplies at the peak of the crisis would have had the severest consequences.[23]

The second conclusion that presents itself is that Malta's offensive in late 1941 owed much to Churchill's constant pressure. Having as a preliminary ordered the strengthening of Malta's defences, he then urged the Air Ministry and Admiralty to build up the island's offensive operations. Pound and Cunningham, only too conscious of the navy's shrinking resources, were both reluctant to send a surface force to Valletta and doubted the effectiveness of such a small force. In the event the Prime Minister's optimism proved more accurate. Indeed, it can be argued that had his view prevailed in August or September rather than in October the further strangulation of Rommel's supply line that might have resulted could have brought about his total defeat in December 1941.

This did not happen. The pendulum of the desert war swung back yet again and for Malta too there was an ominous development in the critical month of December. The *Luftwaffe* had returned to Sicily.

## *Notes*

[1] Lloyd's own account of his experiences in Malta is in *Briefed to Attack: Malta's Part in African Victory* (Hodder & Stoughton, London, 1949).

[2] For details see *The Royal Navy and the Mediterranean, Vol. II,* pp. 149-52.

[3] Gilbert, *War Papers, Vol. III*, p. 1029.

[4] NA AIR 8/500, Ludlow-Hewitt to Portal, 21 July 1941.

[5] Air Marshal Sir Hugh Lloyd, *Briefed to Attack*, p. 13.

[6] NA CAB 69/2, Defence Committee (Operations) (41) 53rd Meeting, 1 August 1941.

[7] Churchill, *Second World War, Vol. III*, p. 364.

[8] F. Hinsley, "Churchill and the Use of Special Intelligence", in R. Blake and W. Louis (eds.), *Churchill* (Oxford University Press, Oxford, 1993), p. 407.

[9] See Tony Spooner, *Supreme Gallantry: Malta's Role in the Allied Victory 1939-1945* (John Murray, London, 1996). Spooner flew one of these ASV Wellingtons between October 1941 and March 1942.

[10] Gilbert, *War Papers, Vol. III,* WSC to Randolph Churchill, 30 October 1941, pp. 1391-2.

[11] H. Macmillan, *The Blast of War: 1939-1945* (Macmillan, London, 1967), p. 424.

[12] Lord Ismay, *The Memoirs of General The Lord Ismay* (Heinemann, London, 1960), pp. 269-70.

[13] Quoted in Churchill, *Second World War, Vol. III*, p. 694.

[14] Ibid., p. 434.

[15] Gilbert, *War Papers, Vol. III,* WSC to Pound, 24 August 1941, p. 1095.

[16] Ibid., WSC to Pound, 3 September 1941, p. 1150.

[17] NA CAB 79/55, COS (41) 27th "O" Meeting, 25 August 1941.

[18] NA PREM 3/274/1, Fols. 6-8, WSC to Pound and latter's reply, 5 October 1941.

[19] British Library, Cunningham Papers, Add. MS. 52561, Pound to Cunningham, 11 October 1941.

[20] NA PREM 3/274/2, Fol. 408, Pound to Cunningham, 23 November 1941.

[21] Gilbert *War Papers, Vol. III,* WSC to Cunningham, 23 November 1941, p. 1493.

[22] Ibid., WSC to Agnew, 27 November 1941, p. 1511.

[23] Quoted by Churchill in *Second World War, Vol. III*, p. 513.

# CHAPTER XII

# The Second Great Siege of Malta, Spring and Summer 1942

*I am deeply anxious about Malta under the increasing bombardment of 450 first-line German aircraft. If the island fortress is to hold out till the June convoy, which is the earliest possible, it must have a continued flow of Spitfires.*

Churchill to President Roosevelt, 22 April 1942

As early as October 1941 Hitler had decided to divert air forces from the Russian front to support Axis operations in the Mediterranean. This decision was given effect in December by his Directive No. 38 which ordered *Fliegerkorps II* to Sicily together with the Headquarters staff of *Luftflotte 2*. At the same time Hitler appointed Field Marshal Kesselring as 'C-in-C South' with instructions to regain control of the central Mediterranean and 'in particular to keep Malta in subjection'. The first German aircraft landed in Sicily later that month and by February 1942 over 400 aircraft had assembled.

As a consequence the Axis onslaught on Malta rose to a new peak of intensity in the spring and summer of 1942. It is estimated that in April 6,700 tons of bombs fell upon Valletta and the surrounding areas, causing many casualties and enormous structural damage. The loss of life might have been greater but for the shelter construction programme which had by then provided some defence for most of the civilian population. This chapter will consider Churchill's reactions to this darkening scene and the decisions that he and the COS took to ensure the survival of Malta as a British operational base.

On 22 December 1941, two weeks after the Japanese attack on Pearl Harbor, Churchill arrived at Washington to discuss with President Roosevelt the plans to be made to defeat Germany and Japan. While he was there he continued to receive full information about developments in the Mediterranean and among these papers was an analysis of a possible invasion of Malta. The COS had already warned the Governor that 'it looks to us that you are next on the list' and Churchill responded to this information by asking: 'I should like to know if anything more is being done to reinforce the fortress and how their reserves of AA ammunition stand.'[1] This led to further discussions with General Dobbie the result of which was a decision that the island should receive substantial additional troops and AA guns.

A further unhappy consequence of the fear of invasion was the decision in February to remove to Uganda forty-two of the Maltese citizens who had been imprisoned since 1940 under the Malta Defence Regulations. Among these were Sir Arturo Mercieca, the former Chief Justice, and Dr. Enrico Mizzi, the leader of the Nationalist Party and a future Prime Minister of Malta.[2] What caused concern and dispute in Malta was not so much the decision to detain these people in 1940 but their deportation in 1942. Three months after their removal the Malta Court of Appeal declared the deportations to be illegal. Stewart Perowne, a member of the Governor's staff who knew many of those deported, later wrote:

> It is a sad story, especially in retrospect. These men were not criminals, nor spies. No charge was ever brought against them. They were victims. The most intelligent of them, who is a friend of mine, has told me that they underwent no cruelty, and very seldom any unkindness. They were honest men with the courage of their convictions; and it was those convictions that convicted them.[3]

Although the author has been able to find no document to which Churchill's name is attached which authorised these deportations this may be because several Colonial Office files are still unavailable for public examination. Nevertheless, it is reasonable to assume that the Governor obtained the approval of the Colonial Secretary, Lord Cranborne, for his proposed action and that Cranborne in turn received Churchill's consent. If this is correct his endorsement of the Governor's actions can only be explained by the alarms and anxieties of the times, which are now, sixty years later, impossible to recapture. These fears, fed by the actions of Vidkun Quisling in Norway and the continuing rumours of a 'fifth column', brought into being legislation in several countries, including the controversial Regulation 18B in Britain, which permitted imprisonment without charge or trial. In a statement to the House of Commons in July 1940 when Britain too faced the threat of invasion Churchill noted that 'the House has accepted numerous regulations which, but for the gravity of the hour, would be extremely repugnant to all our ideas'. He, nevertheless, refused a request to withdraw these regulations. In private, however, he was frequently critical of Regulation 18B and it should be noted that two of Churchill's relatives, one of whom was Lady Mosley, were among 150 prominent persons imprisoned in Britain under this emergency legislation.

Fears of a possible invasion of Malta soon gave way to a growing anxiety that the island might be forced to surrender by a lack of food. Three ships from a convoy of four had delivered 24,000 tons of supplies in mid-January but an attempt to sail a further three-ship convoy from Alexandria in February met with disaster. Two of the freighters were sunk by air attack on 14 February and the remaining ship forced to seek shelter at Tobruk. On 18 February the Governor sent a bleak cable to the War Office commenting on the dwindling food stocks on the island. He warned that a basic minimum of 15,000 tons of supplies were required each month and at this level consumption would be reduced to 'siege conditions'.[4] In a further cable to the Colonial Secretary, Lord Cranborne, on 21 February General Dobbie wrote: 'I feel that we have reached a critical point in the maintenance of Malta', and added that a deterioration in morale was becoming apparent. Cranborne passed this news on to Churchill and went on to write:

This is hardly the place to discuss the consequences likely to follow the loss of Malta, not the least of which would be the surrender of 300,000 most loyal British subjects, who would be then verging on starvation, to the mercy of the enemy.[5]

The Prime Minister had also received on 19 February a telegram from the Middle East C-in-Cs advising that they were 'seriously concerned at the air situation in Malta'.

Churchill immediately asked the COS to review the position and to inform him of the action they proposed to take. The COS considered the whole problem at their meetings on 24 and 27 February and, after obtaining the Prime Minister's agreement, sent a cable to the Middle East C-in-Cs that began:

Our view is that Malta is of such importance both as an air staging point and as an impediment to the enemy reinforcement route that the most drastic steps are justifiable to sustain it. Even if Axis maintain their present scale of attack on Malta thus reducing its value it will continue to be of great importance to war as a whole by containing important enemy air forces during critical months.

They went on to urge that an offensive in Cyrenaica be planned to permit the safe passage of a substantial Malta convoy in April. In the meantime they recommended that a March convoy be attempted, emphasising that 'no consideration of risks to ships themselves need deter you from this. During the progress of this operation it should be regarded as our primary military commitment.'[6]

This makes clear the judgement of the COS that it was Rommel's capture of the airfields around Benghazi that had increased the threat to Malta's supply line. Whereas the January convoy had enjoyed air cover from long-range RAF fighters based near Benghazi these airfields were now held by the German air force. Moreover, the combat-hardened *Luftwaffe* pilots from the Russian front were now deployed in growing numbers in Sicily and re-equipped with the latest version of the Bf109F that outclassed Malta's Hurricane IIs. Finally, the Italian Navy, supplied by Germany with the necessary fuel oil and facing a British Mediterranean fleet that, after the losses in November and December 1941, no longer possessed any battleships or aircraft carriers, presented a formidable surface threat to any convoy to Malta.

If there were any doubts in London about the nature of these risks they were removed by the fate of the March convoy. Although by a brilliant naval action Admiral Sir Philip Vian managed to fend off an Italian battleship force one transport and the naval supply ship, *Breconshire*, were sunk as they approached Malta. Moreover, two other freighters, the *Pampas* and *Talabot*, which did reach Valletta, were subsequently sunk at their moorings after only 5,000 tons of their cargo had been unloaded. Even though a further 2,600 tons was salvaged from these ships the total was far short of Malta's minimum monthly requirement of 15,000 tons.

Before we examine the dramatic events in Malta of April and May 1942 we should step back and consider the key decisions taken in London and Cairo. The fate of the March convoy made abundantly clear that two conditions were essential if Malta was to survive. Firstly, it was necessary for the RAF to regain air superiority without which any merchant ships that succeeded in reaching the island might not be safely unloaded. Secondly, in order that air cover could be provided over the approaches to Malta from the east it was essential to regain the use of the Cyrenaican airfields. The first of these tasks was the prime responsibility of Portal at the Air Ministry; the second depended upon an early and successful offensive by General Auchinleck. Although these two aspects of the problem were inter-related it will be helpful to consider them separately.

By mid-February there was no longer any doubt that Malta's surrender might be brought about by air power alone. The 400 German and 200 Italian aircraft in Sicily, only ten minutes flying time away, had established complete air superiority over Malta and its approaches and were opposed only by the AA guns, whose ammunition had been restricted to fifteen rounds per gun each day, and a dwindling force of Hurricane IIs. The task facing Portal, Tedder and Lloyd was, therefore, nothing less than to build a new air force in Malta under the bombs and guns of the enemy. The accomplishment of this seemingly impossible task within three months must rank as one of the RAF's finest achievements during the war. It was a complex and dangerous process requiring a new type of aircraft, more experienced pilots, improved servicing, repair and handling operations on the ground and an accelerated system for delivering aircraft and pilots to the island. But the cost was high and the names of those airmen who lost their lives in this epic battle are among the 2,301 names inscribed on The Commonwealth Air Forces Memorial outside the walls of Valletta.

On 9 February the Air Ministry advised Tedder and Lloyd that plans had been made for the establishment of five Spitfire squadrons at Malta and the first fifteen Spitfire Vbs was flown to Malta from HMS *Eagle* on 7 March. However, the enemy domination of Malta's skies, demonstrated by the sinking of *Pampas* and *Talabot* in the Grand Harbour on 26 March, led to an urgent plea from AVM Lloyd, supported by the Governor, for much larger and more frequent deliveries of Spitfires. Since the *Eagle* would be out of action for several weeks the COS recommended to Churchill that he ask President Roosevelt for the loan of a large US aircraft carrier. Accordingly, on 1 April Churchill signalled the President:

> Air attack on Malta is very heavy. There are now in Sicily about 400 German and 200 Italian fighters and bombers. Malta can now muster only twenty or thirty serviceable aircraft. We keep feeding Malta with Spitfires in packets of sixteen loosed from *Eagle* carrier from about 600 miles west of Malta. This has worked a good many times quite well, but *Eagle* is now laid up for a month by defects in her steering gear . . . Would you be willing to allow your carrier *Wasp* to do one of these trips provided details are satisfactorily agreed between the Naval Staffs? With her broad lifts, capacity and length, we estimate that *Wasp* could take fifty or more Spitfires.[7]

Two days later the President cabled his agreement and on 20 April *Wasp* flew off 47 Spitfires of 601 and 603 Squadrons in Operation 'Calendar'. Within days, however, such was the intensity of the enemy air attack, this reinforcement had been largely eliminated. On 23 April General Dobbie cabled the Prime Minister to tell him that of the forty-seven Spitfires that had arrived only three days earlier seventeen had been lost and twenty-nine others damaged. The AOC was able to put up a mere six Spitfires. He concluded: 'Situation demands most drastic action and we must think in quite different numbers of Spitfires than we have envisaged heretofore.' On his copy of this signal Churchill wrote: 'CAS. Please speak to me.'[8] The upshot was a second request to the President for the services of *Wasp*. Churchill telegraphed again:

> I am deeply anxious about Malta under the increasing bombardment of 450 first-line German aircraft. If the island fortress is to hold out till the June convoy, which is the earliest possible, it must have a continued flow of Spitfires. The last flying off from WASP was most successful, although unhappily the enemy's attack broke up many after they had landed . . . I shall be grateful if you allow WASP to do a second trip . . . Without this aid I fear Malta will be pounded to bits.[9]

The President's consent was given once more and on 10 May *Wasp* and *Eagle* in Operation 'Bowery' delivered a further sixty-two Spitfires. On this occasion elaborate plans had been made to re-fuel the new aircraft as soon as they landed and many were airborne within ten minutes of their arrival with a Malta-experienced pilot at the controls. On that and the following days a series of furious air battles were joined in the skies of Malta. On 20 May Portal was able to advise the Prime Minister, who had earlier ordered a daily report on Malta air operations, that in the eight days from 10 May sixty-four enemy aircraft had been shot down, forty-five more probably destroyed, and a further seventy-four damaged. He passed on the view of the new Governor, General Lord Gort, that air superiority over Malta had now been recovered.[10]

We must now retrace our steps to early March to consider the fierce arguments that developed around the second of Malta's needs, the recovery of the airfields in Cyrenaica so that eastern convoys could receive air protection. On 27 February, as noted above, the COS, at Churchill's instigation, had sent a signal to the Middle East Commanders recommending an offensive to recover these airfields by mid-April. In early March two lengthy cables from General Auchinleck made clear that he did not think a successful offensive could be launched before June. Churchill was furious and immediately dictated and sent to the COS for consideration a blistering reply which, he said, 'expressed the thoughts which had come into his mind on reading it.' Although this was not the version eventually sent, it shows quite clearly the Prime Minister's forceful insistence that the enemy must be fought and his dismay and anger when he thought that others did not share his determination. Here we may simply quote his conclusion:

> No one is going to stand your remaining in deep peace while Malta is being starved out, while the Russians are fighting like mad and while we are suffering continued disasters in Burma and India at the hands of the Japanese. The whole system of the command will have to be revolutionised. It is imperative that our forces everywhere shall come to grips with the enemy and force him to consume lives, munitions, tanks, and aircraft around the whole circle of his fighting front.[11]

The anger displayed in this draft owed much to the surrender of Singapore on 14 February following which 62,000 British and Commonwealth troops went into a captivity which many did not survive. Churchill was later to call this the 'worst disaster and largest capitulation in British history'[12] and in his draft signal to Auchinleck he wrote: 'I was looking to the 8th Army . . . to repair the shame of Singapore.'

The Defence Committee discussed Auchinleck's worrying appreciation on 2 March. General Brooke noted in his diary that day:

> Another bad Monday. Found PM had drafted a bad wire for Auchinleck in which he poured abuse on him for not attacking sooner, and for sending us an appreciation in which he did not propose to attack till June!![13]

A less abrasive signal was sent in place of Churchill's draft. This stated that 'we are greatly disturbed by your review of the situation. The dominant factor in the Mediterranean and Middle East situation at the present time is Malta.' The signal concluded that an attempt to drive the Germans out of Cyrenaica in the next few weeks was 'imperative for the safety of Malta'. When Auckinleck continued to resist this pressure and declined an invitation to return to London to discuss the matter Churchill instructed Sir Stafford Cripps, who was *en route* to India, to see Auchinleck in Cairo and General Nye, the Vice-Chief of the Imperial General Staff (VCIGS) was also sent out for these discussions. To Churchill's intense annoyance they signalled back that they agreed with Auchinleck's analysis and so with the greatest reluctance the Defence Committee accepted that an offensive with the prospect of success could not be launched before mid-May.[14]

This remained the position until 6 May when Auchinleck cabled once more. He had now decided that in view of his continued inferiority in tanks he would not be able to attack before mid-June. Since, as we shall see below, plans for both an April and a May convoy to Malta had been abandoned the island's survival now rested on a June convoy. The success of this seemed in London to depend on the recapture of the Cyrenaican airfields and Auchinleck's proposed postponement consequently came as a bombshell. The full War Cabinet discussed this development on 8 May and the Prime Minister then cabled to Auchinleck that the War Cabinet had considered his proposals 'with particular regard to Malta, the loss of which would be a disaster of first magnitude to the British Empire, and probably fatal in the long run to the defence of the Nile Valley.' He then went on:

> We are agreed that in spite of the risks you mention you would be right to attack the enemy and fight a major battle, if possible during May, and the sooner the better. We are prepared to take full responsibility for these general directions, leaving you the necessary latitude for their execution. In this you will no doubt have regard to the fact that the enemy may himself be planning to attack you early in June.[15]

A full-scale crisis erupted when two days later Auchinleck refused to accept this 'advice'. Churchill hastily summoned a further meeting of the War Cabinet on the afternoon of Sunday 10 May, the very day on which, unknown to them, Malta's reinforced Spitfire force began to recover air superiority. Auchinleck's cable expressed doubts for the first time about Malta's strategic value. His own view was that 'its fall (much though this would be deplored) would not necessarily be fatal to security of Egypt for a very long period if at all.' In the long discussion that followed Auchinleck's judgement received no support. General Sir Alan Brooke, the Chief of the Imperial General Staff, later observed in his diary that

Auchinleck 'had again stuck his toes in and was refusing to attack till a late date, and had sent in a very bad telegram in which he entirely failed to realize the importance of Malta and over-estimated the danger to Egypt in the event of his being defeated.'[16] After much drafting the Prime Minister sent a signal that read:

> The Chiefs of Staff, the Defence Committee, and the War Cabinet have again considered the whole position. We are determined that Malta shall not be allowed to fall without a battle being fought by your whole army for its retention. The starving out of this fortress would involve the surrender of over 30,000 men, Army and Air Force, together with several hundred guns. Its possession would give the enemy a clear bridge to Africa, with all the consequences flowing from that.[17]

After an uneasy delay the C-in-C bowed to these instructions.

While the Prime Minister and his civil and military colleagues were debating and reaching these decisions that were in their view essential if Malta was not to surrender the news from Malta itself caused them growing anxiety. The delivery in the March convoy of only one half of what General Dobbie considered to be Malta's minimum requirements led at once to the consideration of further convoys. The Governor in two cables at the end of the month painted a grim picture of the worsening outlook in the island as stocks of food were gradually consumed and argued that a 'really strong fighter force' was a 'paramount necessity.'[18] The Prime Minister forwarded these to the COS with the notation: 'This serious report should be considered with a view to action.' The War Office then carried out a further analysis of the food position and the CIGS reported that stocks should with stringent rationing last 'well into June'.[19] Having heard this Churchill reluctantly accepted Admiral Pound's advice that the enemy air and naval strength in the central Mediterranean was such that convoys would not be possible in April from either west or east. When the Governor was advised of this decision he replied with a lengthy and stark cable on 20 April which Churchill circulated to the COS and War Cabinet. The Governor warned that the position had now gone beyond the critical point, writing, 'it is obvious that the very worst must happen if we cannot replenish our vital needs especially flour and ammunition and that very soon . . . If Malta is to be held drastic action is needed now; it is a question of survival.'[20]

To consider what was to be done in this mounting crisis Churchill summoned a full-day meeting of the Defence Committee on 22 April. All the relevant papers were circulated including a report from Sir Walter Monckton, the Acting Minister of State in Cairo, who with Tedder had visited Malta on 13-14 April to assess the situation for themselves.

Compounding the naval difficulties facing the Prime Minister and his colleagues were their existing commitment to seize Madagascar in order to protect Ceylon and India and the provision of a powerful escort for a major Arctic convoy to Russia to guard against the threat of attack from the new German battleship, *Tirpitz*. These commitments ruled out the availability of any battleships or aircraft carriers to protect from Italian naval attack any convoy to Malta from the west. After a very long discussion the Committee approved Churchill's proposal that General Dobbie be advised in the following terms:

> No satisfactory solution of the Malta problem is available in May. The island must, therefore, hold out till the June dark period. This should be possible if a rigorous severity of rationing is imposed from now and the supply of Spitfires by *Wasp* and *Eagle* is maintained.[21]

The Governor at once replied, 'This will be done', and he went on to say that he intended with effect from 5 May to reduce the bread ration by one quarter to 10½ ounces per day. This might, if all stocks of wheat and maize could be milled, allow bread supplies to last until the latter half of July. Nevertheless, he warned, this would 'inevitably reduce working capacity and could not be continued indefinitely.' On his copy of this signal Churchill wrote: 'COS Committee: This looks better than we thought.'[22]

Against this background of worsening conditions in Malta planning for the possibility of one or two convoys in June now continued although the urgent need for AA ammunition was alleviated to a degree by a solo passage by HMS *Welshman*. This ship was a 40-knot, 2,650-ton minelayer which could carry about 300 tons of supplies in her mine deck. On 8 May she left Gibraltar, under the command of Captain W. Friedberger, carrying powdered milk, canned meat, dehydrated foodstuffs, aero-engines, ammunition and smoke canisters designed to conceal the Grand Harbour during unloading operations. On this trip she was disguised as a French destroyer and flew French colours as she proceeded along the Tunisian coast. She docked at Malta at dawn on 10 May and was unloaded within seven hours. However, the risks to an eastern convoy remained and were then increased when, as Churchill had warned in May, Rommel preempted Auchinleck's plan to recapture Cyrenaica by launching his own offensive on 26 May. In the early stages of the resulting battle on 2 June Churchill cabled to Auchinleck and Tedder:

> There is no need for me to stress the vital importance of the safe arrival of our convoys at Malta, and I am sure you will both take all steps to enable the air escorts, and particularly the Beaufighters, to be operated from landing grounds as far west as possible.[23]

Nevertheless, after two weeks of hard fighting Rommel gained the upper hand forcing the 8th Army to retreat and leaving a garrison at Tobruk cut off once more. On the morning of 21 June when Churchill was conferring in Washington with President Roosevelt the President handed him a telegram which read: 'Tobruk has surrendered, with twenty-five thousand men taken prisoners.' As Churchill later wrote: 'This was one of the heaviest blows I can recall during the war . . . I did not attempt to hide from the President the shock I had received. It was a bitter moment. Defeat is one thing; disgrace is another.'[24] The President and General Marshall at once responded by arranging the immediate shipment to the Middle East of 300 new Sherman tanks and 100 self-propelled guns.

While this prolonged desert battle was in progress two convoys sailed to relieve Malta. From Gibraltar Operation 'Harpoon' consisted of five freighters and a tanker, while in Operation 'Vigorous' from Alexandria there were no fewer than eleven cargo ships. In an attempt to compensate for the lack of the Cyrenaican airfields the Air Ministry had sent long-range Beaufighters and Beaufort torpedo bombers to Malta and to Egypt. However, under strong Italian air and naval attack from Sicilian and Sardinian bases only two ships of the western convoy reached Malta and the eastern convoy was forced to turn back when RAF and USAAF attacks failed to stop the approach of a superior Italian battleship force. Malta thus received only 15,000 tons of supplies and a small amount of AA ammunition brought in by HMS *Welshman* on a second independent voyage; barely enough to keep the island from exhaustion for another month.

Before considering in the next chapter the further actions prompted by Churchill to relieve Malta we should take brief note of two decisions taken by the Axis commanders which had a powerful effect upon Malta's fate. Even in April while the German attack on Malta was at its height Churchill's buff despatch box will have contained intelligence which suggested that some German squadrons were leaving Sicily. Later decrypts confirmed this and we now know that in mid-May Kesselring signalled to the German High Command that Malta had been neutralised. Consequently, significant numbers of German aircraft were transferred, some to North Africa and others to the eastern front. This made the recovery of air superiority by the RAF a little easier. Hitler and Mussolini together made the second fateful decision. The two dictators had previously agreed at a meeting at the end of April that after Rommel had advanced to the Egyptian border he would halt his advance to allow the implementation of Operation 'Herkules', the invasion of Malta. Elated, however, by his rapid capture of Tobruk where he acquired large supplies and 2000 lorries Rommel was able to persuade Hitler and Mussolini to allow him to postpone Operation 'Herkules' so that he could pursue a defeated 8th Army to the Nile. As this became clear from other intercepts the danger to Malta was seen to be not one of invasion but of surrender brought about by starvation. It is clear from the large number of minutes, signals and documents in Churchill's Malta files, some of which were subsequently reprinted in his Second World War memoirs, that it was in the first six months of 1942 that he was most concerned about the island and its people. The struggle in the desert, after the setback in January, reached its lowest point when Tobruk surrendered in June. To Churchill it was of paramount importance that Rommel's advance into Egypt should be thrown back and Malta had an essential part to play in this by denying the Axis armies their essential supplies. However, there was another dimension to Churchill's absolute insistence that Malta be sustained, whatever the cost. On 15 April the King announced that he had awarded to Malta the George Cross to honour the bravery of her people. Nothing could more clearly demonstrate that Malta had for Churchill and the British people become a symbol of Britain's determination to fight and overcome the King's enemies. There could be no question of abandoning Malta. The shame of Singapore and Tobruk was not to be repeated.

## Notes

[1] NA PREM 3/266/10A, Fol. 777, WSC to Hollis for COS, 8 January 1942.

[2] For details see P. Vella, *Malta Blitzed*, pp. 87-90.

[3] S. Perowne, *The Siege Within The Walls: Malta 1940-1943* (Hodder and Stoughton, London, 1970), p. 45.

[4] NA CAB 80/34, COS Memorandum (42) 130, Annex II, 18 February 1942.

[5] NA PREM 3/266/2, Fols. 462-3, Cranborne to WSC, 27 February 1942.

[6] NA CAB 79/18, COS (42) 66th Meeting, COS to Middle East C-in-Cs, 27 February 1942.

[7] Quoted in Churchill, *Second World War, Vol. IV*, WSC to Roosevelt, p. 268.

[8] NA PREM 3/266/10A, Fol. 771, Governor to WSC, 23 April 1942.

[9] NA PREM 3/266/2, Fol. 387, WSC to Roosevelt, 22 April 1942.

[10] NA PREM 3/266/4, Fol. 509, Portal to WSC, 20 May 1942.

[11] NA CAB 80/61, Annex III to COS Memorandum (42) 55 (O), 1 March 1942.

[12] Quoted in Churchill, *Second World War, Vol. IV*, p. 81.

[13] A. Danchev and D. Todman (eds), *War Diaries: Field Marshal Lord Alanbrooke* (Weidenfeld & Nicolson, London, 2001), p. 235.

[14] NA CAB 69/4, Defence Committee (Operations) (42) 9th Meeting, 26 March 1942.

[15] Quoted in Churchill, *Second World War, Vol. IV*, WSC to Auchinleck, 8 May 1942, p. 275.

[16] Danchev and Todman, *Alanbrooke Diaries*, p. 256.

[17] Quoted in Churchill, *Second World War, Vol. IV*, WSC to Auchinleck, 10 May 1942, pp. 275-6.

[18] NA PREM 3/266/ 2, Fol. 434, Governor to COS, 1 April 1942.

[19] NA CAB 80/62, COS Memorandum (42) 91 (O), 6 April 1942.

[20] NA CAB 69/4, Governor to COS, 20 April 1942, annexed to minutes of Defence Committee (Operations) (42) 12th Meeting, 22 April 1942.

[21] Ibid., Annex II.

[22] NA PREM 3/266/2, Fol. 376, Governor to COS, 25 April 1942.

[23] Quoted in Churchill, *Second World War, Vol. IV*, p. 323.

[24] Ibid., pp. 343-4.

## CHAPTER XIII

# *Change of Governor and the Relief of Malta*

*The fate of the island is at stake, and if the effort to relieve it is worth making it is worth making on a great scale . . . Gort must be able to tell them: 'The Navy will never abandon Malta'.*

Churchill Minute to Chiefs of Staff, 16 June 1942

General Dobbie had arrived in Malta in May 1940. He was initially appointed as Acting Governor when Sir Charles Bonham-Carter fell ill, and became Governor in May 1941. He was a member of the Plymouth Brethren, an evangelical religious sect whose strongly held Christian beliefs found favour in Malta. In the early months of 1942 as the bombing onslaught on Malta intensified 'Dobbie of Malta' was widely acclaimed in the British press as the epitome of the heroic resistance of the islanders and the garrison. In mid-April he received the following handwritten letter from London:

> The Governor, Malta.
> To honour her brave people I award the George Cross to the Island Fortress of Malta to bear witness to a heroism and devotion that will long be famous in history.
> April 15th, 1942.

George R.I.

Dobbie was then 63 years old and his strength and health had been seriously undermined by two years of increasingly harsh siege conditions and by the restricted Maltese diet which he insisted on sharing. Nevertheless, his many cables, some of which have been quoted in these pages, gave the authorities in London no reason to doubt his continued leadership. The Prime Minister and Lord Cranborne, the Colonial Secretary, were, therefore, shocked and bewildered to receive on 21 April a telegram from the Middle East Defence Committee (MEDC) in Cairo urging that:

> General Dobbie should be relieved as soon as possible on grounds that he is a tired man, has lost his grip of situation, and is no longer capable of affording higher direction and control which is vital (repeat) vital to present situation.[1]

Cranborne voiced to Churchill his consternation at receiving this signal. 'This is a most distressing telegram. I cannot help feeling that the Middle East have treated us very badly.'[2] The MEDC had come to their conclusion after the visit of Sir Walter Monckton, Acting Minister of State in Cairo, and Air Marshal Tedder to Malta on 13-14 April. This visit was prompted in part by a cable from AVM Lloyd at the end of March that was highly critical of the inexcusable failure, as he saw it, to unload the *Pampas* and *Talabot* before they were both sunk on 26 March in the Grand Harbour.

The matter was discussed at the lengthy Defence Committee meeting on 22 April when the Prime Minister was reported as saying:

> He, at first, had been shocked at this proposal to pull down General Dobbie at a time when the gallant resistance of Malta and its Governor was exciting the admiration of the world. On further thought, however, he was inclined to agree with the view expressed to him by the CIGS that the reports from the Middle East seemed to show that General Dobbie's immediate subordinates and superiors had lost faith in his ability to continue to control and stimulate the resistance of the Fortress.[3]

However, before any action could be taken Cranborne received a cable from Dobbie complaining of a 'Strickland intrigue' against him. He alleged that Mabel Strickland, the editor of *The Times* of Malta, had attempted to enlist the support of Lord Mountbatten in seeking his removal.[4] Mabel Strickland was the influential daughter of the former Prime Minister of Malta, Lord Strickland, and a leading member of the generally pro-British Constitutional Party, which her father had founded. Churchill at once cabled the Governor to assure him that:

> You may be quite sure that there shall be no intrigue where you are concerned. Nothing but the public interest must be considered. Mountbatten has not been consulted or had the slightest influence on War Cabinet discussions . . . Naturally we are gravely anxious about Malta. I am therefore, sending Lord Cranborne at once by air to talk everything over with you . . . In all circumstances you may be confident of the gratitude of your countrymen. [5]

In the event it was decided that Richard Casey who was about to leave for Cairo to take up the position of Minister of State should visit the Governor in Malta and investigate the whole matter. When Monckton complained of the delay urging that 'days even hours will count now in sphere of civilian control' Churchill brusquely told him: 'Casey is starting today for Malta to report to Cabinet. Governor has complained of Strickland intrigue. Matter is one of high importance. You should remain in Cairo'[6] Two days later Churchill sent a longer cable to Monckton in which he criticised him strongly for not warning the Cabinet earlier of the MEDC's doubts about Dobbie.[7] Casey saw Dobbie and the local commanders on 2 May and on the following day cabled to Churchill.

> I have no doubt that Dobbie should be replaced by Gort as soon as possible. Dobbie is a man of courage and high character who has set example of steadiness and devotion to duty. He has gone out of his way to make my task easy for me by his generous attitude. I hope that his services and high quality will be publicly recognised. But the team here are not working together and the main reason is that Dobbie is no longer capable of vigorous leadership. He has little grasp of the situation or power of decision and lacks the knowledge and drive which would enable him to guide and, where necessary, impose his will on the forceful commanders under him.[8]

Casey also expressed the view that, although widely respected by the civilian population, Dobbie could have done more to mobilise civilian support for the services. As regards the senior service commanders, General Beak, AVM Lloyd, and Vice-Admiral Leatham, Casey cabled that their assurances of inter-service unity 'may be a little rose-coloured' but he went on, 'they certainly seem to have come to a proper understanding about control in event of invasion.' His only reservation was about the Lieutenant-Governor, Sir Edward Jackson, who did not enjoy the confidence of the service commanders. 'He did not impress me very favourably but he has considerable ability and there is no-one here to replace him.'

He made no reference to the 'Strickland intrigue' that had prompted his visit to the island but he no doubt heard all about this from Dobbie. It appears that Mabel Strickland influenced, it would seem, by AVM Lloyd's criticisms of the Governor, was seeking Dobbie's removal. Moreover, long after the war she added that Dobbie was prepared to surrender the island.[9] This allegation can be dismissed. Casey's judgement is quoted above and Dobbie's numerous cables, while not disguising the mounting crisis in the island, make quite clear his determination to maintain the island's resistance. It need hardly be added that any unauthorised attempt by Dobbie to surrender Malta would have led to his immediate relief.

Upon receipt of Casey's recommendation Churchill on 4 May wrote the following cable to General Dobbie. This deserves to be quoted in full since it demonstrates the authentic Churchillian style that characterises the many shorter quotations reprinted in these pages.

> Pursuant on the report received from Minister of State we have decided that your long and gallantly borne vigil at Malta entitles you to relief and throws new honour on the Island's record. Lord Gort has

been ordered to take over from you at the earliest. I take this occasion of expressing on behalf of His Majesty's Government the high regard in which your conduct of this historic defence stands at home. I shall take the opportunity immediately upon your return of submitting your name to His Majesty for a signal mark of his favour. Let me also thank you for the selfless and high minded spirit in which you have viewed the situation including your own and for your devotion to the public interest.[10]

In reply Dobbie signalled, 'Very grateful for your kind words which I deeply appreciate. Trust I may report to you personally on my return.'[11] Churchill agreed that Dobbie should report to him upon his return to London and promised that he would be kept closely in touch with events in Malta. In a World Broadcast on 10 May after Dobbie's return to London the Prime Minister paid warm tribute to him: 'To-day we welcome back to our shores General Dobbie, for nearly two years the heroic defender of Malta. The burden which he has borne so honourably and for so long entitles him to release and repose.'[12] On the following day, as requested, Dobbie called on Churchill to give him his first-hand account of the worsening situation in Malta. There is no record of this conversation but Churchill will surely have questioned Dobbie closely about the strains among the service commanders. After his meeting with Churchill General Dobbie had an audience with the King who later recorded in his diary:

I knighted him and invested him with the K.C.B., and for his out-standing services in Malta during the last months I invested him with the G.C.M.G... He is a God-fearing man, and lives with a bible in one hand and a sword in the other. He looks very old and tired after his ordeal.[13]

The key to the correct understanding of this crisis is Dobbie's state of health. Like all those living in Malta at that time Dobbie was in a state of semi-starvation. In June, as discussed later in this chapter, two officials of the Ministry of Health, recently returned from Malta, described to the COS the physical and mental lassitude caused in young servicemen by the severely restricted Maltese ration. After the war Mabel Strickland recalled the effects of hunger: 'When you are hungry there is little initiative and you get very lethargic . . . and it is very hard to make a decision.' Churchill himself, when he met General Gort in Cairo in August, was shocked by Gort's physical condition after only four months at Malta. Dobbie had been there for two years and his physical and mental condition must have been immediately obvious to Casey when they met. It was also clear from Casey's signal that the severe strains under which he and all the commanders in Malta were operating had led to a breakdown in mutual confidence. Shortly after Dobbie's return to England his health broke down and he had a serious operation followed by a long period of convalescence. We need look no further for an explanation of the change that had by then become necessary. Churchill's generous post-war tribute to General Dobbie has been quoted in Chapter IX.

General Lord Gort, VC, a former CIGS and the Commander of the British Expeditionary Force in France, had been Governor of Gibraltar since May 1941. When Casey flew there en route to Malta he handed him a letter from the Prime Minister. This read:

> It may be that, as he will explain to you, a change will be required at a most critical juncture in the command of Malta. If this should be so, we all feel you are the man of all others to render this vitally important service. You may be sure that I shall do everything in my power to carry a heavy convoy of supplies into Malta in the latter part of June, and that meanwhile the supply of Spitfires from the west will be continued. Should you be required for this further service you will be equipped with ample powers, and will carry with you the full confidence of His Majesty's Government and of your sincere friend.[14]

Attached to this was a three-page 'Aide Memoire for General Lord Gort' in which the COS set out the situation in detail. After receiving Casey's report the Prime Minister on 4 May ordered Gort to assume command in Malta. 'Every effort,' he wrote, 'must be made to prolong the resistance of the fortress to the utmost limit. We recognise you are taking over a most anxious and dangerous situation at a late stage. We are sure that you are the man to save the fortress and we shall strive hard to sustain you.'[15] There was some press speculation at the time, repeated by several subsequent writers, that Gort also received secret instructions relating to the surrender of the island. However, British Government records contain no such document and all the evidence points firmly in the opposite direction. As plans were made to run two convoys in June the surrender of Malta was clearly not in the minds of the Prime Minister or of his military advisers. Any decision to do so would only have been taken by the War Cabinet if it had proved impossible to get supplies through to the island and the following pages will show Churchill's determination that the island could and would bere-supplied.

Gort flew to Malta on the evening of 7 May and in the middle of an air raid was formally sworn in as Governor. However, Dobbie had a long private conversation with his successor before he and his family returned home in the aircraft that had brought Gort. Apart from a general briefing about conditions in the island it is reasonable to assume that Dobbie recommended that Gort insist on being appointed as Supreme Commander in Malta. Apart from his divided responsibilities to the War Office and the Colonial Office

Dobbie had also suffered from the fact that he could not give direct orders to the naval and air commanders since they reported to their respective C-in-Cs in Cairo. What is certain is that on 10 May Gort cabled to the COS requesting overall command in Malta. The Chiefs were apparently reluctant to do this but Churchill on 16 May, cancelling previous instructions, cabled personally to Gort appointing him as 'Supreme Commander of the Fighting Services and Civil Administration in Malta '.[16]

It seems probable that this decision was influenced by the private meeting that the Prime Minister had with Dobbie on 11 May when, as noted earlier, Dobbie reported to him on his return to London. Churchill must have discussed with Dobbie the command structure in Malta and this may have had a bearing on his cable of 16 May. It also seems likely that it was the tensions among the commanders in Malta, which Casey had noted during his visit and which Churchill also no doubt heard about from Dobbie, that led within the next few months to the replacement of AVM Lloyd and General Beak, who commanded the garrison. Nonetheless, when Lloyd left to take up a senior appointment under Tedder in Cairo Churchill sent him a generous cable: 'I congratulate you on your brilliant fourteen months in Malta, and wish you continued success in your new important command.'[17] In his memoirs Lloyd recorded in the opening sentences the comment of ACM Portal when ordering him to Malta: 'You will be on the Island for six months as a minimum and nine months as a maximum as by that time you will be worn out.'[18] In September Gort also recommended the replacement of Vice-Admiral Leatham, the Vice-Admiral Malta, alleging that 'he is elderly and tired and suffering from the strain of recent months.'[19] However, this change, after a reference to Churchill, was deferred until the following year.

We must now review the deteriorating position in Malta. As soon as the virtual failure of the June convoys became known in London Churchill urged the naval staff to make preparations for a July convoy. On 16 June he sent the COS one of his Action This Day minutes, the conclusion of which is quoted at the beginning of this chapter. He asked that plans be made for a fast convoy of at least a dozen freighters and a powerful escort of battleships and aircraft carriers to fight the convoy through against strong Italian and German attack.[20] On the following day he flew to America for discussions with President Roosevelt but from Washington he found time on 17 June to signal to Clement Attlee, the Deputy Prime Minister:

> We are absolutely bound to save Malta in one way or the other . . .
> I am relying upon you to treat the whole question of the relief of Malta as vitally urgent, and to keep at it with the Admiralty till a solution is reached. Keep me advised so that I can do my best with the President.[21]

The COS duly considered the matter in great detail. They reviewed a report from Gort that indicated that supplies, with even tighter rationing, should last during August and listened on 26 June to a verbal presentation from two Ministry of Health officials, Dr. Drummond and Mr. Wall, about health conditions in Malta.[22] They reported that the troops while 'fit and hard' were steadily losing weight. The civilian population appeared less severely affected probably, they thought, because of the private food stocks that they had been encouraged to accumulate in easier conditions. Any such stocks were, however, dwindling. Nevertheless, since Admiral Pound advised that no aircraft carriers could be made available in July the COS were forced to recommend that the next relief convoy be postponed until August.

Churchill had no choice but to accept this but he cabled Gort on 18 July writing that 'I should be very glad to hear from you how you are getting on.' He added: 'It is a great comfort to me to feel that you are in full control of this vital island fortress. You may be sure we shall do everything to help you.' In his reply Gort commented on the arrival of HMS *Welshman* with an emergency cargo of dried milk and other foodstuffs and advised the Prime Minister that 'the Maltese people remain for the present in good spirits.'[23]

However, in a letter to Cranborne Gort noted that the morale of the population was 'undeniably brittle', and warned that if there were further heavy bombing 'a serious internal situation might easily arise.' On his copy of this letter Churchill wrote, 'A very serious letter.'[24] To a further signal from the Prime Minister the Governor replied in another lengthy letter dated 27 July.

> Morale remains good, but the people have a great deal to put up with ... I have formed a great admiration for the cheerfulness of the Maltese people and their stoical determination to withstand everything that is humanly possible to endure sooner than surrender to the despised Italians.[25]

The four-day battle that engulfed the 'Pedestal' convoy in August 1942 was the climax of Malta's war. Churchill and the COS fully realised that, were it to fail, Malta would surely be compelled to surrender. Such a calamity following the fall of Singapore and Tobruk would have incalculable consequences for the battles now imminent in the Egyptian desert. Admiral Pound, responding to Churchill's declaration that 'the Navy will never abandon Malta', assembled fourteen fast merchant ships including the US-built tanker, *Ohio*, laden with 12,000 tons of fuel. These were given a powerful escort of two battleships, three aircraft carriers, seven cruisers and more than thirty destroyers and support vessels. The whole armada passed the Straits of Gibraltar on the morning of 10 August.

Kesselring, equally aware of the vital importance of this convoy, flew to his bases in Sardinia and Sicily reinforcements from North Africa and Crete which raised his strength to more than 700 German and Italian bombers and fighters. At sea the Italian Navy deployed in the Sicilian narrows submarines, MTBs and E-boats and a cruiser force. To counter these ACM Portal sent additional fighters and torpedo bombers to Malta while HMS *Furious* sailed with the convoy with 38 more Spitfires to be flown on to the island.

The first British loss was the aircraft carrier, *Eagle*, torpedoed on 11 August by the German submarine, *U-37*, and the first air attacks were delivered that evening as the convoy came within range of the Sardinian airfields. In the following three days the convoy faced almost incessant daylight attack and in the dark early morning hours of 13 August an attack by the force of MTBs. British losses steadily mounted and only four of the thirteen cargo ships reached the Grand Harbour. Crucially, however, the *Ohio*, after a series of attacks that on several occasions brought her engines to a halt, reached Malta on 15 August, her decks almost awash and with two destroyers lashed to her sides. Her Master, Captain D. W. Mason, was awarded the George Cross. The remnants of the 'Pedestal' convoy brought to the island 35,000 tons of supplies, enough to provide a breathing space, while the 12,000 tons of fuel enabled the island's air and naval forces to resume their attacks on the enemy supply route to North Africa.

All the British, as well as the German and Italian commanders, followed its preparation and progress closely. In early August the Prime Minister with General Brooke had flown to Cairo and it was there that he decided to relieve General Auchinleck as C-in-C Middle East and replace him with General Alexander. General Montgomery succeeded to the command of the 8th Army. Before leaving Cairo on 10 August to fly on to Moscow for meetings with Stalin the Prime Minister gave instructions that he be informed of the progress of the 'Pedestal' convoy. It was, consequently, at the British Embassy in Moscow that Churchill received signals from Pound announcing the arrival on 14 August of four freighters and, on the following day, of the oil tanker, *Ohio,* from the original convoy of fourteen merchant ships. Churchill immediately signalled to the Admiralty:

Please convey my compliments to Admirals Syfret, Burrough, and Lyster and all officers and men engaged in the magnificent crash through of supplies to Malta, which cannot fail to have an important influence on the immediate future of the war in the Mediterranean.[26]

He followed this with a further signal to Pound in which he concluded, 'prolongation of life of Malta was worth heavy cost.' When on 8 September he spoke in the House of Commons on the war situation he gave an account of the 'Pedestal' operation. He acknowledged the severe costs that had been suffered but went on to say:

But this price, although heavy, was not excessive for the result obtained for Malta is not only as bright a gem as shines in the King's Crown, but its effective action against the enemy's communications with Libya and Egypt is essential to the whole strategic position in the Middle East.[27]

Back in Cairo on his way home from Moscow he met General Gort and his ADC, Lord Munster. He later wrote that although 'they were both very thin and looked rather haggard' they had long talks and 'when we parted I had the Malta picture clearly in my mind.'[28] When researching his memoirs after the war Churchill recalled that when they met in Cairo in August 1942 Gort had told him that if Malta were forced by starvation to surrender he would attempt to lead a force into Sicily to attack the airfields there and then take to the mountains. Churchill recorded that he authorised the necessary plans to be made.[29]

The arrival at Malta of 32,000 tons of general supplies in the 'Pedestal' convoy permitted only a small increase in the rations but gave a breathing space of a month or so. However, the consequence of the arrival in the *Ohio* of 12,000 tons of aviation and fuel oils was to allow the resumption of offensive operations against the Axis supply line to North Africa, a task that had now become urgent. This will be considered in the next chapter but it will be convenient to trace in this chapter Churchill's continuing concern with the food situation in Malta. In the following account it should be borne in mind that when the Prime Minister did not himself chair a COS meeting he always received the subsequent official minutes of the meeting and when he thought his intervention necessary sent a minute of his own to the COS usually through his Chief of Staff, General Ismay. Many of the official COS papers have annexed to them a minute from Churchill. In addition any signal that the COS proposed to send to the Governor and the Middle East C-in-Cs was first sent to the Prime Minister as a draft for his approval or amendment.

After the unloading of the 'Pedestal' supplies it was estimated that Malta was likely to be able to hold out only until mid-December at the very latest and the Admiralty, consequently, made plans for further convoys. However, the problem had now become more complicated by the decision to land an Anglo-American force in North West Africa, Operation 'Torch', D-day for which was finally set for 8 November. This complex amphibious operation, which might be opposed by the French forces in Algeria and Tunisia, required a large concentration of naval warships and transports, pre-empting the powerful naval escort that any western convoy to Malta would need. Nor had the prospects for an eastern convoy improved. To Churchill's dismay the target date for Montgomery's offensive at El Alamein had been postponed until mid-October leaving the Cyrenaican airfields, which controlled the eastern approach to Malta, in German hands. Nevertheless, planning continued and on 7 September the naval staff advised the COS of plans to assemble numerous freighters at both Gibraltar and Alexandria to form possible east and west convoys. The navy expected that one or both of these might need to be fought through in late November.

Disturbing news was then received by the Colonial Secretary, Lord Cranborne. Gort had sent back to London Mr. Rowntree, who was Deputy Director of the Communal Feeding Department in Malta. Prior to his arrival Cranborne circulated his report to the COS with a copy to Churchill. The latter at once signalled to Gort that he had read Rowntree's report and added: 'We are thinking about you every day, and everything in human power will be done. We hope to run some ships through in the flurry of "TORCH".'[30] Rowntree attended the COS meeting on 28 September and was introduced by Sir George Gater, the Permanent Under-Secretary at the Colonial Office, with the comment that they 'had been distressed to find that the food position was much more serious than had been expected.'[31] Rowntree explained that despite a slight increase in the bread ration the calorific value of the ration for adult males stood at 1,360 calories per day and at 1,184 for the general population. The equivalent figures for those using the growing number of communal 'Victory Kitchens' were 1,687 and 1,511 calories.

Since the minimum to sustain life was estimated to be 1,500 calories per day Rowntree observed that an increase must be achieved at the earliest possible moment to avoid 'a general undermining of the health and morale of the population'. He confirmed that existing supplies would be exhausted by the second week in December. The severity of the food problem looming in Malta in the autumn of 1942 can be judged by the fact that the rations in England never at any time during the war fell below a daily value of 2,800 calories.

The Victory Kitchens had been established in January 1942 initially to provide meals for those whose houses and food stocks had been destroyed. As food supplies, public and private, dwindled more and more people subscribed to this emergency service. In June 1942 100,000 were drawing one meal a day, and this figure rose to 175,000 in January 1943. The quality and quantity of the meals inevitably declined, despite a decision to slaughter most of the island's goats and other livestock. The bread ration was barely maintained by adding potato flour and this caused a decline in quality. An appeal by the Bishop of Gozo, Msgr. Gonzi, to the local farmers to release more of their stocks produced some relief but only further convoys could prevent starvation. As the siege came to an end at the end of 1942 an editorial in *The Times* of Malta summed up the experience:

The Victory Kitchens have in fact been 'Siege Kitchens' providing a meagre daily sustenance masquerading as a 'meal' for either lunch or supper . . . The Siege Kitchens of Malta provided the means by which all were hungry together and nobody starved outright.[32]

Four days after the meeting with Rowntree Admiral Pound explained to his fellow Chiefs his plans to assemble as many as 32 freighters to carry 170,000 tons of supplies through to Malta. These would be split between Gibraltar and Alexandria and eight fast ships would be loaded and ready to sail by the end of October. The sailing dates of these convoys would depend on the progress of the Alamein and 'Torch' offensives and the respective western and eastern naval commanders would be left to judge the correct moment.[33] Churchill approved the signal setting out these outline plans. However, in early November Sir Cyril Hurcomb, a senior official at the Ministry of War Transport, attended a COS meeting to explain that the provision of six slow ships required as a follow-up convoy from the west would affect the UK import programme. Since the COS insisted that at least four slow ships be found the matter was referred to Churchill who replied: 'Proceed as you propose. I have spoken to Lord Leathers [Minister of War Transport]. The four ships will cost 32,000 tons of imports.'[34]

The Alamein offensive was launched on 23 October but it was not until 4 November that Rommel began his long retreat into Tunisia. At the other end of the Mediterranean the landings in North West Africa were made on 8 November but, as we shall see in the next chapter, the Germans reacted quickly to block the Allied advance into Tunisia. As these events unfolded it seemed that an eastern convoy to Malta offered the better prospect of success but its safety depended on the 8th Army's capture of airfields as far west as possible. The pressure for an early sailing of the 'Stoneage' convoy to Malta from Alexandria arose not only from the food crisis in the island but also from the increasingly urgent need to release Malta's air and naval forces to attack the German build-up in Tunisia. Until the relief convoy had safely arrived and its cargoes had been unloaded attacks on the Axis supply routes to Tunisia must take second place.

At this critical juncture Churchill intervened with an Action This Day minute to the COS on 12 November:

We cannot divest ourselves of responsibility for the convoy from the east to Malta. If it is to sail on the 15th what arrangements are made to protect it against surface attack by the Italian fleet? . . . This is no time to throw away four fast heavily-laden ships. Will the airfield at Derna be working by the time the convoy gets there? If it is not we ought to wait a few more days till it is. The prospects in Cyrenaica are now so good that that there is no need for forlorn, desperate ventures.[35]

As a result it was not until the evening of 16 November that the four fast freighters of the 'Stoneage' convoy, carrying 35,000 tons of supplies, set sail. Despite air attacks that caused extensive damage to the cruiser HMS *Arethusa* the freighters enjoyed extensive air cover and docked safely in the Grand Harbour on the morning of 20 November. Two weeks later five more cargo ships and a tanker in Operation 'Portcullis' delivered a further 55,000 tons and from then onwards there was a steady stream of ships sailing in pairs from Alexandria. The relief in Malta at the safe arrival of these substantial shipments was surely matched in London where attention could now be concentrated on the difficult situation that had developed in Tunisia.

Although rationing remained in force for some time these shipments effectively ended Malta's long and arduous siege and it may be appropriate, therefore, to end this chapter by quoting the Foreword that Churchill wrote to *The Epic of Malta*. This is a remarkable collection of war photographs of the island that was published at the end of 1942 to raise funds for the Malta Relief Fund. Churchill wrote:

> 10 Downing Street, Whitehall
> Malta is a little island with a great history. The record of the Maltese people throughout that long history is a record of constancy and fortitude. It is with those qualities, matchlessly displayed, that they are now confronting the dark power of the Axis. But it is not given to them, any more than it is to other peoples, to maintain resolute defence without suffering or to escape loss in achieving victory. This book, therefore, is prepared with the aim of serving a double purpose; to contribute in some manner to the alleviation of their suffering and to portray to distant eyes the scene upon which their heroism is enacted.
>
> Winston S. Churchill

## Notes

[1] NA PREM 3/266/1, Fol. 133, MEDC to WSC, 20 April 1942.

[2] Ibid., Fol. 130-1, Cranborne to WSC, 21 April 1942.

[3] NA CAB 69/4, Defence Committee (Operations) (42) 12th Meeting, 22 April 1942.

[4] NA PREM 3/266/1, Fol. 129, Cranborne to WSC, 23 April 1942.

[5] Churchill Archives Centre (CAC), Churchill College, Cambridge, CHAR 20/74/14, WSC to Dobbie, 24 April 1942.

[6] NA PREM 3/266/1, Fol. 121, WSC to Monckton, 24 April 1942.

[7] CAC, CHAR 20/74/37, WSC to Monckton, 26 April 1942.

[8] NA PREM 3/266/1, Fols. 82-3, Casey to WSC, 3 May 1942.

[9] See J. Alexander, *Mabel Strickland* (Progress Press, Valletta, 1996), pp. 121-8.

[10] CAC, CHAR 20/74/116, WSC to Dobbie, 4 May 1942.

[11] CAC, CHAR 20/74/123, Dobbie to WSC 5 May 1942.

[12] Churchill, *War Speeches, Vol. III,* (Cassell, London, 1943), p. 106.

[13] J. Wheeler-Bennett, *King George VI: His Life and Reign* (Macmillan, London, 1958), p. 573.

[14] Quoted in Churchill, *Second World War, Vol. IV*, WSC to Gort, 25 April 1942, p. 274.

[15] CAC, CHAR 20/74/115, WSC to Gort, 4 May 1942.

[16] CAC, CHAR 20/75/37, WSC to Gort, 16 May 1942.

[17] CAC, CHAR 20/78/52, WSC to Lloyd, 25 July 1942.

[18] Lloyd, *Briefed To Attack*, p. 13.

[19] NA PREM 3/266/10A, Fol. 715, Cranborne to WSC, 2 September 1942.

[20] NA CAB 79/12, COS (42) 180th Meeting, 16 June 1942.

[21] NA PREM 3/266/2, Fol. 289, WSC to Attlee, 17 June 1942.

[22] NA CAB 79/21, COS (42) 190th Meeting, 26 June 1942.

[23] NA PREM 3/266/2, Fols. 245-6, WSC to Gort, and Gort to WSC, 18 and 20 July 1942.

[24] NA PREM 3/266/10A, Fol. 742, WSC note of 27 July on Gort to Cranborne, 17 July 1942.

[25] NA PREM 3/266/5, Gort to WSC 27 July 1942.

[26] Quoted in Churchill, *Second World War, Vol. IV*, p. 455.

[27] Churchill, *War Speeches, Vol. III,* p. 164.

[28] Churchill, *Second World War, Vol. IV*, p. 455.

[29] CAC, CHUR 2/149B/232.

[30] CAC, CHAR 20/80/92, WSC to Gort, 26 September 1942.

[31] NA CAB 79/57, COS (42) 130th 'O' Meeting, 28 September 1942.

[32] Vella, *Malta Blitzed*, p. 77.

[33] NA CAB 79/57, COS (42) 135th 'O' Meeting, 2 October 1942.

[34] NA CAB 79/58, COS (42) 170th 'O' Meeting, 3 November 1942.

[35] Ibid., COS (42) 180th 'O' Meeting, 13 November 1942.

CHAPTER XIV

# *Malta's Contribution to Allied Victory in North Africa*

*This is the week of all others when the Malta surface force must strike upon the communications of the Axis forces in Tunis. A week or ten days later will be too late. Infinite harm will be done and the whole battle compromised.*

Churchill to Admiral Pound, 6 December 1942

In the preceding chapter we have followed to the end of 1942 the decisions made and the actions ordered under Churchill's overall direction to ensure that Malta would not be starved into submission, an event that would surely have overshadowed in his mind the surrender of Singapore or Tobruk. However, as Churchill had repeatedly emphasised since war had come to the Mediterranean Malta was to be defended not merely as a matter of imperial duty to an island people under British protection. In British strategic thinking Malta had always been seen as a fortress and the high cost of sustaining the island was borne because of the unique contribution that Malta's offensive forces could make to the defeat of the Axis forces in North Africa. We must now, therefore, return to the desperate days of the summer of 1942 to examine Malta's participation in the two major autumn offensives, the October battle at El Alamein and the November landings in French North West Africa.

Under Kesselring's heavy aerial onslaught in the early months of 1942 Malta's offensive capability had been temporarily eliminated. AVM Lloyd had been compelled to send away all of his remaining bombers, and on 26 April Captain Simpson ordered the submarines of the 10th Flotilla to Alexandria. As a result, although Malta's submarines and aircraft sank fifteen enemy ships, aggregating 69,000 tons, in the first four months of 1942 none was sunk in May and only three in June and July. Thus as Rommel advanced into Egypt large quantities of supplies reached him, with no less than 91,000 tons arriving in July.

We have noted in the preceding chapter Churchill's visit to Cairo in August and the receipt of the news of the arrival of the 'Pedestal' convoy while in Moscow. There he had learned that in addition to the foodstuffs in the convoy the American tanker *Ohio* had brought in 12,000 tons of fuel. Upon his return to Cairo he would have read a COS signal of 19 August to the Malta commanders directing, 'for the next ten days or so supreme importance should be attached to [strike] operations and that considerations of economy in petrol would not justify limiting these operations.'[1]

The urgency of this directive became clear to Churchill when he reviewed with Alexander and Montgomery the abundant Intelligence information that gave details of Rommel's plans. By this time over 4,000 enemy signals a month were being intercepted and decyphered with very little delay and these signals now disclosed details not only of Axis convoy routes and sailing dates but of the cargo carried in each vessel. On 17 August Churchill read a lengthy signal sent two days earlier by Rommel to the German High Command that set out his plan to attack the British position at Alam Halfa on 26 August subject to the receipt of certain reinforcements and a steady flow of supplies.[2]

Submarines of the 10th Flotilla had returned to Malta in late July to provide protection for the 'Pedestal' convoy and the recovery of air superiority around Malta together with the fuel received in the *Ohio* allowed Malta's air and naval forces to mount a sustained campaign against Rommel's urgently needed supplies. Between 17 August and 6 September Malta's aircraft and submarines sank six Axis ships, including two tankers, the *San Andrea* (5,077 tons) and the *Picci Fassio* (2,261 tons). They also damaged two others, the *Pozarica* (7,751 tons) and the *Manara* (7,720 tons), both of which were forced to beach in the Greek islands. The loss of these supplies, as Rommel later admitted, had a major influence on his decision on 2 September to break off his attack on the British position on Alam Halfa ridge and withdraw. Both sides then paused to build up equipment and supplies for the battle that would decide the fate of Egypt and Britain's position in the Middle East.

The inevitable effect of Malta's anti-shipping attacks during the Alam Halfa battle was the depletion of the RAF's reserves of aviation fuel on the island. Although the navy's larger submarines were able to carry in about 200 tons a month, the COS after much discussion had no alternative but to order severe reductions in flying operations and the termination of transit flights through Malta. Moreover, in mid-September Churchill read a worrying Appreciation prepared by the Joint Intelligence Committee.[3] This warned that in view of 'the high percentage of sinkings from attacks by aircraft based on Malta' a renewed attempt by Kesselring to neutralise the island could be expected in October. To defeat any such attack would require a strengthened Spitfire force well supplied with fuel and ammunition. On the other hand it was recognised that the diversion of large numbers of German and Italian aircraft to attack Malta in October would have the advantage of reducing interference with Montgomery's preparations at El Alamein. D-day for Operation 'Lightfoot' had now been set for 23 October.

In the event Kesselring had by 11 October assembled over 600 aircraft in Sicily to carry out what was to prove the last attempt to prevent Malta's interference with the Axis supply line to North Africa. After fierce fighting, during which the RAF claimed to have shot down 126 German and Italian aircraft, Kesselring was forced to call off the raids two weeks later when Montgomery launched his offensive at El Alamein. Moreover, the Axis raids did not curtail Malta's offensive operations and in the month of October the island's forces sank ten Axis supply ships of 33,000 tons, seven of which fell to 10th Flotilla submarines. One of these was the tanker *Louisiana* (2552 tons) of whose loss Rommel subsequently wrote: 'I received the shattering news that the tanker *Louisiana,* which had been sent as a replacement for the *Proserpina,* had been sunk by aerial torpedo. Now we were really up against it.'[4] Several others were damaged and were unable to deliver their cargoes. The consequent shortage of supplies, particularly of petrol and oil, forced Rommel to fight a largely static battle and made a significant contribution to his defeat in the early days of November. Rommel was later to write: 'Malta has the lives of many thousands of German and Italian soldiers on its conscience.'[5]

Churchill with the COS watched all these developments in London and on 26 October received a signal from General Gort in Malta. Gort told him that sixty-four civilians had been killed and sixty-three more injured during this last blitz but added, 'the spirit of resistance has not fallen during the lull of the previous few months'. The Prime Minister at once replied:

> The work you are doing in animating the magnificent resistance of the Island and its effective intervention on the enemy's line of communications commands general admiration.
>
> Your name will be submitted to the King for promotion to the rank of Field Marshal in the New Year Honours List. Every good wish.[6]

While the Governor and the people of Malta were enduring this third heavy blitz and an increasingly anxious wait for the next relief convoy the island's naval and air forces were called upon to participate in a new campaign. On 8 November 1942 American and British forces landed in French North Africa in Operation 'Torch' and when Hitler decided to send a force to Tunisia to resist this invasion Malta was ideally placed for an attack on this new supply route. This complex and fiercely fought six-month campaign has attracted numerous histories (most of which wholly ignore Malta's participation), and we will do no more here than recount several matters involving Malta's forces where Churchill took key decisions.

It was only slowly that Malta's role in 'Torch' emerged. Once President Roosevelt on 30 July had committed American forces detailed planning commenced. On 19 September Admiral Pound warned Admiral Harwood, C-in-C Mediterranean, that 'it will be essential to prevent or delay enemy reinforcements reaching Tunisia before we do. To this end operations will be necessary from Malta on the greatest scale possible.'[7] However, when he asked ten days later about operations from Malta he was surprised to learn from General Brooke that these 'had been shelved when it had been decided to limit the extent of the initial landings.' Nevertheless, the Joint Planning Committee (JPC) on 8 October presented to the COS an Appreciation under the title, 'MALTA—Offensive Operations in Conjunction with a Certain Operation'.[8] This made clear the naval and air operations that could be carried out from the island as long as adequate supplies of fuel oil and aviation spirit had been received before 'Torch' was launched.

However, as we have seen in the previous chapter, the postponement of Montgomery's attack at El Alamein to 23 October and the fierce resistance it then encountered meant that the 'Stoneage' relief convoy was still at anchor at Alexandria when 'Torch' began. This might not have been too serious had the COS been correct in their assumption that the German reaction to the landings would be limited and slow. However, to their alarm Hitler at once ordered Kesselring to send a major German force to Tunisia, including a complete German armoured division. Within days large numbers of German and Italian troops had been flown into Tunisia and on 12 November the first of a steady stream of convoys had left ports in Sicily and Naples. The COS urgently reviewed these unwelcome developments and on 11 November signalled to the Middle East C-in-Cs:

It is important that Malta should take maximum air action against German forces in Tunisia at once. Extent to which they can afford to use up their fuel depends on date of arrival of convoy from your end. Please give us earliest date to which it would be safe for Malta to work.[9]

The shortage of aviation fuel at Malta had been the subject of numerous COS discussions in October and early November, the result of which was that specified amounts were held in reserve to provide air cover for the unloading of the 'Stoneage' convoy. It was fully recognised that it would be disastrous if any ships that reached Malta were sunk in the Grand Harbour as had happened in March. Malta's second priority was to assist the 'Torch' landings, the urgency of which was emphasised by the above cable. At their meeting on 12 November the COS again discussed the problem and decided to leave to the Governor the allocation of the remaining fuel. This did not meet with the Prime Minister's approval and he minuted:

It is of course of the utmost importance that Lord Gort should intervene by Air in Tunis. But I do not think we ought simply to leave the responsibility of using up his petrol to him. What view do the Chiefs of Staff take about the amount he should keep in hand?[10]

In the light of these comments the COS discussed the matter once more and on the following day, with the sailing of the eastern convoy now imminent, recommended that the Governor should use in support of 'Torch' 300 tons of fuel that had been ear-marked for December.[11] They confirmed this advice when several days later the Governor warned that stocks would be exhausted by the end of November.

The arrival of the relief convoy on 20 November and its rapid unloading enabled Gort and his local commanders to implement their plans for attacking the Axis build-up in Tunisia. However, before we consider Churchill's role in this new offensive it will be convenient to examine a controversial proposal that troops from Malta be landed at the port of Sousse 80 miles south of Tunis.

This Operation 'Breastplate' has attracted only a footnote in the official history because it was never executed but it gave rise to numerous debates in the COS and the Defence Committee since it had awkward implications for Anglo-American co-operation.

It was hoped that if the landings in French North Africa were seen to be American-led this might secure the co-operation or, at least, the acquiescence of the French forces there. Consequently, Churchill proposed that the Supreme Commander of the allied force should be General Eisenhower supported by American and British commanders and an Anglo-American staff. While the JPC was considering the role that Malta might play in the 'Torch' campaign a request was received from Eisenhower's staff that an infantry force from Malta be landed at Sousse.[12] When they presented their report to the COS the JPC advised that out of the Malta garrison of fourteen battalions a brigade of three battalions, supported by some field and AA artillery, could be formed for such a purpose. However, they would have no transport, very little in the way of supplies and could not be re-supplied from Malta, at least before the arrival of the relief convoy. Crucially, too, the physical condition of these troops was so poor that an opposed landing or extended operations were precluded. They were simply not fighting fit. The JPC concluded that such an operation would not be justified unless 'it would tip the balance'. The COS endorsed this view and advised General Eisenhower accordingly. The Middle East C-in-Cs were advised of this possible requirement but assured that 'the decision rests with us'.[13]

One week later, however, at a joint conference on 15 October the 'Torch' army commanders renewed the request for a Malta force to be landed by D-Day + 5 on the assumption that the French would co-operate. But when the C-in-Cs were asked about this they replied that they could not send such a force until D-Day + 29. Churchill who had followed this interchange closely at once remarked that 'this was a very pessimistic forecast' and asked for the views of the COS.[14] Brooke agreed with the Prime Minister and told him that planning was still proceeding on the D-Day + 5 assumption. On 27 October Churchill minuted to the COS:

How does the question of the intervention of the Malta force in TORCH now stand? Evidently the prospects of this operation are much improved by what we have heard about the mission of the American Eagle.[15]

This was a reference to General Mark Clark's clandestine visit to Algeria. On 22 October Clark was landed on the coast of Algeria from a British submarine, *P. 219*, for a meeting with General Charles Mast, the Chief of Staff of the French 19th Corps. Mast told Clark that the French forces would only put up a token resistance to any Allied landing. This prompted Eisenhower on 28 October to request that the COS re-consider the matter and he sought authority to order the landing of the Malta force when required.

This request provoked a flurry of cables between the COS, the C-in-Cs in Cairo and the Governor in Malta culminating in a four-page signal from Cairo on 29 October.[16]

This repeated all the C-in-Cs' earlier reservations and added that the removal of these troops from Malta should not be ordered before the 'Stoneage' relief convoy had been safely unloaded. To this the Prime Minister commented: 'They do not know about Eagle's visit yet. Let everything be prepared. We alone can settle when and if to use it.'[17] The result was that Brooke gave a very guarded response to Eisenhower which emphasised that the Malta force could only be sent 'under circumstances amounting to an invitation by the French'. Nevertheless, Churchill thought it right to alert Gort to what was expected:

For yourself alone, an American General of high rank visited "TORCH" area and held long conference with friendly generals. We have every reason to hope, and indeed believe, that very little opposition will be encountered and that powerful aid will be forthcoming. Thus events may move more rapidly—perhaps far more rapidly—than we had planned. . . . Bear all this in mind when thinking about BREASTPLATE.[18]

Preparations in Malta duly went ahead and three days after the initial landings on November 8 the Governor reported that the force could be sailed within 96 hours of orders to do so.

On 16 November as the 'Stoneage' relief convoy left Alexandria for Malta the COS received yet another cable from Eisenhower 'requesting executive authority for ordering Operation 'Breastplate' to be placed in the hands of the Allied C-in-C.' This was referred directly to the Defence Committee where General Brooke pointed out the clash with the expected arrival of the convoy at Valletta. This time it was the Prime Minister who objected:

The arrival and safe unloading of this convoy would be a big event for Malta whereas 'Breastplate' could not hope to do more than divert a few aircraft and the attention of the enemy for a short while from the Allied advance to Tunis. Due regard should be paid to the importance which was attached to the timely arrival of supplies and aviation petrol in Malta. Operation 'Breastplate' might prove to be too big a price to pay for a relatively small diversion of air forces.[19]

The COS, therefore, in their reply to Eisenhower laid down four essential conditions for the execution of 'Breastplate'. These were (a), the safe unloading of the Malta convoy, (b), Sousse was not occupied by Axis forces, (c), a friendly welcome there was assured, and (d), air cover was available.[20] If the COS thought that this ended the matter they were mistaken for on 19 November Eisenhower enquired whether, if airborne troops were first landed at Sousse to secure the area, the Governor could send a single battalion to support a planned advance by General Anderson on 22 November. Both the Governor and the C-in-Cs thought that the landing of such a small, ill-equipped force would have no effect on Anderson's advance but the COS recommended to Churchill that Eisenhower be advised that 'if, in spite of hearing our views, he still wants this small diversion he should have discretion to arrange it direct with the Governor.' In the official records the draft cable advising this proposal bears the notation: 'PM approved attached telegram by telephone from Chequers on 21/11'.[21] To the relief of all the British commanders Eisenhower finally signalled on 22 November that 'all idea of assistance from Malta by modified "Breastplate" will be abandoned.' On his copy of this signal Churchill simply wrote 'Good'.[22]

This cancelled operation has been recounted at some length because it shows how closely the Prime Minister involved himself in a matter affecting Malta's security. Although in the interests of Anglo-American co-operation Churchill and the COS were anxious to meet General Eisenhower's wishes they were not prepared to accept any risk to the relief convoy which was critical for the health and safety of the people and garrison of Malta. On 5 December, as German resistance to General Anderson's advance grew, Churchill minuted to General Brooke: 'It seems to me in view of what has happened that Lord Gort was right not to do the Sousse operation . . . What sort of position would he have been in now if he had acted as was suggested by Eisenhower?'[23]

We must now consider the crisis that had arisen in Tunisia to which all eyes had turned after the safe arrival of 'Stoneage'. While General Anderson's Anglo-American force was struggling eastwards towards Tunisia along poor roads and a single-track railway Kesselring had employed every available ship and transport aircraft, including 400 transferred by Hitler from the Russian front, to gain control of Tunisia. The measure of his success, and of the task now facing the Allies, can be seen in the fact that in the last three weeks of November 25,000 men and 34,000 tons of supplies had reached Tunisia without the loss of a single soldier or ton of supplies. As soon as the aviation fuel from the Malta convoy had been unloaded the COS cabled the Middle East C-in-Cs. After stating that the stoppage of Axis convoys to Tunisia was now of paramount importance they continued:

> Air power can only make its full contribution to this objective if Malta with its limited airfield capacity is exploited to the utmost extent . . . First priority at Malta should be given to torpedo bombers particularly to those able to operate at night and request you consider the immediate move of your two Albacore squadrons and a Beaufort squadron to Malta.[24]

Tedder immediately ordered to Malta as many Wellington bombers, torpedo bombers and fighters as the island's airfields could handle and Churchill saw little need to intervene in these arrangements.

However, as befitted a 'Former Naval Person' he took a closer interest in naval dispositions and the minutes of a meeting of the Defence Committee on 23 November record:

> The Prime Minister enquired what the Admiralty proposed to do to interrupt with surface ships based on Malta the Axis communications to Tunis and Bizerta.[25]

There were now two naval commanders in the Mediterranean. Based at Alexandria was Admiral Sir Henry Harwood, the C-in-C Mediterranean, who at the outset of the war had hounded the *Graf Spee* to destruction. In the west the naval Commander of the 'Torch' Task Force was Admiral Sir Andrew Cunningham who had returned to the Mediterranean he knew so well after several months in a staff appointment in Washington. As noted earlier in this chapter Admiral Pound had warned Admiral Harwood in September that a major naval effort from Malta would be required but in the event the only naval reinforcements to reach Malta before the 'Torch' landings were submarines. Moreover, Captain Simpson deployed his enlarged 10th Flotilla to protect the invasion convoys against any possible attack by the Italian fleet and it was not until 11 November that he received orders to concentrate on the Tunisian passage. The early provision of surface ships at Valletta was then precluded by the paramount need to escort the Malta relief convoy, a task that Pound had already ruled, with Churchill's agreement, must have absolute priority over attacks on enemy shipping.

With this task, if only partly, accomplished Pound was able to reply to the Prime Minister's enquiry that a surface force based at Malta seemed better placed to attack Axis shipping to Tripoli, which was now Rommel's last main port in North Africa. An attack on the new Tunisian route, he advised, could more easily be undertaken by another force based at Bône to the west of Bizerta. On the following day, however, although Harwood signalled that he preferred to retain all his forces to escort the next convoy to Malta, he was instructed to send three cruisers and four destroyers to Malta.[26] These arrived on 27 November to form a new Force K. Three days later Admiral Cunningham established Force Q, comprised of a further three cruisers and two destroyers, at Bône. The power of naval gunnery was quickly demonstrated on two nights in early December when the two Forces, guided by an ASV Wellington from Malta, sank a convoy of four supply ships and two escorting warships.

These losses, however, led Kesselring to suspend night-time crossings and send convoys by day with strong fighter escort, which included the latest version of the Bf109. Despite the greater risks to naval attack in these conditions Churchill nevertheless urged that they be continued. Part of his message to Pound on 6 December relating to Force K at Malta is quoted at the beginning of this chapter but he went on to write:

> This is also the time for Admiral Cunningham to use his cruisers and destroyers, even at heavy risk, against enemy convoys . . . The first duty of the Navy for the next ten days is to stop the reinforcements to Tunisia. This duty should be discharged even at a heavy cost.[27]

Pound consulted Cunningham but then advised the Prime Minister that if Cunningham attempted to attack by day without adequate air cover 'two convoys might be stopped at cost of the whole of Force Q. There are no ships for another.' He elaborated on the problems caused by enemy air superiority and Churchill noted at the foot of Pound's memorandum, 'Thank you for your full explanation of the difficulties. I trust they may be overcome.'[28]

Churchill's hope that the Allies might secure Tunisia by the end of 1942 was, in the event, frustrated. Various unforeseen factors came into play not the least of which was the inability of Malta's air and naval forces to intervene in the new campaign until the relief convoy had been unloaded on 20 November. This gave Kesselring the opportunity to execute Hitler's orders, an opportunity which he seized with characteristic energy and decision. German forces were, consequently, just strong enough to throw back Anderson's weak thrust towards Tunis and Bizerta before torrential rain brought operations to a standstill in late December. Meanwhile in Malta on New Year's Day 1943 the promotion of the Governor, Lord Gort, to the rank of Field Marshal was announced. Churchill at once telegraphed to him: 'Heartiest congratulations on peak promotion. Delighted to hear it. Pray you are now on top and frowns of Fortune all passed.'[29]

Overall Allied strategy in the Mediterranean, and its repercussions on other plans, had ended 1942 on a frustrating note but the position at Malta had been transformed. After the dark days of the spring, summer and autumn air attacks and the growing anxieties caused by the dwindling food stocks, the 'Pedestal' convoy, despite severe losses, had been fought through. 'Stoneage' in November had brought further relief and by the end of December the food position was steadily improving. This and earlier chapters have focused on Churchill's close and continuing involvement in the defence and sustenance of Malta in the midst of all his other concerns. It is, in this writer's view, difficult to avoid the conclusion that without his sustained pressure on his military advisers that Malta must be held so that it could play a full part in the defeat of the enemy forces in North Africa the island and its courageous people might have succumbed.

## Notes

[1] NA CAB 105/10, COS to Middle East C-in-Cs, 19 August 1942.

[2] Hinsley, *British Intelligence, Vol. II*, p. 408.

[3] NA PREM 3/266/10A, Fol. 719, JIC (42) 349, 'Renewal of Air Attacks on Malta', 10 September 1942.

[4] B. Liddell Hart, (ed.), *The Rommel Papers* (Collins, London, 1955), p. 313.

[5] Ibid., p. 286.

[6] NA PREM 3/266/10A, Fols. 674, 677, Gort to WSC and WSC reply, 26 and 28 October 1942.

[7] NA CAB 121/632, Admiralty to C-in-C Mediterranean, 19 September 1942.

[8] NA CAB 79/23, COS Memorandum JP (42) 862, 6 October 1942.

[9] NA CAB 121/632, COS to Middle East C-in-Cs, 11 November 1942.

[10] NA CAB 79/58, WSC minute to COS, 12 November 1942.

[11] NA CAB 79/24, COS (42) 318th Meeting, 17 November 1942.

[12] See Note 8 above.

[13] NA CAB 121/632, COS to Middle East C-in-Cs, 8 October 1942.

[14] Ibid., WSC minute to COS, 21 October 1942.

[15] Ibid., WSC minute to COS, 27 October 1942.

[16] Ibid., Middle East C-in-Cs to COS, 29 October 1942.

[17] Ibid., WSC minute to COS, 30 October 1942.

[18] CAC CHAR 20/81/129, WSC to Gort, 30 October 1942.

[19] NA CAB 69/4, Defence Committee (Operations) (42), 17th Meeting, 16 November 1942.

[20] NA CAB 79/24, COS (42) 319th Meeting, 18 November 1942.

[21] NA CAB 121/632, WSC minute to COS, 21 November 1942.

[22] Ibid., WSC notation on Eisenhower to Governor, 22 November 1942.

[23] Ibid., WSC to CIGS, 5 December 1942.

[24] NA CAB 121/632, COS to Middle East C-in-Cs, 22 November 1942.

[25] NA CAB 69/4, Defence Committee (Operations) (42) 18th Meeting, 23 November 1942.

[26] NA CAB 121/632, Admiralty to C-in-C Mediterranean, 24 November 1942.

[27] Re-printed in Churchill, *Second World War, Vol. IV*, p. 808.

[28] NA ADM 205/27, Pound to WSC, 9 December 1942.

[29] NA PREM 3/266/10A, Fol. 674, WSC to Gort, 1 January 1943.

## CHAPTER XV

# 1943. A Year of Attack and Churchill's Fifth Visit to Malta

*HAD GREAT WELCOME FROM WORKMEN IN MALTA DOCKYARD*
Churchill telegram to Mrs Churchill, 21 November 1943

As previous chapters have shown Churchill had, since Italy's declaration of war in June 1940, paid close attention to events affecting Malta and he had often intervened at critical moments. From the end of 1942, however, after, in Churchill's subsequent words, 'Malta had been revictualled and rearmed and had again sprung into full activity',[1] the island appears less frequently in Churchill's directives and Minutes. Indeed his special series of Malta files, upon which earlier chapters of this study have drawn, come to an end in 1943. There was another reason for this reduced involvement with events in Malta. The victories at El Alamein, Stalingrad and in the Pacific marked a turning point in the war against the Axis powers after which the strategic initiative swung towards the Allies. As Churchill remarked in a speech at the Mansion House when he received the Freedom of the City of London in November 1942, 'Now this is not the end. It is not even the beginning of the end. But it is, perhaps, the end of the beginning.'[2] Moreover, he warned his audience, 'It is very probable there will be heavy fighting in the Mediterranean and elsewhere before the leaves of autumn fall.' However, in Churchill's view, the speedy defeat of the enemy required close co-ordination of strategy and operations, and on critical issues this, in his view, could only be achieved by face-to-face meetings. Hence 1943 was for the Prime Minister a year of extensive travel and this made it more difficult for him to watch day-to-day events in Malta as he had done in the earlier years of the war. Although he continued to receive copies of important telegrams and of the principal Enigma intercepts as well as the Minutes of the COS meetings, his interventions were necessarily more limited. Nevertheless, despite these strategic preoccupations he found time in January 1943 to ask Pound whether it was possible to increase the submarine force at Malta and in May he made a similar enquiry about Malta's Motor Torpedo Boats (MTBs).

The first of Churchill's 1943 journeys in search of victory began on the evening of 12 January when he flew in his special Liberator bomber, 'Commando', to Casablanca where he was joined several days later by

President Roosevelt and the British and American Chiefs of Staff. His son, Randolph, then serving as a Major with the army in Tunisia, also met Churchill there. The newly promoted Governor of Malta might perhaps have joined them there too but ill health had forced Lord Gort to return to London for medical treatment. Among the many decisions taken at the conference was the agreement to invade Sicily as soon as North Africa had been cleared of enemy forces.

Mention has been made in earlier chapters of the great pleasure that Churchill derived from painting and it was after the Casablanca Conference that Churchill painted his only wartime canvas. Before the war he had on several occasions visited Marrakesh to rest and paint and after the Conference had concluded he persuaded President Roosevelt to spend a few days there with him. 'You cannot', he told the President, 'come all this way to North Africa without seeing Marrakesh. Let us spend two days there. I must be with you when you see the sunset on the snows of the Atlas Mountains.'[3] The two leaders accordingly did as Churchill had suggested and on 24 January watched the sunset from the tower of the Villa Taylor. Churchill stayed on for a further two days after the President had left and painted the scene they had observed. He later gave this painting to the President.[4]

The clearance of North Africa was no easy task. As has been observed in the previous chapter, a strong Axis force had been established in Tunisia and it was not until General Montgomery had driven the remnants of Rommel's desert army into Tunisia that General Alexander was able to launch his final offensive. On 13 May, while Churchill was in Washington, he was handed a telegram from Alexander, which read: 'Sir, it is my duty to report that the Tunisian campaign is over. All enemy resistance has ceased. We are masters of the North African shores.'[5] Churchill also received the following telegram from the King:

> Now that the campaign in Africa has reached a glorious conclusion, I wish to tell you how profoundly I appreciate the fact that its initial conception and successful prosecution are largely due to your vision and to your unflinching determination in the face of early difficulties. The African campaign has immeasurably increased the debt that this country, and indeed all the United Nations, owe to you.[6]

Malta's contribution to this final victory in North Africa has been widely ignored but deserves proper recognition. As soon as adequate supplies of oil fuel and aviation spirit had been landed at Malta the island's surface ships, submarines and aircraft launched a continual attack on the flow of Axis troops and supplies to Tunis and Bizerta. Not for nothing did this become known to Italian seamen as the 'death route', the *rotta della morte.* Apart from the many German and Italian aircraft, including many troop-carrying transport aircraft, shot down, Malta's air and sea forces between November 1942 and May 1943 sank 86 ships with an aggregate tonnage of 280,000 tons. This amounts to 50% of Axis shipping losses in the central Mediterranean during this period. Without this major contribution it seems inevitable that German resistance in Tunisia would have been prolonged. As it was, when the German General Warlimont visited Tunisia in February 1943 to assess the situation he quickly concluded that the Axis position resembled a 'house of cards'.[7]

In this long and hard-fought campaign in North Africa Churchill had always believed that Malta should play a valuable part but even he might have been surprised by what was achieved by the defence and sustenance of the island. In the early months of the Mediterranean war it had served as a staging post for air reinforcements for the Middle East and the island's value as a base for air reconnaissance in the central Mediterranean had been demonstrated in the attack on the Italian fleet at Taranto. Its bombers, except in the periods of intense air attack, had continually attacked targets in Italy, Sicily and North Africa. Even the heavy air raids that had caused much loss of life and injury, as well as widespread damage, had nevertheless served the Allied cause by diverting enemy aircraft from North Africa and the Russian front and many of these were destroyed or damaged by Malta's gunners and airmen. But above all it was Malta's task to attack the Axis supply routes from Italy to North Africa, and the most impressive measure of Malta's value can be seen in the number of Axis supply ships sunk by Malta's forces. Between June 1940 and May 1943 Malta's air and naval forces sank 210 ships with an aggregate tonnage of 852,000 tons. This represents 58% of the Axis tonnage sunk in the central Mediterranean during these years. Many other ships were unable to deliver their cargoes because they were damaged or forced to return to port. This was vindication in full measure of Churchill's insistence from the day he became Prime Minister that everything possible be done to sustain Malta as a unique base for offensive operations. The author has suggested elsewhere that British possession and use of Malta may have shortened the Mediterranean war by as much as a year, with incalculable consequences for the war as a whole.[8]

Churchill came very close to visiting Malta in February 1943. After a visit to Turkey and Cyprus, where he inspected his old regiment, the 4th Hussars, of which he was by now the Colonel-in-Chief, he flew to Tripoli. There, on 4 February, he took the salute at a march past of the 8th Army. In his memoirs he then wrote:

> I had planned to fly to Malta, and in consequence of the directions I had given at Cairo all had been set in readiness by Montgomery. As the flight was considered dangerous, on account of the presence of the enemy, I was to go in a small two-seater plane with an escort of half a

dozen Spitfires. However, when I expressed my pleasure and surprise at these excellent arrangements having been made by Montgomery he realised that he had taken what was only my wish as an order. He then began to make objections about the danger of the flight, and finally I deferred to his advice. I am sorry for this, as I should have liked to have a memory of Malta while it was still in its struggle.[9]

It seems appropriate at this point to draw attention to an award he received at this time that must have given him particular pleasure. In March 1943 the Air Council, with the King's approval, had awarded him the Honorary Wings of the Royal Air Force. In Chapter III above we have noted the flying lessons Churchill took in 1912 when he was First Lord of the Admiralty. However, although he flew many dangerous hours he did not achieve a pilot's licence before friends and family persuaded him to stop. The award of Wings in 1943 recognised the many hundreds of hours the Prime Minister had flown during the war, often at altitude in unheated bombers. In writing to accept this honour he recalled the early days of flying in the RNAS and RAF and concluded:

I am honoured to be accorded a place, albeit out of kindness, in that comradeship of the air which guards the life of our island and carries doom to tyrants, whether they flaunt themselves or burrow deep.[10]

From that moment he proudly and deservedly wore his Wings on his Air Commodore's uniform.

In the event it was King George VI who on Sunday 20 June 1943 spent a full day in Malta. He arrived early in the morning on the cruiser, HMS *Aurora*, and a signed copy of a photograph showing the King standing on the cruiser's bridge hangs in Churchill's Study at Chartwell. The King had a busy day. After meeting the Council of Malta and inspecting the George Cross he had awarded to the island the year before he presented the Governor, Lord Gort, with his Field Marshal's baton and knighted the AOC, Air Vice-Marshal Sir Keith Park. Afterwards he moved on to the balcony of the Palace in Valletta to acknowledge the welcome given him by a large crowd. He then left to inspect the dockyard and the surrounding heavily bombed areas before being entertained to lunch by the Governor at Verdala Palace. After lunch he made further inspections of the expanding airfields. As he prepared to leave the island late in the evening the Lieutenant-Governor, David Campbell, told him, 'You have made the people of Malta very happy today, Sir', to which the King replied, 'But I have been the happiest man in Malta today.'[11]

While the Tunisian campaign was entering its final phase planning for the invasion of Sicily, Operation 'Husky', went ahead. On 14 February Admiral Pound presented a memorandum to the COS:

The mounting in the Eastern Mediterranean of the major portion of the Assault for HUSKY will place Malta in the forefront of the largest offensive operation we have yet undertaken and the Island must prepare at once for the part it will be called upon to play.[12]

On his way back to Malta after medical treatment in London Gort attended a COS meeting on 3 March. This gave him the opportunity to discuss in detail the plans for the invasion of Sicily and the role that Malta was expected to play in its launching.[13] In the following weeks and months he and his local commanders received a stream of instructions from the Middle East C-in-Cs about the preparation of the necessary naval and air facilities so that Malta could become an effective advance base. The harbours were cleared of the many wrecks and the docks put back into working order. Several labour battalions were sent to Malta to assist with the expansion of the airfields to accommodate at least twenty-four squadrons and with other engineering work. At the end of March the Governor received instructions to send a brigade of three battalions from the garrison to Egypt to train with the eastern task force.[14] This became the 231st Infantry Brigade and the men wore the Maltese Cross as their brigade sign. By the beginning of July the Governor was able to report that all the necessary work was completed. This included the construction by US engineers of a completely new airfield in Gozo in only seventeen days. As many as thirty-five squadrons were eventually flown from Malta in the opening days of 'Husky'.

In the days before D-Day, 10 July, Generals Eisenhower, Alexander and Montgomery, together with Admiral Cunningham, who for the second time had been appointed C-in-C Mediterranean, arrived in Malta with their staffs and it was there that the final preparations were made. H-Hour for the Sicilian landings was set for 2.45 a.m. and on the night of 9/10 July Churchill was at Chequers awaiting the first news of the landings. His daughter-in-law, Pamela, had stayed up with him and they played bezique while they waited. His thoughts were in Malta and Sicily and she later recalled that at times he put down his cards and said, 'So many brave young men going to their death tonight. It is a grave responsibility.'[15] In the early hours of 10 July when he learned of the success of the initial landings and of the capture of the port of Syracuse he telegraphed to Eisenhower, 'It is a tremendous feat to leap on shore with nearly 200,000 men.'[16] Among the first troops to land were the men of the 231st Brigade. Two days later the first battleships to enter the Grand Harbour since HMS *Warspite's* two-day stay in 1940 anchored there after supporting the landings. They were the Royal Navy's two 16-inch-gunned battleships, HMS *Nelson* and *Rodney*.

Churchill was once again at Chequers on 25 July. There in the evening while with members of his family and staff he was watching a film, news was brought to him that Mussolini had been dismissed. King Victor Emmanuel had assumed control of the Italian armed forces and he had appointed Marshal Badoglio as Prime Minister. Armistice negotiations began at once but on 5 August Churchill boarded the liner *Queen Mary* to begin his fifth wartime transatlantic crossing. Two weeks later in the middle of the Quebec Conference he received a cable from General Alexander telling him that 'the last German soldier was flung out of Sicily and the whole island is now in our hands'.[17] After the Conference Churchill travelled on to Washington and it was there on 8 September that he learned of the Italian surrender. The date 8 September is celebrated in Malta as the day in 1565 when the Turks had abandoned the first Great Siege of Malta. It is also the titular feast day of Senglea, the dockyard community that had become the most heavily bombed place in Malta. On that day in 1943 the statue of Our Lady of Victories, known as *Il-Bambina*, was returned to Senglea from Birkirkara where it had been kept during the bombing. The statue was borne in procession through the ruined streets to the Church of St. Philip and it was there that the parish priest gave the news of Italy's surrender.[18]

At Malta urgent arrangements were made to receive the main units of the Italian fleet which sailed from various Italian ports on 8 September. A German guided bomb sank the Italian flagship, *Roma*, off Sardinia but the remaining battleships and many other naval vessels arrived in Maltese waters on 10 September led by HMS *Warspite*. On the following day Admiral Cunningham signed with Admiral da Zara the surrender documents relating to the Italian fleet. Having done so, he cabled to the Admiralty: 'Be pleased to inform their Lordships that the Italian Battle fleet now lies at anchor under the guns of the fortress of Malta.'[19] In Washington Churchill had followed all these developments closely and on 10 September signalled Cunningham that the Italian ships should be received 'in a kindly and generous manner'.[20] Later with an eye to securing Italian support for joining the Allies he added that 'films should be taken if possible of surrender of Italian Fleet, their courteous reception by the British, and kindly treatment of wounded.'[21] He later wrote: 'The splendid prize of the whole Fleet of what had been a victorious Power of the first rank thus fell into our hands. It must be made to play its part on our side.'[22] Malta, too, was the scene of the last act in the fall of fascist Italy. On 29 September on the decks of HMS *Nelson* in the Grand Harbour Marshal Badoglio was formally received by General Eisenhower, accompanied by Cunningham, Alexander, Tedder and Lord Gort. After the traditional naval formalities Badoglio officially signed the unconditional surrender documents on behalf of Italy. It was entirely fitting that this ceremony should take place at Malta more than three years after the first Italian bombs had fallen on the island in 1940.

Churchill returned to Britain on HMS *Renown* on 19 September and in the House of Commons two days later he gave a lengthy account of the negotiations that had led to Italy's surrender and the sailing of the Italian

Fleet to Malta.[23] On the following day, in reply to a written question, he explained the conditions applying to the award of the proposed Africa Star and went on to state, 'Malta alone of the Mediterranean Islands is included in the award of this Star, by reason of its heavy action and long ordeal.'[24] A month later he gave the House details of the surrendered Italian ships:

> The major part of the Italian Fleet, totalling over 100 warships of all categories is in Allied hands. This includes five out of the six battleships in commission, and eight out of eleven cruisers. More than 150,000 tons of merchant ships have so far been accounted for in ports under Allied control. I can assure my hon. and gallant Friend that the ships will be used to the best possible advantage of the United Nations.[25]

The opportunity Churchill had long sought to re-visit Malta came at last in November. While the Allied armies slowly advanced in Italy against stubborn German resistance it had become imperative to finalise the plans for the invasion of North West Europe. After much discussion it was arranged that the 'Big Three' would meet in Teheran in late November. Prior to that Churchill and Roosevelt agreed to meet in Cairo to concert their own plans and proposals before their meeting with Stalin. Accordingly on 12 November Churchill, nearing his sixty-ninth birthday, once again boarded HMS *Renown*, assuming the cover name 'Colonel Warden'. On this occasion in addition to his usual staff his entourage included his daughter, Sarah, a Section Officer in the WAAF, his son, Randolph, Admiral Sir Andrew Cunningham who had recently been appointed as First Sea Lord upon the death of Admiral Pound on 21 October, Lord Moran, his doctor, and the US Ambassador in London, Gilbert Winant. Harold Macmillan, the British political adviser to General Eisenhower, joined *Renown* in Gibraltar to brief Churchill on the political situation in the Mediterranean theatre. When they put to sea, Captain Pim, who maintained the Prime Minister's Map Room, calculated that Churchill had already travelled 111,000 miles since September 1939. Many more lay in front of him. After a brief stop in Algiers *Renown* sailed on to Malta with a heavy naval and air force escort and anchored in the Grand Harbour in the evening of 17 November. It was disappointing for Churchill and the people of Malta that his long anticipated visit to the island was marred by his having a heavy feverish cold which was exacerbated by inoculations he had been given by Lord Moran against cholera and typhoid. As a result he was compelled to spend much of his three days there in bed.

The Governor, Lord Gort, greeted him on landing and they drove to San Anton Palace. There before dinner Churchill, as he subsequently advised the King, invested Generals Eisenhower and Alexander with the

Africa Star upon the ribbons of which were fastened the emblems '1' and '8'. These were the only two entitled to this honour in recognition of their command of both the 1st and 8th Armies in North Africa.[26] Gort had given up his own bedroom at the palace for the Prime Minister but, still unwell and sleeping badly, Churchill found this too noisy since it was adjacent to a busy road. Lord Moran, his doctor, later recalled that Churchill at one stage opened the window and shouted, 'Go away, will you? Please go away and do not make so much noise.'[27] He also grumbled to General Ismay about the Spartan conditions, the lack of hot water for his bath and the poor food. Nevertheless, he rejected Ismay's suggestion that they return to the comforts of HMS *Renown*. On the following day he summoned the COS and other commanders and held a staff conference in his bedroom. He then learned to his dismay that the Germans had recovered the Greek island of Leros, taking 5,000 British soldiers prisoner. Another unexpected development was a signal from President Roosevelt alleging that their proposed meeting at Cairo was known to the enemy. He suggested, therefore, that the meeting be switched to Khartoum or Malta. Churchill ordered enquiries to be made about facilities in Malta but Ismay reported that the island at that time could not accommodate and feed the large numbers involved.[28] Roosevelt eventually agreed to meet at Cairo as planned.

On the following day, 19 November, Churchill felt well enough to visit Valletta. Wearing the uniform of the Royal Yacht Squadron he toured the dockyard where extensive damage was still all too evident. As he walked about he received a vociferous welcome. His daughter, Sarah, later remembered:

> The people were warm and quite thrilled to see him; he was completely mobbed. Many of the Maltese police forgot that they were supposed to be there to protect him and simply joined the crowd, following him everywhere.[29]

He was given another noisy reception from a large crowd when he went up to the Grand Master's Palace and appeared on the balcony with the Governor. Throughout the war Churchill had made a point of visiting heavily bombed towns in Britain, often arriving while the fires were still being fought and casualties evacuated. His appearances on these occasions usually cheered the survivors and the civil defence workers and there can be no doubt that Churchill himself, although at times reduced to tears by what he saw and learned, gained courage and resolution from the manner in which others had endured their sufferings. The receptions he received in Malta on 19 November had the same uplifting effect on him. After he left the island he thanked the Governor for his hospitality, writing, 'I shall always have the pleasantest memories of my visit and in particular of the moving welcome I received from the brave people of the island.'[30] He also sent a short cable to his wife in which he told her:

HAVE HAD FOR FIVE DAYS BAD COLD ON CHEST NOW DEFINITELY MASTERED. THIS AND BAD WEATHER DECIDED ME TO GO ON IN SHIP AND AM JUST REACHING ALEXANDRIA AFTER SAFE VOYAGE . . . HAD GREAT WELCOME FROM WORKMEN IN MALTA DOCKYARD.'[31]

Churchill boarded HMS *Renown* again on the evening of 19 November and reached Alexandria two days later. Although Churchill did not write at length about his brief stay in Malta the cables to Lord Gort and to his wife suggests that he was pleased at last to see the island that had been much in his thoughts in the previous three years. His visits to the dockyard area and the centre of Valletta would have made clear how much the Maltese had suffered since Italy had entered the war. Had he been in good health or able to stay longer he would surely have wanted to see more of the island and its defenders but the urgent business of fighting the war took him off to Cairo and Teheran.

After the Teheran Conference Churchill planned to fly initially to Algiers to see General Eisenhower and then travel to Italy by air or sea to visit General Alexander. For this purpose many of his staff returned to Malta in the cruiser HMS *Penelope* and it is possible that Churchill might have called there again in December. However, when he arrived at General Eisenhower's headquarters near the ancient city of Carthage on 11 December his heavy cold, exacerbated by the rigours of his long mid-winter travels, turned into a dangerous attack of pneumonia and he had a mild heart attack. This illness ruled out any possibility of visiting Italy. Mrs Churchill flew out from England to be with him and his daughter, Sarah, read to him from *Pride and Prejudice*. Within a week he was recovering and his energy was flowing back. On Christmas Day he entertained to lunch the five C-in-Cs and dictated the doctors' communiqué on his health. Harold Macmillan noted in his diary: 'Although he can be so tiresome and pigheaded, there is no one like him. His devotion to work and duty is quite extraordinary.'[32]

## *Notes*

[1] Churchill, *Second World War, Vol. IV*, p. 643.

[2] Churchill, *War Speeches, Vol. III*, p. 214.

[3] Churchill, *Second World War, Vol. IV*, pp. 621-2.

[4] It is re-produced in M. Soames, *Winston Churchill: His Life As A Painter* (Collins, London, 1990), p. 133.

[5] Churchill, *Second World War, Vol. IV*, p. 698.

[6] Ibid.

[7] General W. Warlimont, *Inside Hitler's Headquarters 1939-1945* (Presidio, Novato, California), p. 311.

[8] Austin, *Malta*, p. 190.

[9] Churchill, *Second World War, Vol. IV*, p. 646.

[10] Churchill, *War Speeches, Vol. IV*, WSC to Air Marshal Sutton, 1 April 1943, p. 67.

[11] Wheeler-Bennett, *King George VI*, p. 578.

[12] NA CAB 80/67, COS (43) 59 'O' Memorandum, 14 February 1943.

[13] NA CAB 79/59, COS (43) 33rd. 'O' Meeting, 3 March 1943.

[14] NA CAB 121/632, Middle East C-in-Cs to Governor, 26 March 1943.

[15] Gilbert, *Churchill: A Life*, pp. 748-9.

[16] Ibid., p. 749.

[17] Ibid., p. 751.

[18] J. Attard, *The Battle of Malta* (Hamlyn Paperbacks, London, 1982), pp. 237-8.

[19] Cunningham, *Odyssey*, p. 565.

[20] Churchill, *Second World War, Vol. V*, p. 102.

[21] CAC, CHAR 20/118/27, WSC to Cunningham and Gort, 10 September 1943.

[22] Churchill, *Second World War, Vol. V*, p. 103.

[23] Churchill, *War Speeches, Vol. IV*, p. 215

[24] Ibid., p. 228.

[25] Ibid., p. 256.

[26] CAC CHAR 20/130/3, WSC to King George VI, 18 November 1943.

[27] Lord Moran, *Winston Churchill: The struggle for survival 1940-1965* (Constable, London, 1966), p. 129.

[28] Ismay, *The Memoirs of General The Lord Ismay* (Heinemann, London, 1960), p. 333.

[29] Sarah Churchill, *Keep On Dancing: An Autobiography* (Weidenfeld and Nicolson, London, 1981), p. 67.

[30] CAC, CHAR 20/125, WSC to Gort, 23 November 1943.

[31] M. Soames, *Speaking For Themselves*, 'Colonel Warden to Mrs. Warden', 21 November 1943, p. 485.

[32] H. Macmillan, *War Diaries* (Macmillan, London, 1984), p. 339.

# CHAPTER XVI

# Churchill's Sixth Visit to Malta, January 1945

*We shall be delighted if you will come to Malta. I shall be waiting on the quay.*
Churchill to President Roosevelt, 1 January 1945

In January 1944 Churchill spent three weeks in the winter sunshine of Marrakesh recovering from the illness that had laid him low in December. On this occasion he did not paint as he had after the Casablanca Conference, and he and his wife enlivened their stay with picnics and lunches, at one of which General and Mme de Gaulle were their guests. He then returned to England on the new battleship, HMS *King George V*, and arrived in London on 18 January. Two hours later he took his place in the House of Commons for Prime Minister's questions and then drove to Buckingham Palace for an audience with the King. The June date for the cross-channel invasion of Normandy, Operation 'Overlord', had been agreed at Teheran and Churchill spent the next six months of the year in England visiting the invasion troops and seeing for himself the enormous and complex preparations.

It took the King's order to prevent his Prime Minister from sailing with the invasion fleet on 6 June but six days later he crossed the Channel in the destroyer, HMS *Kelvin,* and was given a tour of the beachhead area by General Montgomery. Afterwards he re-boarded *Kelvin* and sailed along the invasion coast. At his request the destroyer then joined in the bombardment of enemy positions inland before returning to England. In the distance he may have seen once again the battleship HMS *Warspite* which was assigned a bombardment position at the extreme eastern end of the invasion area. *Warspite* had been heavily damaged by a German guided bomb while supporting the Allied landings at Salerno in the autumn of 1943 and had been towed back to England for extensive repairs. One of her 15-inch turrets was not repaired but her other guns made her a formidable floating battery. Her last action in the war came in November when she provided fire support for amphibious landings on the island of Walcheren in the Scheldt estuary.

Meanwhile in Italy General Alexander, whose forces had been reduced by the demands of 'Overlord', advanced slowly north against stubborn German opposition and it was not until 5 June that he was able to signal

Churchill that his troops had entered Rome. On that day Alexander was promoted to Field Marshal. Malta's long ordeal was now over and convoys were able to reach Malta safely. Nevertheless, conditions remained difficult. Although there was a relaxation in the food rations many commodities, all imported, remained in short supply. Between October 1943 and August 1944 there were no more than eight air raid alerts and no casualties or damage resulted. The last 'All Clear' sounded at 9 p.m. on 28 August 1944. Three weeks earlier on 5 August Field Marshal Lord Gort relinquished his appointment as Governor to become High Commissioner in Palestine. On the eve of his departure a large crowd assembled in the town of Zebbug to witness the presentation to him of a Sword of Honour. The blade of the sword bore the inscription:

> Presented by the band and Allied Clubs in Malta and Ghawdex, interpreters of the People's admiration, gratitude, devotion and love to H. E. Field-Marshal The Viscount Gort, V.C., their leader and Governor during the Second Siege of Malta.[1]

In the last six months of 1944 Churchill embarked on a veritable Odyssey of sea and air travel. Duty demanded this arduous programme but Churchill, at the age of 69, still retained a fascination for the harsh realities of front-line warfare and was always eager to see men in action. After a second three-day visit to Normandy in July he flew to Italy on 10 August and spent the next three weeks visiting Alexander's forces and the invasion coast in southern France. As Alexander later recalled:

> I took him right up to the front line. You could see the tanks moving up and firing and the machine guns in action a few hundred yards ahead of us. There were quite a lot of shells flying about, and land mines were all over the place. He absolutely loved it. It fascinated him—the real warrior at heart.[2]

Churchill also visited General Mark Clark's Fifth Army and Clark presented to him the first Union Flag to be raised over Rome after its capture on 5 June.[3] This flag now hangs in the rafters of Churchill's Study at Chartwell.

A week after his return to England the *Queen Mary* once again hosted the Prime Minister's party *en route* to the second Quebec Conference. A month later Churchill was in Moscow seeking to agree with an unresponsive Stalin the post-war settlement of Germany and Eastern Europe. Finally, on Christmas Eve when a family party had already assembled at Chequers Churchill announced to a tearful Clementine that he intended to fly on the following day to Athens. There a full-scale civil war seemed about to erupt as the communist ELAS guerrilla forces attempted to seize control of the country. For five days in bitterly cold weather and often under fire Churchill presided over discussions that resulted in the formation under the regency of Archbishop Damaskinos of a non-communist government.

By the end of 1944 the British and American armies were fighting hard to halt and turn back the surprise armoured offensive that Hitler had launched through the Ardennes in mid-December while in the east the massive Russian forces stood on a line reaching from Lithuania through Poland east of Warsaw to the Carpathian Mountains in the south. In order to co-ordinate strategy for the final advance into Germany and in a further attempt to reach some agreement on the post-war settlement in eastern Europe Churchill was convinced that a further 'Big Three' meeting was necessary. Since Stalin absolutely refused to leave Russian soil it was with considerable misgivings, soon proved to be well founded, that Churchill and Roosevelt agreed to meet him at Yalta in the Crimean Peninsular in February 1945. Churchill later told Harry Hopkins, Roosevelt's special adviser, that 'we could not have found a worse place for a meeting if we had spent ten years on research'.[4] Roosevelt who had in November 1944 been re-elected to a fourth term as President but was in poor health had initially planned to travel by sea to Naples and then fly to the Crimea. However, when advised by his doctors not to risk a high altitude flight over the Balkan mountains he decided to sail first to Malta before flying on to Yalta. When Churchill learned of this he at once telegraphed to Roosevelt:

> We shall be delighted if you will come to Malta. I shall be waiting on the quay. You will also see the inscription of your noble message to Malta a year ago. Everything can be arranged to your convenience. No more let us falter! From Malta to Yalta! Let nobody alter![5]

The reference to Roosevelt's message recalled the President's visit to Malta in December 1943 when, on his return from the Teheran Conference, he had presented to the Governor an illuminated scroll with a tribute to the heroism of the people and defenders of Malta. The text of this message is now inscribed on a marble plaque fixed to the walls of the Grand Master's Palace in Valletta alongside the inscription of King George VI's letter awarding the George Cross.

Churchill was anxious that he and Roosevelt and their advisers spend several days together in Malta to consider in detail their approach to their meeting with Stalin and on 10 January 1945 he telegraphed to Roosevelt:

> Eden has particularly asked me to suggest that Stettinius might come on forty-eight hours earlier to Malta with the United States Chiefs of Staff, so that he can run over the agenda with him beforehand

... I do not see any other way of realizing our hopes about World Organisation in five or six days. Even the Almighty took seven.[6]

The President agreed to this and sent ahead the American Joint Chiefs of Staff for preliminary discussions with their British counterparts and Edward Stettinius, recently appointed US Secretary of State, also arrived for diplomatic talks with Anthony Eden. It was finally settled that Churchill would fly to Malta on 29 January 1945 and that Roosevelt would arrive by sea on 2 February.

Churchill, on this occasion travelling as 'Colonel Kent', took a large party with him on his sixth visit to the island of Malta. Many of his companions, among them Eden, Ismay, Brooke, Cunningham, his daughter, Sarah, his doctor, Lord Moran, and even his secretary, Elizabeth Layton, later wrote about this visit. The following account, therefore, draws on these recollections and on the telegrams and letters that Churchill sent home to 'Mrs Kent' from Malta. After several delays Churchill's immediate party took off in a new Skymaster aircraft late in the evening of 29 January. Once again, perhaps as a result of the medication prescribed for him by Lord Moran, Churchill developed a high temperature and when the aircraft landed at Luqa at 4.30 a.m. on the following day he decided to remain asleep on board. His naval aide, Commander 'Tommy' Thompson, had signalled that in view of Churchill's late departure from London he did not expect to be met. However, to Thompson's horror he found when he got out of the aircraft that the signal had not been received and that the new Governor, General Sir Edmond Schreiber, and numerous officers and officials were waiting on the airfield. As Thompson later related: 'Surrounded by this bunch of nearly explosive V.I.P.s, I felt I was lucky to regain the Skymaster without being torn limb from limb!'[7] A long shadow of tragedy later fell on the party when news came in that one of the aircraft carrying twenty of the staff had crashed off Pantelleria and that there were only seven survivors.

Perhaps recalling his uncomfortable stay at St. Anton Palace a year earlier Churchill had decided on this visit to take up quarters in the relative comfort of a naval warship. On the morning, therefore, of 30 January with his temperature only somewhat lower Churchill was driven to the Grand Harbour where he boarded the cruiser, HMS *Orion*, moored in French Creek. After inspecting the office prepared by his secretaries in the Admiral's quarters Churchill went to bed again, although only after the bed had been moved 'the right way round'. Elizabeth Layton has described how disconcerted the Captain was to learn that he also had to provide accommodation for two female secretaries and Churchill's travelling office.[8] Churchill under Moran's orders stayed in bed for much of the day but later held conferences with General Brooke and Eden to discuss matters to be reviewed with the US Joint Chiefs of Staff. In the evening he presided over dinner on board *Orion*. Afterwards, as Lord Moran later wrote, 'when it was nearly midnight, he demanded cards and began to play bezique with Harriman. Damn the fellow, will he never give himself a chance?'[9] Averell Harriman had earlier in the war been President Roosevelt's Special Representative in London and in October 1943 had become US Ambassador in Moscow.

Churchill spent most of the next day on *Orion* where General Marshall, Chairman of the US Joint Chiefs of Staff, was his luncheon guest. In the evening, however, he went ashore to join a large dinner hosted by the Governor, General Sir Edmond Schreiber, at San Anton Palace. On 1 February he remained on board his cruiser and found time to write a lengthy letter to his wife, telling her that his health had much improved.[10] He also wrote that he had had his photo taken with the whole crew of the *Orion*. Afterwards, perhaps viewing the scene with his painter's eye, he went on, 'I lingered on the deck as the Malta sunshine was very pleasant, and the shattered buildings which encompass us at every side, for we are in one of the creeks, showed their fine warm yellow-ochre shapes.' The American Admiral King came to lunch that day and in the evening he entertained Eden, Stettinius and Harry Hopkins who had just arrived from Naples.

Throughout this period he received regular reports about the diplomatic and military discussions that had been taking place at various places in Valletta. Eden and Stettinius soon reached agreement on most of their agenda but the meetings of the Combined Chiefs were by all accounts much more torrid. Eisenhower was not in Malta but had presented, through his Chief of Staff, General Bedell Smith, his 'broad-front' strategy for the advance into Germany. Brooke found this highly unsatisfactory. General Ismay, who attended all these meetings, later wrote that 'the altercation which ensued was vehement and at times acrimonious'. Nevertheless, he went on to write, 'there is a good deal to be said for Churchill's advice that there should be no "smoothings or smirchings" to disguise one's true feelings.'[11] Since, as he added, 'General Marshall stood four-square behind Eisenhower', the British Chiefs had no choice but to accept his plan. In none of these discussions was Malta itself on the agenda since the island was no longer in danger and its role was that of a repair yard for damaged ships and landing craft.

The Combined Chiefs, after completing their work, were taken for a tour of Valletta visiting the Palace, the Library and St. John's Co-Cathedral. Brooke in his diary described this as 'most successful'.[12] That evening they were all guests at a dinner given by Admiral Sir John Cunningham, C-in-C of the Mediterranean Fleet. This was held at Admiralty House in Valletta where in January 1927 Churchill had stayed as the guest of Admiral Sir Roger Keyes. Commander Thompson, Churchill's naval aide, later described the scene. As the guests 'mounted the wide staircase on their way to dinner they saw above them the great marble scrolls bearing the names of every British C-in-C in the Mediterranean for one hundred and fifty years, Hood and St.Vincent, Nelson and Collingwood among them.'[13]

On the morning of 2 February the President arrived at Malta on the heavy cruiser, USS *Quincy*. Crowds lined the battered ramparts of the Grand Harbour, bands played the national anthems, sailors stood to attention and the President and Prime Minister saluted each other as *Quincy* slowly passed *Orion* to her moorings. Later Churchill with his daughter, Sarah, joined the President and his daughter, Mrs. Anna Boettiger, for lunch. Although Churchill signalled to 'Mrs Kent' that he had found the President 'in the best of health and spirits',[14] this was not the view of most of those who saw him that day. Sarah later wrote that she was shocked at the 'terrible change in him since I had last seen him at the Teheran Conference', and went on to write:

It was quite obvious that he was a very sick man; the bright charm and the brave, expansive heart were there but his appearance gravely distressed my father and, indeed, everyone.[15]

Despite this Roosevelt went for a drive around Malta in the afternoon visiting Mdina and inspecting on the walls of the Grand Master's Palace in Valletta the inscription of the tribute he had paid to the people of Malta on his previous visit in December 1943. In the afternoon Churchill received a deputation from the Malta Chamber of Commerce and was presented with a bronze model of a medieval Maltese cannon.[16] This is now one of the many gifts to Churchill kept at Chartwell. Thirty-five years earlier, as recounted in Chapter I, the Chamber had presented a silver model of a Gozitan fishing boat to Churchill and his wife as a wedding gift.

Roosevelt and Churchill jointly presided at a formal meeting of the Combined Chiefs of Staff on *Quincy* before dinner and were told of the matters that had been agreed during their three days of meetings. Eden, however, observed that the President refused to enter into discussions of any substantive issues and at the final dinner that evening no further progress was made. Eden noted in his diary for that day:

Impossible even to get near business. I spoke pretty sharply to Harry [Hopkins] about it, when he came in later, pointing out that we were going in to a decisive conference and had so far neither agreed what we would discuss nor how to handle matters with a Bear who would certainly know his mind.[17]

Later that evening the President and the US party left in a stream of aircraft closely followed by the British group. Churchill was not airborne until the early hours of 3 February and before leaving the *Orion* he went into the wardroom for a farewell drink with the ship's officers. Elizabeth Layton later remembered his saying, 'I hope you have looked after my two young ladies. They go everywhere with me and don't mind putting up with my bad temper.'[18]

This brought to an end Churchill's sixth visit to Malta. As in 1943 he had not been well enough to make an extensive tour of the island but such was his concern for the harsh realities of war that he would surely have done so had he been in better health. The people of the island, therefore, had only brief glimpses of Churchill on what was to be his last visit. At the end of the Yalta conference he gave some thought to returning from the Crimea by ship calling in again at Malta but first he decided to make a quick visit to Athens. There, two months after his last difficult meetings under gunfire, he found that Archbishop Damaskinos had restored order and, travelling in an open car with the Archbishop, he received a vociferous welcome. Before leaving he gave an impromptu speech in Constitution Square to a crowd estimated to be as large as 40,000. He later cabled from Cairo to his wife: 'Athens was a most marvellous experience. I have never seen anything like the size of the crowd or so much enthusiasm.'[19] In recognition of Churchill's role in helping to restore peace in Greece the Archbishop presented him with a Greek icon depicting St. John the Baptist and this now hangs in the corner of Churchill's Library at Chartwell.

Churchill flew from Athens to Alexandria and there on 15 February he had his last meeting with President Roosevelt on board *Quincy*. As he later recalled: 'The President seemed placid and frail. I felt that he had a slender contact with life. I was not to see him again. We bade affectionate farewells. That afternoon the Presidential party sailed for home.'[20] Churchill then signalled to the Governor of Malta, General Sir Edmond Schreiber, that the need to return quickly to England and favourable weather conditions precluded a further visit to the island and he left Egypt in the early hours of 19 February. Fourteen hours later he landed in England.

In May 1945 another Churchill briefly set foot on Malta. This was Mrs Churchill on her return from a long and tiring visit to Russia. In October 1941, three months after the German invasion of Russia, Mrs Churchill had agreed to become Chairman of the Red Cross Aid to Russia Fund. In the following years she devoted much of her time to this and in March 1945 she was invited to Russia to see some of the medical facilities that had been financed by the Fund. She left for Moscow on 27 March and spent five weeks in Russia visiting many cities. Shortly before her return she was made a Member of the Order of the Red Banner of Labour and was the guest of honour at a gala performance at the Bolshoi Ballet.[21] As she prepared to return to London it was expected that she would make a brief stop at Malta and Churchill alerted the Governor to this possibility.

Mrs Churchill left Moscow on 11 May and landed at Malta later that day. However, since the weather forecast was favourable and she was understandably anxious to get home her aircraft took off again later that night and she arrived at Northolt airport at 7 a.m. on 12 May. The insignia of Mrs Churchill's Russian decoration are on display at Chartwell.

Shortly before his wife's return Churchill was told that the German army leaders had signed surrender terms to become effective at midnight on 8 May. Although Churchill warned in his broadcast that day that the war against Japan had still to be won, the end of the war in Europe was the occasion for great celebration around the world. In the following days hundreds of messages of congratulation were received by Churchill and among them was a telegram from the naval dockyard in Malta. This read:

On Thursday 24<sup>th</sup> May at a fully authorised Victory March through yard in the dinner hour a motion was passed by acclamation from between four and five thousand workmen begins:

'We desire that a telegram be forwarded to the Prime Minister, Mr. Winston Churchill, who has visited this dockyard and is well acquainted with our circumstances, conveying our congratulations for the Great Victory in Europe and Malta Dockyard pledge of unshaken loyalty to our Beloved King and the British Cause.'[22]

A reply to this message was sent on 1 June:

The Prime Minister has received your message and wishes his warm thanks to be conveyed to all concerned.

Churchill had wished the coalition government to continue in office until the defeat of Japan but, although Attlee was prepared to accept this, the Labour Party Conference on 21 May rejected the proposal. As a result Churchill resigned as Prime Minister and was then invited by the King to form a caretaker administration until a General Election could be called. Polling day was 5 July but in order to allow time to count all the overseas service votes the results were not announced until 26 July. On the previous day both Churchill and Attlee returned from the Potsdam Conference to await the results. By noon on the 26 July it was clear that Labour would win by a landslide. When his wife, attempting to ease Churchill's pain at this unexpected rejection, said to him that the defeat might be a 'blessing in disguise' he famously replied, 'At the moment it seems quite effectively disguised.'[23]

# *Notes*

[1] P. Vella, *Malta Blitzed*, p. 201.

[2] *Churchill, Vol. VII*, p. 915.

[3] Ibid., p. 904.

[4] R. Sherwood, *The White House Papers of Harry L. Hopkins, Vol. II* (Eyre & Spottiswoode, London, 1949), p. 839.

[5] *Churchill, Vol. VII*, p. 1138.

[6] Ibid.

[7] G. Pawle, *The War and Colonel Warden* (George G. Harrap, London, 1963), p. 349. See also the account in S. Churchill, *Keep On Dancing*, p. 72.

[8] E. Nel (née Layton), *Mr. Churchill's Secretary* (Hodder and Stoughton, London, 1958), p. 165.

[9] Moran, *Churchill*, p. 217.

[10] M. Soames, *Speaking for Themselves*, WSC to CSC, 1 February 1945, p. 511-3.

[11] Ismay, *Memoirs*, p. 385.

[12] A. Danchev and D. Todman, (eds.), *Alanbrooke Diaries*, p. 654.

[13] Pawle, *The War and Colonel Warden*, p. 350.

[14] M. Soames, *Speaking for Themselves*, WSC to CSC, 2 February 1945, p. 513.

[15] S. Churchill, *A Thread in the Tapestry* (Andre Deutsch, London, 1967), p. 76.

[16] Vella, *Malta Blitzed*, p. 203.

[17] Earl of Avon, *The Eden Memoirs: The Reckoning* (Cassell, London, 1965), p. 512.

[18] E. Nel, *Churchill's Secretary*, p. 166.

[19] M. Soames, *Speaking for Themselves*, WSC to CSC, 16 February 1945, p. 518.

[20] Churchill, *Second World War, Vol. VI*, p. 348.

[21] This visit is described by her daughter, Lady Soames, in M. Soames, *Clementine Churchill* (Doubleday, London, 2002), pp. 403-15.

[22] CAC, CHAR 20/229A, pp. 56-7.

[23] Churchill, *Second World War, Vol. VI*, p. 583.

# CHAPTER XVII

# *The Post-War Years*

*I am indeed moved by this gift from the people of Malta who suffered the strokes of war so long and with such admirable tenacity.*
                    Churchill to Justice Montanaro-Gauci, 9 August 1955

On the evening of 26 July 1945 Churchill was driven to Buckingham Palace to tender his resignation as Prime Minister. By then the results of the election held on 5 July had become clear. The Labour Party had won 393 seats in the new Parliament and the Conservatives only 213. However, Churchill was returned for his Woodford constituency by a majority of more than 17,000 votes and thus, at the age of seventy, became for the first time Leader of His Majesty's Opposition. This quite unexpected result meant that the hopes and plans that Churchill had been developing for post-war recovery and reconstruction were set aside. Among these were two matters of major importance for Malta and its citizens.

In an earlier chapter it has been observed that during the war Churchill considered his overriding responsibility as Prime Minister and Minister of Defence to be the defeat of the enemy. Other matters must be delegated to the relevant Ministers. Thus, when in October 1942 Lord Cranborne, the Colonial Secretary, forwarded to him a telegram from Lord Gort setting out his ideas for the post-war reconstruction of Malta Churchill wrote on it: 'I don't wonder you are puzzled. For my part I am going to get on with the war.'[1] Consequently, much in the civil sphere relating to post-war policy affecting Malta was left to the Deputy Prime Minister, Clement Attlee, to the Colonial Secretary and to the Chancellor of the Exchequer. Nevertheless, while the Maltese people and the island's garrison were enduring the darkest days of the war Churchill's Cabinet took two far-reaching decisions.

Firstly, on 10 November 1942 in the House of Commons Sir Kingsley Wood, the Chancellor of the Exchequer, after noting that the repair of war damage in Malta would be beyond the resources of the Maltese government, went on to say:

There will be general agreement that the outstanding gallantry shown by the people of Malta in the face of enemy attacks of unprecedented length calls for some special recognition. In view, therefore, of the unique position of Malta and the extraordinary sufferings which it has so gallantly undergone, His Majesty's Government proposes to seek the approval of parliament for a free gift of £10,000,000 to the Government of Malta to be used for the purposes of restoration of war damage and the rebuilding of Malta after the war.[2]

Provision was made for the initial sum to be increased and eventually the grant rose to £30,000,000.

Secondly, on 7 July of the following year, shortly after the King's visit to the island and as a result of representations from all the elected members of the Council of Government, the Secretary of State rose in the House of Commons to make a statement about the future constitutional development of Malta. After recognising that the 'steadfastness and fortitude' of the Maltese people and garrison had 'rendered service of incalculable value to the Allied cause' he went on to say:

It is the policy of His Majesty's Government that Responsible Government in the same sphere [i.e. the 1921 Constitution] should again be granted to Malta after the war . . . It is the intention of His Majesty's Government that as soon as hostilities are brought to an end these matters should be pursued without delay and that steps should be taken to consult responsible opinion in Malta with a view to giving expression as far as possible to the wishes of the Maltese people regarding the form which the new Constitution might take.[3]

There can be no doubt that, despite Churchill's pre-occupation with military matters, both these promises carried Churchill's full support. The repair of war damage was the least that Britain could do for a people for whose courage Churchill had so often expressed admiration. On the wider issue of constitutional development we have seen in earlier chapters his support for the principle of self-government with minimal interference from London. However, his 1945 defeat meant that it fell to the Labour Government to honour these wartime pledges and to establish the new Malta Constitution in 1947.

Churchill naturally found it very difficult to accept his sudden relegation from wartime leader and one of the 'Big Three' to Leader of the Opposition. On the day of defeat his youngest daughter, Mary, wrote in her diary, 'We lunched in Stygian gloom. Papa struggled to accept this terrible blow—this unforeseen landslide . . . But not for one moment in this awful day did papa flinch or waver. "It is the will of the people".'[4] When several days later he said farewell to his three Chiefs of Staff, General Brooke noted in his diary, 'It was a very sad and very moving little meeting at which I found myself unable to say much for fear of breaking down. He was standing the blow wonderfully well.'[5] The process of adjustment took a significant step forward in September when Field Marshal Alexander invited Churchill to join him on a painting holiday at the villa on Lake Como that Alexander had made his HQ. There, as in 1915, the Muse of Painting came to his rescue. He painted several scenes and on one occasion he and Alexander sat side by side painting a lakeside view. Both these paintings now hang on the walls of Chartwell. His daughter, Sarah, who was with him, wrote to her mother: 'I really think he is settling down—he said last night—"I've had a happy day". I haven't heard that for I don't know how long.'[6]

In the six years of opposition that followed the 1945 election defeat the affairs of Malta rarely engaged Churchill's attention. The new 1947 Constitution for Malta received bi-partisan support and Churchill did not make a speech on that occasion. Rather, as the world's Elder Statesman he applied his undiminished energy, his experience, and his eloquence and imagination to the strengthening of the western democracies and the need, vividly illuminated by his 'Iron Curtain' speech at Fulton, Missouri, to resist what he saw as Russian imperialism. As he embarked on these weighty affairs of state Churchill was clearly delighted to receive in July 1946 Mr. Edward Ceravolo's gift of the Malta Shield, the story of which has been recounted in the Preface to this volume. It still hangs in the quiet of Churchill's medieval-timbered Study at Chartwell, the coat of arms of Grand Master Jean de la Valette and the weapons of the Great Siege of 1565 gleaming in the warm light.

By the end of 1946 Churchill had decided to write his war memoirs. In the first volume, published in March 1948, there are few references to Malta. However, increasingly frequent mention is made of the island in the following three volumes, published between 1949 and 1951, as Churchill recounted his recollections of the war in the Mediterranean. Chapter 22 in Volume III, now entitled 'The Mediterranean Passage' originally bore the provisional title 'Malta, the Navy and the Air', while Chapter 17 in Volume IV bears the title 'Malta and the Desert'. It was Churchill's habit to dictate, pacing to and fro in his Study, his own first draft version of each chapter based on the relevant papers and signals assembled by his research team. In these years, therefore, while he was reliving almost on a day-to-day basis the critical events of the Mediterranean war, it is perhaps not too fanciful to imagine that he may have paused at times to gaze at Edward Ceravolo's splendid tribute to his concern for the people of Malta during the dark days of the island's second Great Siege.

By the summer of 1951 the Labour Government of Clement Attlee had lost public support and in the ensuing election in October the Conservative Party gained 321 seats against 295 for Labour. On the evening of 26 October, a month before his seventy-seventh birthday, Churchill was invited by the King to form an administration. This second Churchill government was to last a further three and a half years in the course of which he became the first 80-year-old Prime Minister since

Gladstone. Even more than as Leader of the Opposition he concentrated his slowly diminishing energies on attempts to strengthen the western alliance and to ease east-west tension. However, his pleas for a summit conference with the Russian leaders who had succeeded Stalin upon the latter's death in March 1953 were rejected by Eisenhower, who had become US President in November 1952. In June 1953 Churchill suffered a serious stroke and although he made a remarkable recovery his energies were further reduced.

The affairs of Malta rarely claimed his attention during these final years of office. Although the wish in Malta for full independence was gaining strength it was not until Dom Mintoff had in February 1955 succeeded Borg Olivier as Maltese Prime Minister that the constitutional problem entered a period of considerable turmoil and difficulty. By then Churchill no longer stood at the head of affairs. On 5 April 1955, in his eighty-first year, he resigned as Prime Minister. Although he continued to be the Member of Parliament for Woodford until the year before his death in January 1965, his resignation as Prime Minister effectively brought to a close fifty-five years of public service. A week later he and Clementine with a few friends went to Sicily for a two-week holiday and although the spring sunshine was fleeting Churchill painted quite happily. There he was only 60 miles from Malta but he did not cross over to the island. However, one of the canvases from this holiday is a of a scene in Syracuse from the harbour of which on an October evening in 1907 he had embarked on the steamship, *Carola*, on his first visit to Malta. This canvas now hangs in his Studio in the grounds of Chartwell.

Malta briefly came to his notice in March 1956 when the House of Commons was due to debate the Government's declared intention to move forward with a plan, first proposed by the Maltese Prime Minister, Dom Mintoff, to 'integrate' Malta with the United Kingdom. This would have provided seats in the House for three elected Maltese Members. There were grounds for believing that there were doubts about this novel proposal in Malta itself, and many British MPs thought that to grant such a representation to Malta would set a precedent that other colonies would seek to follow. Churchill was one of those who shared these doubts. He was on holiday in the south of France when the debate was due and Edward Heath, the Government Chief Whip, wrote to him there to ask if he would be willing to be paired in support of the Government. Churchill declined replying to Heath: 'I am convinced this is a wrong and mistaken thing to do, and it will inflict lasting injury upon the character of the House of Commons.'[7] In the event no vote was taken after the debate and for complex reasons that lie outside the scope of this study the idea of Maltese representation at Westminster was abandoned. There are no other papers that might shed further light on his views in this matter. However, it should be remembered that since his first election to the House in 1900 there had been no firmer supporter of the House of Commons than Churchill. He believed it to be the cornerstone of British democracy and it seems clear that he thought the Government's intentions would weaken that structure.

In the years that followed Churchill was often the guest of Aristotle Onassis whose yacht, *Christina*, took him on eight voyages around the Mediterranean and the West Indies. One evening in April 1962 the ship passed to the south of Malta *en route* to Libya but did not call there. This may have been Churchill's last sight of the island he first saw on his way to India in September 1896.

It may be appropriate to conclude this account of Churchill's long involvement with the island and people of Malta by briefly describing three tributes paid to him in the closing years of his life. Upon his eightieth birthday on 30 November 1954 he received very many letters and telegrams of congratulation. Among these was one from Mr. G. Borg Olivier, Prime Minister of Malta. This read:

> It is my privilege and great pleasure to convey to you on behalf of the Government and people of these Islands warm congratulations on your 80th Birthday together with sincere wishes that you may long be spared to enjoy health and happiness.[8]

Upon his retirement as Prime Minister on 5 April 1955 it was Malta's newly elected Prime Minister, Mr. Dom Mintoff, who sent the following message:

> On your well-earned retirement after a very full life spent in serving the Commonwealth and in shaping contemporary history the Maltese Government and People recall the inspiration you gave them during the war years and pray God that he may spare your life and endow it with happiness and peace for many years to come.[9]

A more tangible and lasting mark of Malta's regard for Churchill is the bronze bust of him that now stands in the Upper Barrakka Gardens at Valletta alongside those of others who have played a part in Malta's long history. Just before his 80th birthday in November 1954 Churchill received a letter from Justice A. J. Montanaro-Gauci writing in his capacity as President of the Malta Society of Arts, Manufacturers and Commerce. Montanaro-Gauci's letter began by 'recognising the great debt we owe to you personally in the steps which you took in the war to ensure the protection of Malta and its ultimate relief at a time when the risk of invasion seemed very real.' He went on to tell Churchill that a fund had been raised in Malta to provide a suitable birthday gift to him and it had been decided to ask if he would be prepared to have his bust sculpted by a leading Maltese artist, Mr. Vincent

Apap. He concluded by writing that 'your acceptance of this offer from the people of Malta will give unbounded pleasure to your many admirers and friends throughout the islands of Malta and Gozo.'[10] Churchill at once replied that he would be glad to accept this offer and expressed the wish that after the finished bust had been presented to him it should be returned to Malta for permanent display there.

In December Vincent Apap came to London and Churchill sat for him at 10 Downing Street on two occasions on 9 and 10 December. These were short sessions between Cabinet meetings after one of which Apap has recorded that Churchill was so pleased with the work that he called in some of his Cabinet colleagues to see the early results. Apap then returned to Malta to complete the bust but it was not until July 1955, after Churchill's resignation, that the bronze bust was ready for presentation. Montanaro-Gauci and Apap then brought the bust to London and it was presented to Churchill at his London house at 28 Hyde Park Gate on Wednesday 3 August. Churchill was also given an elaborately illuminated Presentation Volume.

After the presentation ceremony Churchill wrote to Justice Montanaro-Gauci in the following terms:

> My dear Judge
>
> Your visit on August 3, and the gracious and complimentary remarks you made, gave me the greatest pleasure. Would you please express my warm thanks to all the donors of the bust? I am indeed moved by this gift from the people of Malta, who suffered the strokes of war so long and with such admirable tenacity. Would you please also convey my compliments on their work to the sculptor, Mr. Apap, and to those who executed the beautiful presentation book?
>
> I am happy to know that the bust will overlook the Grand Harbour at Malta, the scene of so many pages of history.
>
> Yours very sincerely,
> Winston Churchill[11]

Churchill also sent to Justice Montanaro-Gauci a signed photograph of himself together with an inscribed set of his biography of his ancestor, the first Duke of Marlborough. After its return to Malta the bust was placed in the Upper Barrakka Gardens and formally unveiled on 5 May 1956 by the Governor Sir Robert Laycock. Justice Montanaro-Gauci sent Churchill a photograph of the ceremony and wrote:

> You may be interested to hear that a very imposing ceremony was held on that occasion, and it was attended by all the high personalities of Malta, comprising the Archbishop of Malta, the Bishop of Tralles, the heads of the three services, representatives of NATO,

foreign Consuls and representatives of practically all constituted bodies of the island ... The bust stands proudly in a very conspicuous place overlooking the Grand Harbour, and people and tourists stop to look at it.

It was a very kind gesture on your part to ask that your bust be kept in Malta, where you rightly enjoy the admiration, gratitude and affection of her people.[12]

There are statues, busts and memorials to Sir Winston Churchill in many countries and it is fitting that one should stand overlooking the Grand Harbour in Valletta. Across the harbour, glowing in the warm light, is the fortress of St. Angelo where Grand Master Jean de la Valette victoriously led the Knights of St. John and the Maltese people in the Siege of 1565. Behind rise the tiered buildings of Senglea, Vittoriosa and Cospicua so heavily devastated during the bombing raids of 1941-43 while towards the open sea is the Siege Bell Memorial dedicated to those who lost their lives in the wartime Malta convoys. It is among these historic scenes that the bust of Sir Winston Churchill now stands as a reminder to resident and visitor that he too played a part on the brightly lit stage of Malta's long history.

## Notes

[1] NA PREM 3/266/10A, Fol. 671, WSC to Cranborne, 30 October 1942.

[2] H. Frendo, (ed.), *Maltese Political Development 1798-1964* (Valletta, 1993), p. 552.

[3] Re-printed in J. Cremona, *Maltese Constitution*, pp. 168-9.

[4] M. Soames, *Clementine Churchill* (Doubleday, London, 2002), p. 424.

[5] Danchev and Todman, *Alanbrooke*, p. 712.

[6] M. Soames, *Clementine Churchill*, p. 431.

[7] *Churchill, Vol. VIII*, WSC to Heath, 24 March 1956, p. 1189.

[8] CAC, CHUR 2/470A, Fols. 92-3, Borg Olivier to WSC, 29 November 1954.

[9] CAC, CHUR 2/481D, Fols. 191-2, Mintoff to WSC, 6 April 1955.

[10] CAC, CHUR 2/425, [no Fol. Nos.] Montanaro-Gauci to WSC, 10 November 1954.

[11] CAC, CHUR 2/341, Fol. 72, WSC to Montanaro-Gauci, 7 August 1955.

[12] CAC, CHUR 2/558B, Fol. 132, Montanaro-Gauci to WSC, 17 August 1956.

# Bibliography

## I  Records at the National Archives, Kew

Records of the following series of official British government papers have been consulted: Admiralty (ADM 1, 116, 205); Air Ministry (AIR 2, 8, 9, 23, 41); Committee of Imperial Defence (CAB 2, 4, 5); Oversea Defence Committee (CAB 7, 8); Cabinet Papers to September 1939 (CAB 23, 24); Joint Oversea and Home Defence Committee (CAB 36); Chiefs of Staff Committee to September 1939 (CAB 53, 54); War Cabinet (CAB 65, 66); Defence Committee (Operations) (CAB 69); Wartime Chiefs of Staff Committee (CAB 79, 80); Prime Minister's Operational Papers (PREM 3); Prime Minister's Operational Papers relating to Malta (PREM 3/266/1-10A); Colonial Office (CO 158, 355): War Office (32, 106).

## II  Churchill Archives Centre

The Churchill Papers, a very large collection of Sir Winston Churchill's private papers, are now lodged in the Churchill Archive Centre (CAC) at Churchill College, Cambridge. Many of these documents have been re-printed in the Companion volumes that accompany the eight volumes of the official biography.

## III  Unpublished Private Papers

Admiral of the Fleet Viscount Cunningham, British Library.
Admiral of the Fleet Lord Chatfield, National Maritime Museum.

## IV  Published Documents

Cannadine, D. (ed.), *The Speeches of Winston Churchill* (Penguin Books, London, 1990).
Eade, C. (ed.), *War Speeches by the Right Hon. Winston S. Churchill, Vols I-VI* (Cassell, London, 1942-46).
Rhodes James, R. *Churchill Speaks: Winston Churchill in Peace and War. Collected Speeches, 1897-1963* (Windward, London, 1981).

## V  Books and Newspapers

This is an abbreviated list of the principal works consulted.
Alexander, J. *Mabel Strickland* (Progress Press, Valletta, 1996).

Amery, L. S. *My Political Life, Vol. II, War and Peace 1914-1929* (Hutchinson, London, 1953).

Arnold-Forster, M. *The World at War* (Collins, London, 1975).

Attard, J. *The Battle of Malta* (Hamlyn Paperbacks, London, 1982).

— , *Britain and Malta: The Story of an Era* (Publishers Enterprises, Valletta, 1988).

Austin, D. *Malta and British Strategic Policy 1925-1943* (Frank Cass, London, 2004).

Avon, Earl of, *The Eden Memoirs: The Reckoning* (Cassell, London, 1965).

Badoglio, P. *Italy in the Second World War: Memories and Documents* (Oxford University Press, London, 1948).

Baer, G. *The Coming of the Italian-Ethiopian War* (Harvard University Press, Cambridge, Mass., 1967).

Barnett, C. *Engage The Enemy More Closely: The Royal Navy in the Second World War* (Penguin Books, London, 2000).

Best, G. *Churchill: A Study in Greatness* (Hambledon and London, London, 2001).

Bialer, U. *The Shadow of the Bomber* (Royal Historical Society, London, 1980).

Blake, R. and Louis, W. (eds.), *Churchill* (Oxford University Press, Oxford, 1993).

Blouet, B. *The Story of Malta* (Progress Press, Malta, 2004).

Boffa, C. *The Second Great Siege: Malta 1940-1943* (Progress Press, Valletta, 1992).

Bonham-Carter, Violet, *Winston Churchill As I Knew Him* (Eyre & Spottiswoode and Collins, London, 1965).

Bragadin, Commander M. A. *The Italian Navy in World War II* (United States Naval Institute, Annapolis, 1957).

Brodhurst, R. *Churchill's Anchor: Admiral of the Fleet Sir Dudley Pound* (Leo Cooper, Barnsley, 2000).

Cameron, I. *Red Duster, White Ensign: The Story Of Malta and the Malta Convoys* (Bantam Books, London, 1983).

Casey, Lord, *Personal Experience 1939-1946* (Constable, London, 1962).

Churchill, R. *Winston S. Churchill, Vols I-II* and associated *Companion Volumes* (Heinemann, London, 1966-67).

— , *Twenty-One Years* (Weidenfeld and Nicolson, London, 1964).

Churchill, S. *A Thread in the Tapestry* (Andre Deutsch, London, 1967).

— , *Keep on Dancing: An Autobiography* (Weidenfeld and Nicolson, London, 1981).

Churchill, Sir W. *The World Crisis* 6 Vols (Thornton Butterworth, London, 1923-27).

— , *The Second World War*, 6 Vols (Cassell, London, 1948-54).

— , *Great Contemporaries* (Macmillan, London, 1943).

— , *My Early Life: A Roving Commission* (Thornton Butterworth, London, 1930).

— , *Painting as a Pastime* (Odhams Press, London, 1948).

— , (Foreword) *The Epic of Malta* (Odhams Press, London, n.d., c. October 1942).

— , *Thoughts and Adventures* (Odhams Press, London, 1947).

Ciano, G. *Ciano's Diary 1937-1938* (Methuen, London, 1952).

Colville, J. *Man of Valour: The Life of Field-Marshal The Viscount Gort, V.C.* (Collins, London,1972).

— , *The Fringes of Power: Downing Street Diaries 1939-1955* (Hodder and Stoughton, London, 1985).

Corbett, Sir J. *History of The Great War: Naval Operations, Vol. I* (Longmans, Green & Co., London, 1920).

Cremona, J. *The Maltese Constitution and Constitutional History Since 1813* (Publishers Enterprise Group, Malta, 1994).

Cunningham, Admiral of the Fleet Viscount, *A Sailor's Odyssey* (Hutchinson, London, 1951).

*Daily Malta Chronicle*.

Danchev, A. and Todman, D. *War Diaries 1939-1945: Field Marshal Lord Alanbrooke* (Weidenfeld & Nicolson, London, 2001).

Dobbie, S. *Faith and Fortitude: The Life and Work of General Sir William Dobbie* (privately printed, 1979).

Esher, Viscount (ed.), *Journals and Letters of Reginald Viscount Esher, Vol. 3, 1910-1915* (Ivor Nicholson & Watson, London, 1938).

Frendo, H. *Party Politics in a Fortress Colony: The Maltese Experience* (Midsea Publications, Valletta, 1991).

— , (ed.), *Maltese Political Development 1798-1964* (Valletta, 1993).

Gilbert, M. *Winston S. Churchill: Volumes III-VIII; and related Companion Volumes* (Heinemann, London, 1971- ).

— , *Churchill: A Life* (Heinemann, London, 1991).

Gretton, Admiral Sir P. *Former Naval Person: Winston Churchill and the Royal Navy* (Cassell, London, 1968).

Guedalla, P. *Mr. Churchill: A Portrait* (Hodder and Stoughton, London, 1941).

Halpern, P. (ed.), *The Keyes Papers, Vol. II, 1919-1938* (Navy Records Society, London, 1980).

— , *A Naval History of World War I* (UCL Press, London, 1995).

Hancock, W. *Survey of British Commonwealth Affairs, Vol. I, Problems of Nationality* (Oxford University Press, London, 1937).

Hassall, C. *Edward Marsh: Patron of The Arts* (Longmans, London, 1959).

Hinsley, F. et al, *British Intelligence in the Second World War*, 5 Vols (HMSO, London, 1979-90).

Hoare, Sir Samuel (Viscount Templewood), *Nine Troubled Years* (Collins, London, 1954).

Hough, R. *The Great War at Sea 1914-1918* (Oxford University Press, Oxford, 1983).

Hyam, R. *Elgin and Churchill at the Colonial Office 1905-1908* (Macmillan, London, 1968).

Ismay, Lord, *The Memoirs of General The Lord Ismay* (Heinemann, London, 1960).

Jacob, Sir I. *Churchill By His Contemporaries: An "Observer" Appreciation* (Hodder and Stoughton, London, 1965).

Jenkins, R. *Churchill* (Macmillan, London, 2001).

Knox, M. *Mussolini Unleashed: Politics and Strategy in Fascist Italy's Last War* (Cambridge University Press, Cambridge, 1988).

— , *Hitler's Italian Allies* (Cambridge University Press, Cambridge, 2000).

Laferla, A. *British Malta* (Aquilina & Co., Malta, 1947).

Lamb, R. *Mussolini and the British* (John Murray, London, 1997).

Liddell Hart, B. *The Rommel Papers* (Collins, London, 1955).

Lloyd, Air Marshal Sir Hugh, *Briefed to Attack: Malta's Part in African Victory* (Hodder & Stoughton, London, 1949).

Lukacs, J. *Five Days in London May 1940* (Yale University Press, New Haven, 1999).

Lucas, L. *Malta: The Thorn in Rommel's Side* (Stanley Paul, London, 1992).

Lumby, E., *Policy and Operations in the Mediterranean 1912-14* (Navy Records Society, London, 1970).

MacCallum Scott, A., *Winston Spencer Churchill* (Methuen, London, 1905).

Macintyre, D. *The Battle for the Mediterranean* (Batsford, London, 1964).

Macmillan, H. *The Blast of War: 1939-1945* (Macmillan, London, 1967).

Manduca, J. (ed.), *The Bonham-Carter Diaries 1936-1940* (Publishers Enterprise Group, Malta, 2004).

Massie, R. *Dreadnought: Britain, Germany and The Coming of The Great War* (Pimlico, London, 2004).

— , *Castles of Steel: Britain, Germany and the Winning of The Great War at Sea* (Pimlico, London, 2005).

Middlemas, K. and Barnes, J. *Baldwin: A Biography* (Weidenfeld and Nicolson, London, 1969).

Ministry of Information, *The Air Battle of Malta: The Official Account of the RAF in Malta, June 1940 to November 1942* (HMSO, London, 1944).

Montague Browne, A. *Long Sunset: Memoirs of Winston Churchill's Last Private Secretary* (Cassell, London, 1995).

# BIBLIOGRAPHY

Moran, Lord, *Winston Churchill: The struggle for survival 1940-1965* (Constable, London, 1966).

Muggeridge, M. (ed.), *Ciano's Diary 1939-1943* (Heinemann, London, 1947).

Nel (née Layton), E. *Mr. Churchill's Secretary* (Hodder and Stoughton, London, 1958).

Nicolson, H. *King George The Fifth: His Life and Reign* (Constable, London, 1952).

Nicolson, N. (ed.), *Harold Nicolson: Diaries and Letters 1930-1939* (Collins, London, 1966).

Pawle, G. *The War and Colonel Warden* (George G. Harrap, London, 1963).

Perowne, S. *The Siege Within The Walls: Malta 1940-1943* (Hodder & Stoughton, London, 1970).

Playfair, General I. et al, *The Mediterranean and Middle East*, 6 Vols (HMSO, London, 1954-73).

Roberts, A. *'The Holy Fox': A Biography of Lord Halifax* (Weidenfeld & Nicolson, London, 1991).

Rogers, A., (ed.), *185: The Malta Squadron* (Spellmount, Staplehurst, Kent, 2005).

Rollo, D. *The Guns and Gunners of Malta* (Mondial Publishers, Malta, 1999).

Roskill, S. *The War at Sea*, 3 Vols (HMSO, London, 1954-1961).

— ,*The Navy At War 1939-1945* (Collins, London, 1960).

— , *Naval Policy Between the Wars*, 2 Vols (Collins, London, 1968, 1981).

— , *Churchill and the Admirals* (Collins, London, 1977).

— , *H.M.S. Warspite* (William Collins & Sons, London, 1957).

Sherwood, R. *The White House Papers of Harry L. Hopkins, Vol. II* (Eyre & Spottiswoode, London, 1949).

Shores, C., Cull, B. with Malizia, N. *Malta: The Hurricane Years 1940-41* (Grub Street, London, 1987).

— , *Malta: The Spitfire Year 1942* (Grub Street, London, 1991).

Simpson, Rear-Admiral G. *Periscope View* (Macmillan, London, 1972).

Soames, M. (ed.) *Speaking for Themselves: The Personal Letters of Winston and Clementine Churchill* (Doubleday, London, 1998).

— , *Winston Churchill: His Life As A Painter* (Collins, London, 1990).

— , *Clementine Churchill* (Doubleday, London, 2002).

Spooner, T. *Supreme Gallantry: Malta's Role in the Allied Victory 1939-1945* (John Murray, London, 1996).

Tedder, Marshal of the Royal Air Force Lord, *With Prejudice* (Cassell, London, 1966).

The National Trust, *Chartwell*, 1999 edition.

*The Royal Navy and the Mediterranean: Vol. II, November 1940-December 1941* (Whitehall History Publishing, London, 2002).

*The Times*, London.

*The Times*, Malta.

Trevor-Roper, H. (ed.), *Hitler's War Directives 1939-1945* (Pan Books Edition, London, 1966).

Van der Vat, D. *The Ship That Changed The World* (Hodder and Stoughton, London, 1985).

Vella, P. *Malta: Blitzed But Not Beaten* (Progress Press, Valletta, 1985).

Warlimont, General W. *Inside Hitler's Headquarters 1939-1945* (Presidio, Novato, California, n.d.).

Wheeler-Bennett, Sir J. (ed.), *Action This Day: Working with Churchill: Memoirs by Lord Normanbrook, John Colville, Sir John Martin, Sir Ian Jacob, Lord Bridges, Sir Leslie Rowan* (Macmillan, London, 1968).

— , *King George VI: His Life and Reign* (Macmillan, London, 1958).

Wingate, J. *The Fighting Tenth: The Tenth Submarine Flotilla and the Siege of Malta* (Leo Cooper, London, 1991).

Woodman, R. *Malta Convoys: 1940-1943* (John Murray, London, 2000).

# Index